The Bishop Is In a Hurry!

Letters of A Well-Traveled
Ambassador for Christ

Bishop Arthur J. Moore

Compiled and Edited by
Robert E. Daniel

Arthur J. Moore Methodist Museum
St. Simons Island, Georgia

ISBN: 978-1-954617-49-0 paperback edition
ISBN: 978-1-954617-50-6 hardcover edition
ISBN: 978-1-954617-51-3 eBook edition

In Memory of
Martha Tabitha McDonald Moore
(1884-1964)

"To a brave and gracious wife throughout the long years of my incessant world travels has always supported and encouraged me by her prayers and affection I render my grateful praise. If, at the end of my earthly way the Heavenly Father has any praise or reward to bestow, to her will certainly go the greater part."

Arthur J. Moore
Wesleyan Christian Advocate
November 4, 1948

In Honor of
Elaine Noles Daniel

"Set me as a seal upon your heart, as a seal upon your arm, for love is strong as death, jealousy is cruel as the grave. Many waters cannot quench love, neither can floods drown it."
Song of Solomon 8:6-7

Thank you for the ultimate journey, forty years of one glorious adventure, one after the other.

Dona Nobis Pacem
Robert E. Daniel

PREFACE

Our church today struggles with its identity. This ecclesiastical tug-of-war is not unique. It was true of the church in which Arthur J. Moore found himself when he gave his life to Jesus Christ at a revival meeting in Waycross, Georgia in 1909. The church had splintered over temporal issues and had endured the Civil War and its economic aftermath. By the time he began his ministry, splintered Methodism was looking for ways to honor Christ and forging a road that would lead to a more perfect union.

The church had excellent leadership. However, it was an aging clergy whose message was strongly laced with overtones of pessimism: God was a punishing deity, the world is bad and getting worse and the way out was to accept Christ and receive your reward in Heaven. There was very little optimism to be found in those days.

Arthur J. Moore came to Christ with a very different outlook. He said, "No man can believe in the supremacy of God and not believe in the ultimate supremacy of righteousness in the world." He brought to the pulpit a positive, optimistic view of God and religion. He did not believe that we had to die and go to Heaven to experience the joy of a life lived for Jesus Christ. Thousands responded to his positive message about a loving, forgiving God. New converts were received into old established churches and where there was no church, new churches were organized.

The articles in this book, written by Bishop Moore, give an insight into the splintered world in which he had his most important and challenging ministry. He looked for avenues of conversation with temporal leaders, as well as church officials, to preserve long-standing ministries of The Methodist Church both at home and around the world. In Ralph McGill's article, *"The Bishop's In a Hurry!"* he discusses the cleaver ways that Bishop Moore helped countless thousands in war-torn countries to find relief. He was an extraordinary leader who perfected the art of "getting to know the people."

I first became interested in Bishop Moore as a student at the Candler School of Theology, Emory University. Someone had given me a copy of Bishop Moore's autobiography *Bishop to All Peoples*. It was such a fascinating story that I began to interview professors and staff that knew him. I flew to New York to interview Mr. Arthur J. Moore, Jr. about his father's life and ministry. Mr. Moore, Jr., by that time, was Editor of *New World Outlook,* a periodical published by the Board of Global Ministries of The United Methodist Church. Many of the photographs in this book were gifts of Arthur Moore, Jr. I interviewed the Bishop's son, Wardlaw, the Treasurer of the North Georgia Conference. Also, Bishop Nolan B. Harmon, invited me to his home where he discussed the episcopal career of Bishop Moore. The common denominator of the interviews was that Bishop Arthur J. Moore gave of himself without reservation. He traveled constantly for the church, whether dedicating churches in his episcopal area or presiding over Conferences on four continents.

The focus of this project was to allow Bishop Moore to speak to a new audience through his writings. In June 2021, Anne Packard, Director of the Arthur J. Moore Museum, St. Simons Island, Georgia expressed an interest in publishing a new book about Bishop Moore. In this volume, Bishop Moore would tell his story through articles that were published in *World Outlook* and the *Wesleyan Christian Advocate*, the newspaper of the North and South Georgia Conferences of The Methodist Church. The articles and letters were altered only to correct spelling, or to explain the meaning of phrases that are no longer in common usage. Thank you for your interest in Bishop Moore's life and ministry.

This book was begun while I was a student at the Candler School of Theology. By the time I finished it, no one was interested in publishing it. So, it was filed with my Arthur Moore collection as time passed. In 2012, a minister of an Annual Conference asked to borrow the manuscript, I agreed, and that was the last I saw of my manuscript.

Forward to 2021, I was diagnosed with Mantle Cell Lymphoma and was looking at several months in quarantine, due to Covid and my compromised immune system. Thanks to the encouragement of Dr. Anne Packard, I reconstructed the manuscript. I've always said that nothing happens without a reason. This book is more in-depth due to the material that was made available through the Special Collections at Pitts Theology Library, Emory University, Atlanta, Georgia and the General Commission of Archives and History, located at Drew University, Madison, New Jersey. Thanks to those archives and individuals, named below, who went beyond the norm to make this retelling of Bishop Moore's life abroad as complete as possible.

Special Thanks

- Elaine N. Daniel, typing, proofreading, and the best caregiver!
- Dr. Anne Packard. Curator
  Arthur J. Moore Methodist Museum
- Dr. Brandon C. Wason,
  Head of Special Collections
  Pitts Theology Library, Emory University
- Frances Lyons, Reference Archivist
  General Commission on Archines and History.
  The United Methodist Church
- Joan Osborne, Collection Services Director
  R.T. Jones Memorial Library, Canton, Georgia
- Doctors and Nurses, Bone Marrow Transplant Group, Northside Hospital, Atlanta and Georgia Cancer Specialists, Best Cancer Care Ever!
- The "BEAST", for their prayers and culinary care

Robert E Daniel
June 26, 2022

Bishop Arthur J. Moore, 1940

Bishop Moore in Asia, undated

TABLE OF CONTENTS

In Memorium

CHAPTER ONE

The Bishop's In a Hurry!
by Ralph McGill

In 1935, in the Central Belgian Congo village called after its chief, Wembo Nyama, a Methodist missionary bishop named Arthur James Moore was approached by the tall, massive tribal ruler, closely followed by a retinue of twenty-three wives, reduced to that low figure from some 160 odd by the Christian influence, and certain members of the royal family. As an influential ally and convert of the church, the chief occupied a special status. And he had a request to make. For some time he had been watching the ease with which missionaries rode their bicycles, and the chief wished for one with all the yearning of a small boy.

A month later in a town some 400 miles away, the bishop found a red bicycle of French make and purchased it for his friend. It was duly presented, though not without some trepidation. Before the admiring eyes of the village, the delighted chief swung his great bulk upon the saddle and pushed off down the slight slope before his house. He careened forward a few yards and then fell in a wild tangle of legs and wheels, to the accompaniment of gasps from the court and shrill cries of alarm from his wives. He disentangled himself and, with great dignity and never a glance at the treacherous vehicle, the bishop or the wives, retired to his house.

Soon thereafter, a worried bishop, who was calculating the trouble a hostile chief could create, received a letter from the chief, written by a graduate of the mission school who served as a scribe to the tribal ruler. It was short and to the point: "Dear Friend-Chief: you have given me a bicycle which will not stand up. Please send one that will."

The bishop brooded unhappily over this, and it was some months before a stroke of luck enabled him to make good. It was the sight of a large and sturdy invalid's chair on a ship at a coastal port that inspired him to inquire as to its origin and to order a duplicate from a New York department store. Weeks later it arrived, was uncrated, demonstrated, and presented to the chief, who beamed not at all, but looked on, as did the anxious wives and the royal court.

But when the chair was pushed before him, he lowered his bulk into it and, having noted the demonstration with care, called imperiously to his wives to push. With great glee and delighted clucking and giggling, they worked in relays to wheel the chief about the village and back before the bishop. The chief stepped out, beaming. "This," he said to the bishop, "is a true bicycle that knows how to stand up."

Since April 1909 when Arthur James Moore, as a young flagman for the Atlantic Coastline Railroad, was converted at a service in Waycross, Georgia, his admirers say that the man who now is president of the Council of Bishops of the Methodist Church and its more than fifty different fields in Asia, Africa, Latin America, and Europe has been giving to all peoples who hear him vehicles of faith that will stand up.

At sixty-two, sturdy and stocky, with a young face and boundless enthusiasm and stamina, he is something of a living legend in the Methodist Church, which is, since the union in 1939 of the Methodist Episcopal Church, the Methodist Episcopal Church, South and the Methodist Protestant Church, the largest Protestant group in America.

In the service of this church, the President of bishops has been a circuit rider, evangelist with nationwide assignments, pastor of outstanding churches, a member of the Council of Bishops since 1930, president of the Board of Mission since 1932, with oversight of church affairs in fifty-two countries, and president of the Council since early 1951.

From 1934 to 1940, he went more or less breathlessly up and down the world, doing the work previously done by three missionary bishops. For six years his schedule placed him with the churches in China, Japan, and Korea from September to April; in Poland, Czechoslovakia, and Belgium through May, June, and July; and the rest of each year in the Congo. He began flying when to do so was an event. Thomas and Jan Masaryk, Eduard Benes, Josef Pilsudski, Leopold III, Generalissimo

Chiang Kai-shek, Gen. Douglas MacArthur, Gens. Jiro Minami and Iwane Matsui, of the Japanese war party, Ambassador Hiroshi Saito, and others of the Japanese military and civil life were either friends or well-known acquaintances made during those years.

In the post-war years, his official duties have sent him on trouble-shooting jobs to most of the countries of Europe and the islands of the Pacific, including a journey to the state of Sarawak, in Borneo. There he ate dinner with a new convert who had swinging from the rafters a net of dried human heads. "Mostly Japanese," he said modestly to the inquiring bishop.

When he went to the First Methodist Church at Waycross for the spring revival service in 1909, Moore was twenty years old, a railroad flagman since eighteen, married at eighteen and a half, father of a son, and on the threshold of his young life's most coveted goal – promotion to the full-time freight conductor's job. He was not an irreligious man, but he had given to the church only routine attendance.

In fact, at fourteen he had been "readout" of the Baptist Church in his hometown of Glenmore, near Waycross, where his father, an Atlantic Coastline section foreman, then lived. In those days all small, rural towns frowned on the simple pleasure of dancing. One-night young Arthur Moore, in company with other curious boys of the town, was drawn to the home of a non-churchgoing citizen where a dance was in progress. Boy like, they peered through a porch window at the goings-on. For this sampling of worldly joys, he was summoned by the board of the Baptist church to explain his erring ways. Resenting what seemed to him an unfair accusation, the boy, who had never then nor since danced a step, refused to go. His name was removed from the list of members of the church.

So, on this night of the eventful service of 1909, preached by Dr. Charles Dunaway, now in retirement in California, the young railroader had no sense of impending change. Yet something in the sermon moved him to go down to the altar and seek membership in the church on confession of faith. For years, now, a bronze plaque at the church has commemorated that conversion. The young convert had no thought then of becoming a minister. But his job no longer interested him. He became a lay worker, seeing to it, for example, that the church was cleaned and that cooking fires at the summer camp meetings were supplied with wood.

Bishop Moore was born at Argyle, Georgia, one of the small towns on his father's railroad section, on December 26, 1888. It is in the flat wire-grass and piney-woods area not far from the great Okefenokee Swamp. His father, John Spencer Moore, was first-generation Irish, the son of an immigrant who came over from North Ireland and took up land in Clinch County, South Georgia, a few years before the outbreak of the Civil War. When volunteers were called, he joined the 26th Georgia infantry and died in a charge at Gaines' Mill, one of the grim struggles of the Seven Days Battles.

The grandfather had come alone to Georgia. He had been married but a few years when he went to war. "My grandmother knew little of her husband's life in Ireland except that it had been hard and he had left the poverty of it to seek opportunity in America," says Bishop Moore. "She was left a widow in what was almost frontier country and had a cruel, hard time of it with her young son, my father. When the railroad came, he took a job with the construction crews and then stayed on as a section foreman."

Arthur Moore's first memories center on Brookfield, another town in the section. It was at this town that he met, at the age of eleven, the granddaughter of a Waycross Methodist minister, visiting in an uncle's home. This was Martha McDonald, his first and only sweetheart. They were married on April 26, 1906. They have three sons and a daughter. The eldest son, Harry, is a minister who has triumphed over blindness which came to him about five years ago. Wardlaw, the second son, is a businessman in Corpus Christi, Texas, and the third son, Arthur, is with the Columbia University Press. The daughter, Alice Evelyn, is Mrs. Lowell V. Means, of San Antonio.

"I was always deeply interested in church membership," Mrs. Moore recalls, "and I wanted to be completely proud of my husband. I tried quietly but persistently to bring him to membership, and I will never forget my joy and pride the night he rose and went down to the altar." In August of that year, while Arthur was still with the railroad, the Presiding Elder sent for him. Down at St. Marys, Georgia, an old pre-revolutionary seaport town at the mouth of the river of the same name, an elderly minister named John W. Simmons was critically ill. "I want you to go down there and preach in Dr. Simmons' place," the Presiding Elder told him. "You got it in you. Pray with Dr. Simmons and preach."

So, at twenty years of age, possessed of only a common-school education, an unlicensed layman, he obtained leave from his job and preached for six weeks at St. Marys.

Bishop Moore has had many experiences and satisfaction, but he recalls those at St. Marys as among the superior ones. When he presented himself before the conference in late October to request a license, there was also before the bishops a request from the St. Marys' congregation to send back the young preacher. He received the license, but the assignment was a circuit of seven isolated rural churches in agricultural McIntosh County.

Arthur and Martha "Mattie" Moore in the early days of their marriage.

The Moores remember those days well. Their parsonage consisted of two rented upstairs rooms, one of them a kitchen. Mrs. Moore, who is a small person, recalls that she had to carry water, wood, and supplies up the steps – the circuit rider was gone most of the time. But it was a happy year. The people were kind. The doctor was a Baptist, but he sent no bills. The neighbors provided frequent gifts of milk, butter, chickens, and vegetables.

The seven towns echo yet the preaching of the young circuit rider. He was a sort of ministerial Paul Bunyan. Elisha Thorpe, of Townsend, had lent him an old, half-blind white horse that would not step over logs – a handicap on a circuit where much of the riding was through woods with years of accumulated logs felled by age and storm. But Moore went everywhere. There are men there yet who recall the young preacher walking up and down beside plowmen in the fields, talking to them about the Gospels. He and his old horse would arrive at a lonely clearing at dusk. The minister would chop wood, help to milk, and that night about the fire or, if in summer, out in the yard in straight kitchen chairs, he would talk of God's mercy, to the family about him.

He visited every house in his wide circuit, seeking out lonely cabins and distant clearings. The first time he preached at Jackson's Chapel, twenty-three persons joined the church. He never got another member there. Every unsaved soul in the community joined that first night. It was that way in all towns. Great crowds came long distances on Sundays to hear him preach. He was, as his listeners said, "on fire with the Word." Until his conversion, he had never made a talk in his life. Now the cabin clearings and the schoolhouses were filled with his eloquent, moving exhortations.

"It was a miracle to me to hear him," says Mrs. Moore. "All I can believe is that God gave it to him that night before the altar at Waycross."

Toward the end of the year, the Thorpes, who admired him mightily, came to him and said, "Brother Moore, you ought to go to Oxford College." (Old Oxford, at Oxford, Georgia, now Emory University, near Atlanta.)

Brother Moore, who by then was the father of two children, thought it was a good idea, but on $440 a year there didn't seem to be much chance. The Thorpes offered to donate $25 a month to the cause, and so the Moores unhesitatingly picked up and moved to Oxford and Emory College, a small Methodist school about 35 miles east of Atlanta.

There was neither time nor background for a routine beginning. The college wisely assisted Moore to select certain necessary courses. A four-room house was found, as were students who would rent two of the rooms and thereby add to the meager income. Lights regularly burned late as the young man attacked his texts with the inadequate tools of the poor-grade schooling offered in rural communities in his day. He did find time to play on the baseball team and to take up tennis, which he enjoyed more because it could be played at odd hours. He liked best the hour before dinner in the evening. He would take the two babies with him to the tennis court, put them on a blanket in one corner, and by this method of babysitting have his game and also give the misses more time to prepare their evening meal.

The college rules required church attendance each Sunday. Student Moore met this by preaching in nearby towns, where he soon was in great demand. Flocks of fellow classmen accompanied him, and the congregations of the small rural churches often complained that if they did not arrive early, Moore's mobile congregation took all the seats.

At the end of two work-packed years, he knew more about preaching and people than any other student, but less Greek. He also faced a decision. When he had quit railroading to preach at $440 per year, he had left some debts behind. He had gone to each person he owed – and they were but few - and told them his story. He wanted to preach. If he did, he could not be sure when they would get their money, but he promised that they would in time receive it. Now three years had passed at school with no income at all beyond bare subsistence. There was a demand for his services in the church's field of evangelism, so, reluctantly, he gave up the idea of more schooling.

Today, he is an unusually well-educated man. He has never ceased to study, read and learn. He is the author of several scholarly religious books and is a careful researcher and student in all addresses, sermons, and writings. He has accepted only a few of the many honorary degrees offered to him.

On leaving college, he was appointed a district revivalist, and as such took a tent and went to preaching. He followed his old custom of going to backwoods towns and communities, where preaching had been scarce. He organized almost 100 churches and won thousands of converts.

Dr. William N. Ainsworth, the pastor of the large Mulberry Street Methodist Church in Macon, Georgia, sent for him on the basis of the enthusiasm he had aroused about the state and had him pitch his tent on the outskirts of Macon at a place called Cherokee Heights. Thousands came, and a church was organized. Today it is one of the largest congregations in the state, numbering well over 2000, and the church plant is a large and efficient one. The word began to get around that when Arthur Moore converted someone, it "took." Dr. Ainsworth began to tell laymen and ministers that he had never before met a man with the power of preaching that the district evangelist had.

The next step was that of a general evangelist – a post that enabled him to preach in more than two-thirds of the forty-eight states. It was not at all uncommon for special trains to be run to his meetings and it was almost a rule that when he had completed a revival the people of that town would follow him onto the next.

In the fall of 1920, Dr. Ainsworth, then bishop, wired him at San Angelo, Texas, where a typical Moore revival was at its height, saying, "Arthur, the time has come for you to take a church. I am today appointing you to Travis Park Church in San Antonio." This was, and is, one of the largest and most successful churches in the Methodist domain.

Moore was there for six years. In a church that seated 2400, there was rarely a service, day or night, when there were not many persons standing. In those six years, an average of twelve persons joined the membership each Sunday.

In 1926, Dr. George R. Stuart, one of the great preachers of Southern Methodism, died suddenly of a heart attack. Bishop Warren A. Candler, who had taught Moore at Emory College, moved him from San Antonio to fill Stuart's pulpit at Birmingham, Alabama. In four years there he duplicated his San Antonio success. In the ten years at the two pastorates, he received more than 6000 persons in the church membership. The man who had been so convincing in the cabin clearings and the weather-beaten one-room schoolhouses of McIntosh County was just as effective in the large city churches.

In 1930 at the General Conference in Dallas, Texas, the pastor of Birmingham's First Methodist Church was proposed for election to a bishop. It is not unusual for 200 or 300 ballots to be taken in such deliberations. Pastor Moore was elected overwhelmingly on the very first ballot, a rare and glowing compliment.

Arthur J. Moore upon his election to the episcopacy.

He was sent to the frontier of Methodism in America – the Western states of Arizona, Montana, California, Washington, and Oregon. His salary was about half what it was when he was pastor, but he was happy on a familiar assignment. It has always seemed to him that lonely people are lonely chiefly for the word of God. The distant ranch houses, the wagons of sheepherders, the small Western towns, sun-baked in summer and raw-cold in winter, as well as the cities, came to know his voice. He used automobiles and he rode horseback. He attended roundups and rodeos. He founded churches and revived old ones. He lived with the people, and it is no figure of speech to say they loved him. There was, and is, much tangible evidence of it everywhere he has been. A well-known minister spoke of this at a dinner tendered to the Bishop on the occasion of his election as president of the council. "While the rest of us were learning Greek and Hebrew, Arthur was learning how to reach the hearts of people," he said.

At the General Conference of 1934 at Jackson, Mississippi, the financial problems of the church were pressing. The world depression was at its worst. The Board of Missions was heavily in debt. Of the council of sixteen bishops, two had died and three had reached the age of retirement. It was determined to ask eleven to do the work which sixteen had been doing before. Prior to 1934, there had been three bishops in the foreign field. One was based in Shanghai, serving China, Japan, and Korea. A second minister to Poland, Belgium, and Czechoslovakia, and the third was in charge of the vast mission developments in the Belgian Congo.

"Let's leave them all to Arthur," said one of the bishops. And they did. For six years he moved constantly about a world preparing for its second great war.

China and Japan were already at war. In Korea, the Japanese were ruthlessly squeezing out the Christian church. Everywhere there was growing fear and concern. One of the problems Bishop Moore faced then was the same one that confronts the Christian church in the Russian satellite countries today. There was pressure in those years in Korea to resist the Japanese antichurch moves, even if it meant being sent out of the country or arrested, and the closing of the churches. In Korea, for example, the Japanese required all the children, those of Christian schools included, to bow before the Shinto shrines and gods. They had shrewdly ordered this on two grounds – religious and patriotic. Failure to bow could be classified as unpatriotic and subversive. Bishop Moore, with the hardheaded practical sense that has characterized his career, said, "We'll stay. Let the children bow. Would they not be required to bow if we left? As long as we are here, we can continue to teach the truth."

General Jiro Minami was governor-general of Korea in those days. Bishop Moore's able diplomacy and always-good-natured resistance interested him. They became well acquainted and were, in a sense, friendly enemies. In 1950, at a dinner with his good friend, General Douglas MacArthur, in Tokyo, Bishop Moore asked what had been the disposition of General Minami, who had been one of the war criminals and who had received a life sentence. "Did you know him?" asked the astonished General MacArthur. "Well," said the bishop.

The next day a quiet interview was arranged. Bishop Moore waited in a room at the end of a prison corridor. Soon he saw a shuffling figure, clad in a prisoner-of-war uniform, come down the hall, not at all resembling the glittering governor of a few years before.

"We talked about forty-five minutes," said Bishop Moore. "I recalled to him something that had happened in Korea. He had imposed a restriction on us because of an offense by another religious group. I protested, and he said, 'Bishop, you must suffer for the sins of others. I told him that, in my opinion, he was doing just that, and that I had prayed for him and forgiven him. He did an unusual thing for a Japanese," the bishop continued. "He put his arms about me and held me tightly and wept."

To this day, Bishop Moore regards as a sort of minor miracle the fact that he was not jailed in Japan. In those years he was going back and forth between China and the Emperor's domain. One of his books, extremely critical of the Japanese, had been published. But even after severe fighting between China and Japan had begun and the Japanese had taken Shanghai, he was able somehow to do much of his job. A shadow crosses his face as he recalls the International Settlement, jammed with refugees in those days when the Imperial Army clique had launched its determined invasion of China. Thousands died of hunger and disease. At least 250 bodies were picked up off the streets each morning, in addition to the hundreds who died elsewhere.

Japanese officials refused him permission to visit churches outside Shanghai. He particularly needed to go to Soochow (Wuhsien), about fifty-five miles west of Shanghai.

One day while trying to break down official resistance, the bishop recalled a letter that had been most helpful on numerous occasions in Japan. Two years earlier he had visited his friend, Ambassador Hiroshi Saito, in Washington and requested a letter that would facilitate travel in Japan. He had obtained a generously worded letter in which the ambassador vouched for him and urged all those to whom the document might be presented to give the bishop full co-operation in travel. The ambassador had put his personal "chop" on the letter, as well as the official Imperial seal. It was an impressive-looking document.

The bishop plucked it from his files. He then put on his cutaway coat and striped pants and approached the sentry at the Soochow Creek Bridge – presenting the letter with a flourish. The troubled sentry read it, sucked air through his teeth, and called the officer in charge. This soldier, too, read it with care and was also greatly troubled. As he stood in doubt and irresolution, the bishop took the letter, said "thank you," and walked by.

At General Matsui's headquarters, they were also astonished to see him and disturbed by the letter. There was a great scurrying, but at last, the letter and the bishop were sent in to the general. The general appeared dubious, and the bishop said he would be most unhappy to report to America that the Japanese refused to allow inspection of church property. Since they were not quite ready for Pearl Harbor, the general, at last, consented for the bishop "and his entourage" to make the journey under escort. The bishop, of course, had no entourage, but he supplied one, taking along other missionaries as "clerks" and "chauffeurs." They were escorted by a Colonel Oka, who slept lightly in the room with the bishop at each stop. From Colonel Oka, the bishop learned, with some discouragement, of how the winebibbers of the earth have been able to spread an obscure Biblical verse about the world to annoy good Methodists, who emphatically do not look with favor upon wine or strong drink. One cold night, as they sat around a fire near Soochow, the Colonel obtained some sake and offered a drink to the bishop. "No, thank you," said the bishop. "Doesn't your Bible say to take a little wine for the stomach's sake?" asked the grinning Shinto sinner. When the party returned to Shanghai, the bishop felt that prestige, custom, and appreciation called for a dinner. Colonel Oka was among those invited. Naturally, no wines were served. The Colonel arrived in a jovial mood, smelling loudly of sake. About midway through the meal, he had lost his edge, and the bishop was startled to hear him call, "Oh, beesh-opp. There is something wrong with my stomach."

Some years later, General Matsui, chief guest at that dinner, was hanged as a war criminal in Tokyo.

Bishop Moore is a firm admirer and old friend of General Chiang Kai-shek. He believes him to be a sincere Christian. In one of his rare ventures into the political controversy, he was outspoken in his support of the Chiang government and has endorsed continued aid to an alliance with the Generalissimo. He has visited Chiang on Formosa and believes the Army there is loyal and that it and Chiang merit confidence.

Chiang was baptized a Christian and a Methodist by a Chinese bishop, Kiang Chang-Chuan, who apologized a few months ago for having performed this symbolic ritual. In the course of the speech on behalf of the new organization of the church in China under communist direction, Bishop Kiang also denounced Chiang as a tool of imperialists and an enemy of the Chinese people.

Bishop Kiang and Bishop Moore were warm friends and associates, and although greatly distressed by the reported speech, the president of the Council of Bishops refuses to pass judgment on its maker.

"I will retain confidence in Bishop Kiang and all others in his position in other countries under communist rule until we know the facts," he says. "We do not know what pressures they are under. I recall my own less arduous days in Korea."

Recently the bishop received a letter smuggled out of China. It was from a young Chinese minister whom the bishop had confirmed and started on his way.

"Do not send any letters, cables, or literature to any of us in China," the letter said. "When the General Conference meets, do not seat any Chinese in America as representing the church in China."

That letter has meaning far beyond the instructions, he believes. "Until we can get behind those curtains and know the truth," he says, "We must not cease to believe in the men whom we knew and love." The bishop does not believe either the Chinese or Russian communists will be able to conquer forever the Christian, democratic spirit in the countries they now control. He was in Czechoslovakia when the Germans took the Sudetenland. He went to call on his friend, Eduard Benes. The Czech president, in deep sorrow and foreseeing the agony ahead, told him he had that morning gone to the grave of Thomas Masaryk and prayed there.

"Tell the world that Masaryk and I did our best to build here a democratic nation with a free religious life," he said as they parted.

"The world is poorer because the Czech flame is temporarily extinguished," Moore said, "but it is not gone forever. It burns in the hearts of millions in that unhappy country. The Christian, democratic spirit is immortal."

One of his greatest thrills came at a conference held in Frankfurt, Germany in 1946, the first after the war's end. Representatives were there from all over Europe. Many German pastors had been imprisoned, and fifty-two had lost their lives during the war. The conference opened with a hymn that begins, "And are we yet alive, and see each other's face?"

"It was a magnificent, emotional moment. Most of those singing had tears in their eyes, but triumph in their voices and hearts. A great revival has continued in Germany ever since, and much of it is in the Russian Zone. "I believe the Christians of the communist-held countries will one day be able to meet with their old comrades and brothers and sing the same hymn," says Bishop Moore. "If any man has had a chance to see these monstrous forces which have been turned loose in the world which threaten us today, I am that man. I hold tenaciously and triumphantly that out of this insanity and horror will come to a better world. I believe this because I believe in the character and sovereignty of God. He has not abdicated. He will not allow the folly of man to rule forever. One day God will break in on that folly. This is not the end of things."

Saturday Evening Post, November 10, 1951, p. 34.

Editor's Note:
Throughout Bishop Moore's episcopal career publicity stated that Arthur J. Moore was elected to the episcopacy on the first ballot. In a close examination of the Journal of the General Conference 1930, there was *no election* on the first ballot. On the second ballot, there were 446 ballots cast, 221were required for an election. Arthur J. Moore received 209. There was no election on the second ballot. However, on the third ballot 441 ballots were cast, and 217 were required for an election. Arthur J. Moore received 233 votes and was elected on the third ballot.

CHAPTER TWO

A Missionary Journey to Europe and the Belgian Congo
February – April 1936

My assignment by the General Conference in Jackson, [Mississippi] to live and labor in seven of the important mission fields of the world marked a distinct epoch in my life. That commission ushered me across the threshold of a new world – a world filled with hungering, aspiring people alternating between hope and despair; I have tried faithfully to administer the work of our church in all these lands – so different in a thousand ways and yet so alike in their need of the life-giving and transforming power of the Christian gospel.

Because of the vast distances between fields and the demands of the work in the Orient and Europe, it was February 1936 before I could start the long journey to our mission in the heart of the Belgian Congo. A sea voyage of twenty-five days from Shanghai allowed some rest after seven busy and happy months in the Orient. I took advantage of a month's stay in Europe to visit our missions in Belgium, Czechoslovakia, and Poland. It was my third sojourn in these fields, I am beginning to feel very much at home. Recent governmental interference with our work in Poland made the visit to that country timely. The Christian movement has always had to battle with age-old human passions, but in these modern days, the forces of racial prejudice and narrow nationalism have come forth to oppose its teaching and hinder its progress.

In many lands, we see the hand of the state with dirty fingernails reaching for the garments of the bride of Christ. The mad militarists would not only demand that the youth of the world follow them in the stupidity of war, but they also seek to conscript human freedom. Rulers seem more interested in building up their reputations and exaggerating their importance than in producing a safe and friendly world.

Having completed the visit to our European fields, I crossed the English Channel to London to meet my good friend, Homer Rodeheaver, who has agreed to accompany me on the journey to Africa. He is paying all his expenses and is going because of his love for the people. To have sufficient time to study the problem confronting the missionaries in the Congo, visit all the stations and preside over the Annual Mission Meeting, it seems necessary to make the journey by air. Both the English and Belgian lines from Europe to Africa are equipped with modern planes designed especially for service in that land of desert and jungle. Some of my friends seem to think I have chosen the airplane because of its novelty. Such is not the case. Three conferences in the Orient in the autumn and three in Europe in the summer make air travel a necessity if one is to have sufficient time to know the field. The airplanes are here. They may be used to drop bombs on defenseless villages or to carry mail, medicines, and missionaries.

Africa is second in size only to Asia. If one will get out a map and measure the distance from Brussels, where we begin our flight, to Luluaberg, where we leave the plane, he will discover it to be approximately seven thousand miles. The Belgian Air Service crosses the Mediterranean Sea and follows a course over Western Africa. When Bishop Walter Lambuth, accompanied by the faithful John Wesley Gilbert, went to the Congo in 1912, they traveled on foot along native paths or elsewhere carried in hammocks by scores of black men, who relieved one another at frequent intervals. These pioneers were lucky to make ten or fifteen miles a day. Here, I am twenty-four years later going in by air, making a thousand to fifteen hundred miles a day, and accomplishing in six days what would require forty days by other means of travel. In these articles, I am attempting to write down in a general but intimate way, something of my experiences on the journey.

It is no longer necessary, in the language of David Livingstone, to "beg to direct your attention to Africa." The nations of the world are disputing over Africa. The peace of the world is involved in what is happening there. If these notes of mine help the Methodists of America to consider Africa, I shall be glad.

Here we are, on April 24, in the home of Rev. W. G. Thonger, Superintendent of our work in Belgium. We have spent some days outfitting ourselves. I doubt whether our American friends would recognize us in these boots and helmets and some days "hickory" shirts and khaki trousers. The journey will not be without danger. The knowledge that we are on the King's business assures us of His protecting care.

Saturday, April 25, 1936

We were called by Thonger at 3:00 a.m. After a cup of coffee, we motored about five miles to the airport. It is quite large, with waiting rooms and every facility for travel. There were those last-minute formalities, such as weighing both passengers and baggage. We are allowed only forty-five pounds of baggage, and although I had reduced mine to the lowest possible amount, it was seven pounds in excess.

The weather is very foggy and "the ceiling" is very low. A huge mail plane from Berlin has been flying over our heads for some minutes trying to find the landing field. Our plane is now in front of the waiting room and the three motors are being tested. It is a Fokker with a wingspan of more than seventy feet.

There are seats for only three passengers, as much of this space is reserved for mail and express going to the Congo. There are three officers in the plane – a first pilot, a second pilot, and a radio mechanic. They are all trim young fellows, and much to our delight, we discover they speak some English.

The order to go onboard has come. The roar of these mighty engines makes it difficult to be heard as we try to say goodbye. We leave the ground without a jar, and in less than five minutes we are in that thick fog which caused the German plane so much trouble. It is not yet daylight – and we climb up to seven thousand feet as we leave Brussels. It is impossible to describe the glorious sunrise as we see it up here. Slowly the light dispels the darkness, dries the fog away and we catch our first bird's eye view of beautiful little Belgium. How green and peaceful it appears.

We have now crossed the French border, making for Marseilles on the Mediterranean. The Argonne Forest is below us. Mile upon mile of trenches used in the World War can be seen. There were some of the fiercest fights of the war. Our American boys held a large sector of this line. In other sections of France, the trenches have long since been filled, but as there is little farming here, they have been allowed to remain as the boys left them in November 1918.

Never did I expect to see the Alps from above, but these lines are being written at an altitude of eight thousand feet above the French Alps. Down the beautiful Rhone River Valley and over the city of Lyons, and at 9:05 a.m., we are on the field of Marseilles taking gas. Here we start a six-hundred-mile flight, practically all of it over the sea. This is a landplane, and what would we do in case of an accident is not quite clear. We are not far from the coast of Spain, near enough, to look down upon the beautiful city of Barcelona.

We have said goodbye to land until we catch sight of northern Africa. The beautiful Mediterranean has a charm of its own. Now and then we catch sight of a ship, but I will feel better with some kind of land beneath us. Exactly at 2:30 p.m., we sight Africa – and soon we are down on an airfield in Oran, Algeria. In this city is the [greatest] mixture of races I have seen. We have been in the air for eleven hours and traveled eleven hundred and forty miles. We find a modern hotel with [enormous] prices, and after a warm bath and a good dinner, we go to bed – tomorrow we plunge into the Sahara Desert.

Sunday, April 26, 1936

What a strange Sabbath! In the air in Africa above the Sahara! We left Oran at 5:00 a.m., and in less than an hour all the beauty and fertility of the Mediterranean coast have disappeared and we are far out over the sandy wastes of this great desert. I am very surprised to find rugged mountains – so high that we had to climb up to seven thousand feet to pass over.

It is now afternoon. I began these notes while on the plane this morning, but the air became so rough that our plane rose and fell like a tiny vessel on a stormy sea. Sandstorms such as I had never seen filled the skies and we were "flying blind." Now and then we would catch sight of that endless stretch of sand beneath. Here and there could be seen lonely caravans with many camels. Where they were going and why they had chosen such a lonely road, I know not. Perhaps their journey and destination were as important to them as ours to us.

Rodeheaver and I have not talked much today. The truth is we have both been airsick. The continuous rise and fall of the plane have made us wish for terra-firma.

Believe it or not, right out in the center of the desert we found a little city of four thousand inhabitants. Its name is Columbo-Bechar. It was at this place only a week ago that Amy Mollison, the famous English woman flyer, crashed and wrecked her plane. She was attempting to recapture the record for the fastest trip from London to Cape Town. In her attempts to take off with an extra load of gasoline, she struck a dune and destroyed her plane. The mechanic who had come out from London to repair it was a nice chap and a Methodist.

After thirty minutes at Columbo-Bechar, we left for Raggan, where we are spending the night. We had four more hours of that same treacherous, nauseating "choppy" air, but at last caught sight of an oasis with a few palm trees, a soldiers' barracks, and this rest house where we now are. Never have I seen a tree appear so lovely as these palms growing out here in this land of desolation.

We had much difficulty at supper tonight convincing our host that we drank water only. Wine and whiskey were much more plentiful, but after some persuasion, mineral water was brought forth, and we paid a good deal more for it than the price of wine. Rodeheaver got out his famous, much-traveled trombone and played "When you come to the end of a perfect day." Why he thought that appropriate is beyond me. So, to bed to end the strangest Sabbath of my life. Well, I have enough for one day. Good night!

Monday, April 27, 1936

We are up long before daylight to start our flight at the very first appearance of dawn. This is to be our second day in the desert. I am hopeful that it will be smoother than yesterday. Well, like yesterday, these notes were started early in the morning but were laid aside before we had been up an hour. We had another terrific day over that awful, overheated, windswept land of desolation. Through vast stretches, there are no landmarks by which the pilot can determine his course. He must depend absolutely on his compass. You fly for hours with nothing but sand beneath dust storms sweep up and hide the sun.

It is necessary to refuel the plane during the day. The Shell Oil Company has installed a gasoline station in the very heart of the desert. It is the loneliest spot I know anywhere in the world. Two men compose the entire population of Bison-Sank, as it is called. We drop down out of a dust storm to make a perfect landing. How the aviator ever found that spot is a miracle.

Leaving Bison-Sank, we were off for our longest single hop of the entire flight – from 9:05 a.m. until 4:55 p.m. without the sight of a living thing. Almost halfway the company has erected in the desert a white cross. It is the one guidepost in that wilderness of sand. Find that cross and all is well. Miss it and you are lost. I have no word to describe our thrill when we sighted it at about 2:00 p.m. Our pilot made a circle about it and then took a straight course for Niamey, where we are spending the night. What a parable of life! The way of the cross leads home.

Tuesday, April 28, 1936

The heat last night was terrible. We had little sleep. The hotel hardly deserves the name. We had our evening meal outside, dressed only in pajamas because of the intense heat. Once more we were off at dawn. Except for a storm in the late afternoon, which I shall describe later, this has been an average day.

We usually have a cup of coffee early in the morning and no other food until night. Fortunately, I brought along some dried figs and milk chocolate. They have been lifesavers. There is no opportunity for small talk during the flight. Our ears are stopped with cotton to soften the everlasting hum of the three motors. We can read some, but after four days, my nerves are on edge and I cannot concentrate on my book.

At 3:00 p.m., we had our most thrilling and certainly our most dangerous experience. We flew head-on into an African tornado. The lightning flashed and the wind handled our huge plane like a leaf. We were blown sideways – lifted upward – and dropped into huge air pockets. How long it would last or what would be the end no one knew. We were all frightened, and when an hour later we were able to land safely at Fort Lamey, gratitude to God filled our hearts.

We are now out of the desert. While not yet in the Belgian Congo, sand has given way to jungles. After landing this afternoon, Rodeheaver and I took a walk through the village to quiet our nerves and see how the natives live. We saw hundreds of black men and women with but little or no clothing. Somehow it does not shock as much as you would expect. A simple loincloth constitutes their entire wardrobe – and frequently they discard even that.

We asked if there were any missionaries near, and were directed to the mission of the Reverend Mr. Alley, a New Zealander. He had been out [here] for seventeen years without a furlough, has mastered four dialects, and is doing splendid work. Most of the people in this section are Moslems, and converting them to Christianity is most difficult.

Wednesday, April 29, 1936

The world beneath us has completely changed. The desert with its wind and dust has given place to a dense jungle and wide rivers. The air currents are no longer unruly. We were up for eight and a half hours today – floating through space at the rate of one hundred twenty miles an hour – the blue sky above – endless swamps below. We have been flying all day either directly above or else within sight of one of Africa's numerous rivers. Within twenty-four hours, I have seen more wild animals than in all the balance of my life – herds of antelope, giraffes, elephants, gazelles, ostriches, hippopotamuses bathing in the river, with literally hundreds of monkeys in the forests and crocodiles splashing into the water from the riverbanks. A circus menagerie will always seem drab and pitiful after the wonderful game we have seen today.

Tonight, is our first in the Belgian Congo. Since last Saturday morning, we have been flying over French territory. This line is being written at Coquilhatville, a town situated right on the equator. The Congo River is its only connection with the outside world except for the air service. The rain is falling outside in such volume as I have never seen before. Tomorrow, if all goes well, we are due at our Congo mission. What distance have we come in these days!

Travel in Africa has made such progress. When Bishop Lambuth came to open our mission he traveled on foot, with scores of men carrying his hammock, making ten or fifteen miles a day. Even as late as Bishop [James] Cannon's visit a few years ago, that kind of travel was the best Africa had to offer.

The distance from Brussels to Luluaberg, where we leave the plane, is approximately seven thousand miles. We have made the journey in less than six days – more than a thousand miles a day. Certainly, the world has changed, even in Africa! And now for that quinine which the doctor has ordered each day to combat malaria, and I'll say good night. Tomorrow night I expect to sleep in the comfortable bed of some missionary friend.

Thursday, April 30, 1936

We were glad to get an early start on the last day of our air journey. The rain of last night had left low cloud banks which made our take-off a bit difficult. We soared up through the clouds and for three hours look down only on white without the sight of the ground. At 10:00 a.m. we left the plane which had been our home for nearly a week and took another plane that flew from Leopardville to Elizabethville.

We regretfully said goodbye to the pilots and radio officer. Their skill over desert and jungle, through cloud and storm, cannot be overpraised. Now we are on another plane. Instead of three passengers, we are now seven. Across the aisle are two fellow missionaries – Miss Miller, of the Presbyterian mission at Lusbo, and Miss Mary Foreman, of our own Congo mission, returning from a furlough visit to her home at Amarillo, Texas. Miss Miller also resuming her labors in the Congo after furlough in America. Although this is their first air journey, they act like veterans. They are thrilled at the thought of "getting home."

Promptly at 3:30 p.m., we sighted Luluaberg. The pilot circled the airport twice to give Rodeheaver a chance to get some good movies of the field. Down there on the ground, I caught sight of Dr. and Mrs. W. B. Lewis, of our hospital at Runda; Rev. J. J. Davis, an old boyhood friend now at Minga; Joe Maw, who has charge of our transport service; and Mr. Crane, of the Presbyterian mission. They had driven 200 miles to welcome us to the Congo.

We are on the ground – out of the air into the warm hospitality of God's people. This poor heart of mine is filled with gratitude to God for journeying mercies, for Christian friends, and for the privilege of coming to this continent to have a small share in building the Kingdom.

We hurry over to the radio station to start a cable to the loved ones beyond the swelling seas, saying "safe and well." Into automobiles for a four-hour drive to Lubondai, where our Southern Presbyterian friends are doing such magnificent work. Although it was 9:00 p.m. when we arrived, the missionaries were out to welcome us – a good Southern dinner, which included fried chicken. I don't know how soon this feeling of being up in the air in the hum of those motors will leave me, but tonight I am happy with friends and a task to perform.

Editor's Notes:
1. A hickory shirt is made of strong twilled cotton fabric with vertical stripes and is used especially for work clothing. From the early 1940s until the mid-1980s the Lee Company was the industry standard for the Hickory shirt, button-front, or zip. It also is called the railroad shirt and the fabric is known as hickory fabric, a relative of denim and as durable as hickory wood. One could say this is the shirt that built this country.
2. Today known as Mbandaka (pronounced mba-nda-ka.) It is a city on the Congo in the Democratic Republic of Congo, located near the confluence of the Congo and Ruki rivers.

Editor's Note: This manuscript is from the Bishop's files housed at the Pitts Theology Library, Emory University, Atlanta, Georgia.

Bishop Moore with Chief Wembo Nyama at the Methodist Mission in the
Belgian Congo.

CHAPTER THREE
Experiences and Impressions in China 1937-1938

December 22, 1937

Shanghai has been called the "city with two souls" because in this international metropolis one finds a strange mixture of Western civilization and Oriental antiquity. But the Shanghai I found on my arrival was not the one I left ten months ago. Since the thirteenth day of August, one of the fiercest battles of history has gone on in and around this city of more than 3 million inhabitants. Vast areas of fine buildings have been destroyed. Hundreds of thousands of men have died, and while the armies have now gone further inland the city remains a war zone. Practically every street corner has sandbag fortifications and barbed wire entanglements. Much of the city is under martial law and the Japanese troops go swaggering through the main thoroughfares. The widest rumors are running like electric currents throughout the whole population, but one does not need rumors because the facts are bad enough.

The gallant stand of the Chinese army ended at last in a retreat. Even the Japanese bear testimony to their heroism. The key cities of Soochow, Changchow, and Nanking have fallen. The Chinese government has been removed to Chungking, seven hundred fifty miles west of Nanking. Without a Declaration of War, Japan is conducting a major military operation that is in direct violation of treaties in which she has solemnly promised to respect Chinese territorial integrity.

When I was in Africa strange stories of death and destruction in Ethiopia reached my ears, but this is even worse. Old and proud cities have come under the most devastating shell fire and bombing. Thousands of innocent and helpless men, women, and children have been ruthlessly slaughtered. The prospects of religion, the teaching of philosophers, and even the primary resolutions against needless bloodshed seem to have all been swept aside to satisfy the greed and ambition of the god of war.

December 25, 1937

Today is Christmas, the season of peace and goodwill among all men, but it is hard to develop the Christmas spirit here. Outside my window are several hundred hungry refugees waiting to enter Moore Memorial Church for a bowl of rice. This is their total food supply. I was in a refugee camp this morning where there were seventeen thousand sick, hungry, and homeless people. The total number in Shanghai alone is above three hundred thousand. The weather is very cold and heating these camps is out of the question. One might finally adjust himself to the horrors of the battlefields, but the bitter agony of the suffering civilians tends to depress one spirit. One wonders if our scientific age has invented mechanical devices that we are unable to control. The unending reception of bad news in the sight of all the suffering tries one's soul almost beyond endurance.

At 11:00 a.m. today, I stood to preach to a congregation of approximately fourteen hundred Chinese people. Nothing I had said before seemed appropriate for this kind of situation. I took for my text Isaiah 53:1, 2 – "he was a man of sorrow and acquainted with grief." My message had to do with Christ's identification with the struggles and sorrows of his children. Having known sorrow, he can comfort all who mourn.

This afternoon we had a long and interesting conference with the Japanese Consul General. In substance this is what we said to the highest Japanese authority we could reach: "The recent hostilities and occupation of this region by the Japanese Armed Forces have greatly affected mission work. We are under the necessity of reporting fully to our home churches, not only about the present conditions of the work but also about the prospects for the immediate future. We cannot avoid expressing to you our deep grief and disappointment at the way mission work has been interfered with by the Japanese Armed Forces. We have been led to expect the Japanese soldiers would give due consideration to all noncombatants, and the nations on friendly terms with the Imperial Japanese government, instead of such consideration we have seen many of our American owned churches, hospitals, schools, private residences, and other buildings occupied and looted or destroyed by uniform Japanese soldiers. This happened not only during the fighting but even after the Japanese occupation has been established. Yet even this loss of property we consider slight in comparison with the lack of consideration shown to our efforts to relieve the sufferings of countless civilians, especially the women. We earnestly hope, given the recent assurance given the American government, that from now on such occupation of our property and interference with our legitimate work will cease."

At the close of our Conference, the Consul General suggested that he arrange a meeting for us with General Matsui, who is in charge of military operations. We will see what we see. In the meantime, I am besieging them to permit me to visit our centers in the war zone.

January 10, 1938

Imagine my delight when the Japanese authorities announced their willingness for me to visit the occupied areas. With W. B. Burke, R. T. Henry, and J. H. Berekmann of our mission, we left Shanghai last Friday for Sungkiang. Sentries challenged us time and time again but our military passes got us through. We found the roads almost impassable and it required hours to cover a short distance. We reached our destination about four in the afternoon to find ancient and lovely old Sungkiang where Burke had labored for fifty years in ashes. Our mission buildings have been bombed and completely looted. Two large school buildings have been burned to the ground. A city of eighty thousand population had been reduced to six thousand. Never have I seen such destruction. Here it was war at its worst.

As we drove into the city, the few people remaining were surprised, as we were the first people except enemies to visit them in months. Soon someone spied Burke and began to shout his Chinese name in a loud voice. Out from the debris old men, women, and children climbed together around and shouted his name, exclaiming, "If you have been here this sorrow would not have come to us." It was one of the most moving sights of my life. We pressed our way through narrow streets, followed by the entire population. One old man said, "Brother Burke has returned, and his three sons came to bring him." What does being a bishop amount to when you can be regarded as the son of a missionary who by love dominates the entire city?

January 16, 1938

We have been to Soochow, and what we saw has increased my sorrow. I feel years older than when I wrote my notes a week ago. We were allowed to travel to Sungkiang alone, but Soochow was something different. We were given a high military officer and a member of the Japanese Embassy as escorts. They did not fail to impress us with the danger of such a journey. We were traveling in territory held by thousands of armed Japanese troops where there are also bands of Chinese troops left. One was in danger of being fired on at any moment.

From Shanghai to Soochow is about sixty miles, and the whole area was the scene of the most stubborn fighting. Scarcely a house is left standing. The villages are all empty. The roadside is lined with trucks, tanks, trenches, and concrete machine-gun nests. Not all the dead bodies have been buried. It is a land of desolation and destruction.

Our church has in Soochow, a university, a normal school for women, a hospital, three large churches, and another half dozen primary and middle schools. These, coupled with a dozen missionary residences, made it the "Capital of Southern Methodism in China." In all our institutions we have approximately a hundred buildings. We found that four of these buildings have been bombed, all buildings, including missionary residences, looted of everything of value, and that most of our property was occupied by Japanese soldiers. The beautiful new Laura Haygood Chapel has been converted into a stable for horses. While most of the buildings are standing it will take money, and a great deal of patience to make them usable again. The missionaries have spent long years accumulating lovely things for their residences. I never saw a dresser or trunk that was not open, nearly all doors broken in, and everything of value stolen. When they return they must start all over again. It was hard to hold one's tongue in the presence of such a scene.

But the destruction of property is insignificant compared to the suffering of the population. The Japanese estimated there were eighty thousand people in the city, but the normal population is about three hundred thousand. Where are the others? What has become of the women?

It is well-nigh impossible to exaggerate the orgy of looting, murder, and rape that took place following the entrance of Japanese soldiers into the conquered territory. While defeated Chinese soldiers staged their share of looting before evacuation, there was a virtual collapse of discipline in certain sections of the Japanese army, and harbors were perpetuated which exceeded those attributed to the worst bandits China has ever known. Some of us believe the Japanese troops would at least bring order out of chaos. Imagine our grief when well-authenticated reports from Nanking, written by foreign newspaper correspondence and missionaries, stated: "the whole outlook was ruined by frequent murders, wholesale looting, and uncontrolled disturbance of private homes, including offenses against the security of women. Foreigners who were permitted to travel about the city counted at least one dead civilian in every city block. People who ran in fear and excitement were caught in the streets by roving patrols and were killed on the spot. Shooting and bayoneting went on in the safety zones as well as elsewhere. Squads of men picked out as former Japanese soldiers were tied together and shot in bunches by rifle and machine gunfire. From one building in the refugee zone 400 men were singled out and were tied in bunches of 50 and marched off between lines of machine gunners. There was no doubt as to their fate. There was no trace of prisoners in Japanese hands other than the groups on the way to execution grounds, except those compelled to carry loot and equipment for the Japanese militarists. The general conduct of the Japanese troops which included the plundering of thousands of private homes and even robbery of refugees created a feeling of nausea on the part of foreigners who have read the statements of suave Japanese military [leaders.]"

January 17, 1938

Yesterday was a quiet Sunday and I went to hear Ms. Muriel Lester of Kingsley Hall, London preach. Her text was "Be of good cheer, I have overcome the world." Surely Christ can help us keep our heads and our hearts in a world like this. Despite all I see around me, the dream of the coming of the Kingdom of

God on earth is not a dream but a solid reality beneath my feet. I do believe in the ultimate supremacy of goodness.

January 24, 1938

The China Annual Conference closed last night. The attendance was small, but the spirit was good. Only one-third of the membership could reach Shanghai on account of war conditions. A few Chinese preachers, at great risk of life, made their way through the Japanese lines and answered roll call.

In some Conferences, where I have presided, the making of reports was a most uninteresting item of business. Not so here. Practically every person present – missionaries and Chinese – has been under the deadly machine-gun fire of airplanes. All had fled for their lives. Some had spent considerable time in the dugouts before the fiercest fighting drove them out. Some while traveling the open country roads have been forced to flee into the wet rice fields and stretch themselves on the ground to escape the reign of death. All have seen their personal belongings swept away as their residences have been either been looted or destroyed. Families have been separated from each other. Parents were looking for children and children begging for parents. Alas, some will not be found. The old Methodist Conference hymn, "And Are We Yet Alive" must have been written for the China Conference this year.

The date had been postponed to allow scattered workers to gather if possible. It is well-nigh impossible and certainly unwise for the Chinese to travel. On one road a few weeks ago, I counted a dozen dead bodies in a distance of less than half a mile. Missionaries are not permitted to leave Shanghai for their stations in the interior. We have been able to gather but little information touching the fate of mission properties in many cities and villages where we have worked.

The Conference devoted three days to a very earnest study of our present position, problems, and possibilities in evangelism, Christian education, and medical work. It is hard to forecast the future. In some ways, we are back where the pioneers were in the beginning. Equipment in schools and hospitals is gone, and students and congregations are scattered. The future will demand not only courage to face difficulties, but wisdom to find ways and means of carrying on.

For some time, it will be dangerous for the Chinese to travel and it is hoped the Japanese will relax and permit missionaries to minister to the people. The morale of the workers is high. The Chinese people are not given to wailing over what is happened. They take a long look and set in the belief that conditions will right themselves.

The appointments were read Sunday night. The Sacrament of the Lord's Supper was administered. All those to be appointed gathered about the altar of the church to sing, "Faith of Our Fathers." In another twelve hours pastors, dressed in the garb of the very poor, were out on the roads and canals trying to work their way through the enemy's lines, to reach their scattered congregations.

How I wish the church in America could see what their gifts are doing in China in this time of need. But for the help from America these pastors, teachers, doctors, nurses, and multiplied thousands of church members would be without the absolute necessities of life. My plea to all who read these lines is, to send a gift to the Board of Missions for relief work in China. Large funds must be found somewhere to reestablish and reinforce our many activities.

In a few days, I must leave China for Korea and then on to Japan. The church is facing perplexing problems in all these countries. It is hard to leave China at this time, as these people need and appreciate the help so much. There are some things I can never forget:

The long line of frightened, helpless people feels her safety.

The eagerness of missionaries to return to their places of work.

The refugees, numbering more than three hundred thousand crowded and poorly equipped camps in Shanghai.

The dead bodies on the roadside, the overturned trucks, and the terrible amount of wreckage after the armies passed on.

The vast stretches of ruins in certain cities where war has done its worst.

The people in the streets especially little children looked frightened whenever an airplane appeared in the sky.

The few old people left in the fields trying to patch up their burned homes and grow a little something to eat.

The look of fear on the faces of Chinese people, especially women, in the areas dominated by the Japanese.

The long hours I spent pleading, flattering, scolding Japanese for their foolish delays in permitting us to visit our property.

The indignation I felt when I found all missionary residences looted in the beautiful chapel of Laura Haygood school and suture out being used as a stable.

The struggle I have had to believe that mankind is civilized when it allows stupid aggression like this to go unchallenged.

The thrill in my heart while Christian people's possessions have been taken and for whom the future was uncertain stood to sing triumphantly – "Faith of our fathers living still despite dungeon fire and sword – we will be true to Thee."

March 22, 1938

After the thought and reflections on these days in America, I'm writing this plea. I am at home and rejoicing in the fellowship of friends and the beautiful atmosphere of Christian – yes, by comparison, to me still 'Christian America! – America." But I am aware that much of my real self I have left behind. All the sympathy of which my heart is capable is there. My deep concern and wish for them by way of the Throne keeps turning back. I have been saying these things to the Church. I, knowing nothing more to say than to give you the facts. But let me in the best human way that I can command call to you on behalf of China.

I beg you to remember the missionaries. I have no words to describe the courage, endurance, and heroic loyalty of the missionaries in a time like this. Your missionaries expect your understanding and support. Our own Chinese Christians, in their sense of utter desolation, look to us, to the good God through us, for relief and help. This great nation of people, four hundred million, five hundred million – who knows how many – vastly beyond count, overrun, trampled underfoot, violated, and bleeding.

The few leaders, brave and noble, are still hopeful, and dare to believe that their Methodist comrades in America will not desert them now. I have made my appeal to the Board of Missions. I make it again to the members of the General Conference. What to do – who knows? Beyond all these, dark and distressing conditions are the eternal and inexhaustible resources of the Living Christ. God is still on the throne, maybe in all this He is guiding, maybe opening up the way to give Methodism a new opportunity to take its place and bear witness still to both China and Japan.

Missionaries will not be withdrawn, bound as they are to their Chinese colleagues, through a fellowship of suffering; rather their number should be strengthened. The church cannot falter now, it will pit against the forces of evil and destruction all that it has – the ministry of Christian service and the example of brotherly love. There must be even greater ministrations to the body, the mind, and the heart. We must keep alive the belief of the individual and his value as a child of God; we must foster a love for justice, and fire it with a living hope for its ultimate consummation; above and beyond everything else we must discover and appropriate the resources of the Eternal Christ as the one enduring hope of is sorely tried and needy world.

Editor's Notes:
1. From the papers of Bishop Moore, Pitts Theology Library, Emory University, Atlanta, Georgia

2. Sungkiang or Songjiang was a province (c.32,000 sq mi/82,880 km) of the Republic of China. Mudanjiang was the capital. It was one of nine provinces created in Manchuria by the Chinese Nationalist government after World War I. It was bordered on the east by the USSR, and along part of the southern border ran the Nen (Nonni) and Songhua Rivers.

3. A letter to Bishop Moore from the Chinese Executive Committee, Z. T. Kaung, J. H. Berkman, and S. R. Anderson, detailing the damage to Methodist Episcopal Church, South property in several cities can be seen on page 485 of the addendum.

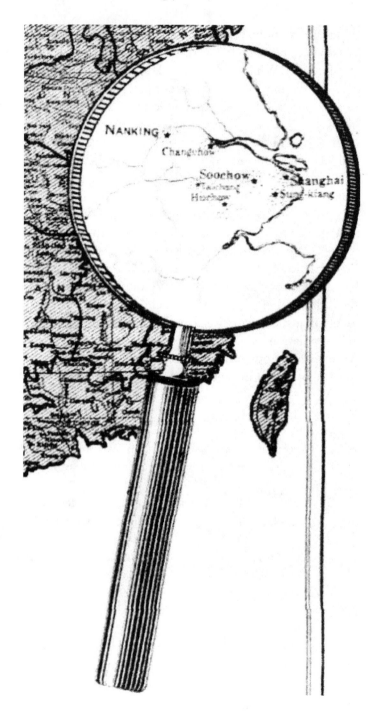

CHAPTER FOUR

Bishop Moore's Report to the General Conference of the Methodist Episcopal Church, South, Birmingham, Alabama, 1938

Throughout this quadrennium, I have had the privilege and responsibility of participating in the Christian missionary enterprise around the world. I am humbly grateful for the privilege of sharing in a movement that has made and is making such notable contributions to the welfare of the human family.

During these four years, I have traveled constantly to Africa, Belgium, China, Czechoslovakia, Japan, Korea, and Poland. In all these nations I have found rare friendships, and unique opportunities, and had the high honor of sharing in the creative enterprises of the kingdom of God. It has been my serious purpose to be a faithful administrator of the work of our Church in a complex and critical period of human history.

It was my privilege to succeed Bishop U.V.W. Darlington in Europe, Bishop James Cannon, Jr., in Africa, and Bishop Paul B. Kern in the Oriental fields. Everywhere I have found evidence of their efficient administration. They are much beloved by the people of the fields over which they presided.

My task has been made easier because of their continued interests and helpful assistance. In this connection, let me record my appreciation of the unfailing and constructive assistance of Dr. W.G. Cram, the General Secretary of the Board of Mission, Dr. A.W. Wasson, Foreign Secretary, General Section, and Miss Sallie Lou McKinnon, Foreign Secretary, Women's Section.

Their intimate knowledge of their fields, coupled with wise and sympathetic administration, makes it a joy to labor with them.

Our Missionaries

It has been an enriching experience to know and labor with our missionaries. In every field, I have found them enthusiastically loyal to Christ and the Church. They have identified themselves beautifully and sacrificially with the aspirations and struggles of the people to whom they have gone. They feel the cruel burdens that rest upon their brothers and sisters as though they rested upon their shoulders. They are occupied with the proclamations of a great gospel – a gospel adequate to satisfy the deepest longings and highest aspirations of the human race. They have let loose in the world a stream of understanding and sympathy for the underprivileged. Through their sacrificial labors, uncounted numbers have found in Christ forgiveness of sins and a new life in God.

The most inspiring and comforting thing I have seen around the world is this army of devout, patient, courageous men and women. In moral character and unselfish devotion to the welfare of others, they rank as high or higher than any group in the world. I salute them for their noble fortitude and invincible good temper. It is the solemn duty of the Church in America to give not less but more in both personnel and money. Choice young men and women of unquestioned consecration and outstanding talents with special training should be sent forth to reinforce our missionaries in every field. As a result of the Bishops' Crusade, our Board of Missions has already been able to stop the retreat, but we must have sufficient force to attempt a bold offensive on every battlefront.

The General Situation

In practically every part of the world, the situation is chaotic, confused, and admittedly critical. No one will deny that we live in a fateful hour.

Running loose in the world are the rampant forces of racial prejudice, assertive nationalism, blind economics, coupled with the age-old passions and lusts of unregenerate humanity. One does not need a chart of the future to feel that the world is at a crossroads.

Not in my memory have there been so many sinister forces contesting the progress of Christianity. On every hand, the powerful anti-religious movements, with able leadership and generous financial support, have unfurled their banners and announced their purpose to drive the Church of Jesus Christ from the field of battle. Our missionaries and national Christian leaders live and labor at the very center of this critical world situation. They face a combination of problems such as would baffle the wisest counselors and challenge the boldest leadership. Only a united and courageous Church can meet the demands of such a situation.

However, the situation is not without encouragement. The steady progress of Christianity in these lands makes stirring reading and calls for gratitude. The books are not closed and many a golden page for the history of Christian Missions is being written. I have a deepened assurance of the adequacy and universality of the Christian message.

We may be in a time of transformation, but not of defeat. The growing complexity and difficulty of the work may call for reconsideration and restatement of plans and programs, but I was never so sure that in all the turmoil and confusion of individuals and nations Christ's uncompromising conquest goes on. The missionary enterprise rests not upon our human frailty and shifting economic conditions, but upon God's unchanging purpose and Christ's unwearied compassion for all men. In my heart is the assured hope of final and glorious success.

I am unable adequately to give here a detailed report on that far-flung enterprise to which you have sent your sons and daughters, your gifts, and your prayers. It is enough to say, the Church is being abundantly repaid for its sons and daughters who have gladly invested their lives in this great venture with Christ, and all the dollars appropriated across the years have yielded a large dividend.

In May 1937, the supervision of the Baltimore, Virginia, and Western Virginia Conferences were added to my responsibilities. Bishop Edwin D. Mouzon labored up to the very hour of his translation. Everywhere in these Conferences, I have found abundant evidence of his wise, sympathetic, and constructive leadership.

In these three Conferences, we have a strong Methodism, rich in Christian experience and historic background. In love for

Christ and loyal devotion to the program of the Church, these Conferences are unsurpassed. Here Methodism stands upright in the power of an assured faith in the teachings of Christ which expresses itself in zeal for all the redemptive enterprises of the kingdom of God. The kindly forbearance of our preachers and laymen and the friendship manifested by them during this brief but happy ministry will be gratefully cherished as one of the happiest and most inspiring memories of my ministry.

Contemplating the work with which Christ has charged His Church, I would summons us all to a more heroic practice of the gospel. Once more we must proclaim the message of Christ in supreme confidence. Admitting all the ugly facts, we must go forth facing every situation with courage. With a new vision of the conquering Savior, a more perfect allegiance to His will, and a new yielding to His passion to redeem all men, we must speedily lay the claim of Christ upon all the unoccupied areas of the world and human life.

Editor's Note: This report is from the papers of
  Bishop Arthur J. Moore, Pitts Theology Library,
  Emory University, Atlanta, Georgia.

Bishop Nagimiga of Japan, Bishop Moore,
and Bishop Ryang of Korea.
Bishop Ryang was captured by the Japanese, tortured and not
released at the end of the war and is presumed dead.

CHAPTER FIVE

The Flag of Faith is Never Furled

At some hour in the not-too-distant future, the order to "ceasefire" will be heard across the battlefields of the earth. Flags will be furled, armies demobilized, and the nations of the earth will turn again to the pursuits of peace.

Immediately thereafter, the Christian church will face an incomparable opportunity and a terrible responsibility. It will be met with a challenge that will demand all the devotion, farsightedness, and generosity of which it is capable. The postwar problems associated with the relief of human misery and the rehabilitation of missionary work will demand vision and sacrifice as great as those we are now making for the successful prosecution of the war. The church will stand on trial at the bar of mankind as perhaps never before. We are therefore to be under the logical and inescapable necessity of gathering together all the inspirations the past can yield, heeding the lessons of past defeats, so that the church, inspired by the spirit of the living Christ, may demonstrate that it is the instrument of God's will and the redemption of the world. There is a great need for renewed and fearless study of the mind of Christ so that we may ascertain the duty of the church to this day and generation.

It would be a gesture of insincerity and artificiality to deny or ignore the implications the present world situation holds for the church. Like every other worthy institution, it must re-examine its commission, define its standards, the defendant's teachings, and justify its existence.

Some cynic has declared, "The state of the church suggests the predicament of a referee who has swallowed his whistle and is, therefore, unable either to direct or stop the game." Always in times of great tension men began to ask: "What is the church doing?" Before long some fearful people declare that the church as an agency for world redemption is ineffective.

No one would deny that the world has been too much with the church. Too often the church has been tepid and full of compromise. More than one crisis has found it lacking in spiritual discernment and incapable of courageous action. But it is equally true that in most of the great crises of human history Christianity has exercised a powerful influence on affairs, whether human, national, or international. No one can imagine what the present state of the world would be if the Christian church had not been planted throughout the earth. The church has more than once moved against the evils of the world and its force has been irresistible. It has produced an unaccounted multitude of sincere, Christlike men and women who strive to see that the intentions of God are carried out.

Some writer has declared: "the eighteenth century believed, the nineteenth hoped, but the twentieth does neither." This statement is quoted not because one agrees, but to emphasize that mankind has been caught in the undertow of scientific materialism which has produced a philosophy of life in which there has been little room for God and spiritual ideals. Christians throughout the world are being stabbed awake by this hopelessness and chaos. Dr. H. Kraemer, in his *The Christian Message in a Non-Christian World,* declares: "The Tempest of contemporary history is forcing back the Christian church to fundamentals, to such a radically religious conception of life as is revealed to us in the Bible. We are exploring again the simple but revolutionary meaning of faith.
The Christian church is awakening to its responsibility to give clear and unequivocal answers to the questions that arise out of the thunder of events."

The inescapable conclusion of all this is that we must begin now to prepare for an extraordinary missionary offensive.
Otherwise, we are in danger of being enveloped by the inevitable reaction which always follows a long and costly war. Either we surrender to apathy or plan and execute a bold advance. Certainly, we cannot invade the challenge of the postwar situation. Here is as bracing and emancipating a challenge as was ever offered to Christians in any century.

Recently the writer was engaged in serious conversation with a devout layman. The subject of our conversation was the worldwide need for all Christianity offers. When I finished my part of the conversation this thoughtful layman looked at me and said: "Do you think the church is ready to play its part in this world situation?" Upon the answer to that question hangs the missionary ardor and the evangelistic passion of the church, and it is the secret to a safe, friendly, redeemed world. Surely we must give serious concern to the true nature of our faith if the church is to be the salt of the earth and the light of the world.

It is not difficult to envision the situation as we will face it at the end of the war. Europe and China and other vast sections of the earth will be a ghastly combination of poor house and cemetery. There will be burned buildings; scorched earth; many churches destroyed or damaged; our Christian constituency scattered, homeless, and starving; our schools, hospitals, and other institutions crippled; and beyond all this – famine, disease, and agony on a wider scale than has been known in recent centuries. We must rehabilitate our Methodist work and take our part in the general reconstruction of the world.

At the close of the last war, the demand was so great that it called forth the Centenary movement, in the course of which our churches gave close to $100 million to serve the world. At the close of this war, the demand will be much greater. Will we be ready to meet it? Will we be ready to gather the facts, develop the procedure, and to lead our people in a great redemptive crusade?

There is always a temptation to relax and swing back to isolationism and self-centered materialism. This is true of the nations. This is what occurred at the end of the last war, and it goes far to explain the present war. Some people think they discern public trends in that direction now. This may also be true of the church. The provincialism, the indifference to everybody and everything outside of our congregations, the anti-missionary attitude in some sections of our church – this all grew up after the end of World War I. Will there be another such reaction now?

Here is a sinister danger immediately before us. We must at any cost avoid it in the Methodist Church. We cannot keep it out of the Methodist Church unless we keep it out of the nation. To do this will require all our wisdom, but the cause is worth it. This also is evangelism. The Christianization of the last man in the last corner of the globe is the essence of the gospel of Jesus Christ. And provincialism, a selfish and anti-missionary attitude that prevents this, would eventually destroy the Christian movement.

To follow Jesus Christ, therefore, in a time like this is to face the future not only without despair but with an un-decaying hope in the heart. The church must have its institutions, ministers, teachers, sacraments, and rites, but in the end, these will all fail unless the whole body of men and women who claim Christ as Lord moves with measured, un-hastening, but irresistible advance in the way He leads.

Pearl Buck, in her story "Fighting Angel," presents a stirring picture of these men and women who went forth and other days to declare in no uncertain terms the Christian message of hope encourage: "These early missionaries were born warriors and very great men, or in those days religion was still a banner under which to fight."

No weak or timid soul could sail the seas of foreign lands and defy danger and death unless he did carry his religion as a banner under which even death would be a glorious end....To go forth, to cry out, to warn, to save others – these were frightful urgencies upon the soul already saved. There was a very and agony of salvation." The flag of faith must never be furled!

World Outlook, January 1944, P. 13

Bishop Moore with ministers and their families.

Bishop Moore with ministers in Asia.

CHAPTER SIX

The Methodist Church in Korea
1946

Soon after my arrival in Korea a few months ago a prominent Korean handed me this quotation, "If you wish to make a new world we have the material ready. The first world was made out of chaos." While there I came more and more to appreciate the significance of that statement certainly the perplexing problems confronting both the government and the church in Korea cannot be understood unless they are viewed against the long and tortuous history of these people. The task of liquidating the disastrous results of the vicious Japanese domination, the reestablishment of Korea as an independent state, and the creation of conditions for developing the country on democratic principles is of such magnitude that they can be accomplished only when approached in the spirit of genuine cooperation and unprejudiced intelligence.

The liberation of Korea has thrust this country into the international limelight. Especially are the eyes of all small nations focused on what happens there. Generalissimo Chiang Kai-shek has said, "Korea's failure to achieve independence, freedom, and equality would be equal to China's failure to achieve independence, freedom, and equality. If Korea is not independent – the piece of East Asia and the world cannot be secure."

In August 1945, the Emperor of Japan announced the surrender of Japan to the Allied armies. To facilitate the disarming of the Japanese Army, Korea was divided by the Russian and American forces at the 38th parallel. In the American Zone, south of the 38th parallel, are found seventeen million people, living in the nation's breadbasket. Here is produced most of the rice, wheat, and other cereal crops. North of the 38th parallel is another seven million inhabitants living in the over which the Russians assumed authority. Here are to be found the bulk of the industrial resources. Whatever the political or military expediency responsible for this arbitrary division, it served to make Korea a sort of international football.

Today the question on the lips of all thinking Koreans, representing every shade of political opinion, is this, "Why has our country been divided?" "Is Korea being held as a hostage in international politics?" While one seeks to allay these fears with the usual explanation about time being needed to set up a stable government, etc. It cannot be denied that inherent in the present situation is the danger of producing here, not a united and happy nation, but an unhappy nation was torn into parts, irreconcilable in ideology, facing each other across the 38th parallel.

My main mission in Korea was to the Christian churches and especially to the Methodist Church of Korea. It has been my responsibility and other days to labor for the defense and preservation of the church while powerful forces set themselves against everything for which the church stood. But never have I found a situation so puzzling and so difficult as the present situation in Korea.

Long before the missionaries were compelled to leave Korea in 1940, the heavy hand of the official opposition was upon the church but their withdrawal marked the beginning of the worst scourge of Japanese militarism. The church became the special target of unrelenting persecution. Properties were confiscated, and ministers and laymen were carried away to prison to suffer indescribable torture.

It is a story of attempted extermination. The Korean National Christian Counsel, the Sunday School Association, the Young Men's Christian Association, and other organizations linking Korea to the worldwide church were completely abolished or reshaped to the Japanese pattern. At one time more than three hundred pastors and laymen representing the Protestant churches were thrown into prison. Some died of torture and others did not survive their prison sentences. One cannot understand the near extinguishment of the Christian flame in this land until he watches the unfolding of this pattern of persecution. The method was changed from time to time but the continuing purpose to destroy the Christian influence was never abandoned.

In October 1940, a small group of prominent leaders introduced a Program of Reform in the Methodist Church. It is now evident that this was supported by the Japanese police and military authorities. On October 14, a special session of the General Conference of the Japanese Methodist Church was convened in Tokyo. At that time the Japanese Methodist Church proposed union with the Korean Methodist Church and a plan was adopted but the government authorities in Korea objected. Apparently, the police authorities had their plan for dealing with the church.

In February 1941, to promote the so-called "Reform Program," a special session of the General Conference was called. Some preachers and laymen protested and the conference was adjourned without transacting any business. The police called in those who objected to this illegal conference and ordered them not to make any more trouble.

In February 1942 the so-called "Chong Chin Hoi" or "Forward Association" was organized under the sponsorship of the Police Bureau of the Government General. The main object of this Association, according to the reports, was the investigation of the "thoughts" of the Korean Christian leaders. It was a terrible movement and the Christian leaders were like sheep before the wolf. At this time there was a rumor to the effect that the Japanese military had a plan to kill about thirty thousand Korean Christians, but the organization of this Association deferred its execution, hoping that the Christians would change their attitude and be more willing to collaborate with the Japanese.

In April 1943, a special session of the General Conference was opened in Seoul which authorized the union of the Methodist Church with the Seoul Presbytery of the Korean Presbyterian Church. On the next day, the representatives met and organized the so-called "Korean Reformed Church," but, after a few days, the members of the Seoul Presbytery met and announced that the members had never voted to unite with The Methodist Church.

Then Dr. Pyen, Bishop of the Methodist Church, and his followers demanded the reorganization of the Korean Methodist Church. After a month or so the Police Bureau recognized the non-existence of the so-called Union. But at the same time, the police forced Dr. Pyen to resign. The police had plans and were now determined to make the Korean Methodist Church into a "Reformed Church." A part of this program was to discard the Old Testament Scriptures and to place a Shinto shrine in every churchyard.

In April 1944, several thousand yen were spent in the establishment of a Shinto shrine in the Sang Dong church in Seoul, which shrine was styled "the Civilized Hall of the Imperial Way." A four-day ceremony for the opening of this hall lasted from September 26-29. A regular Shinto priest came and perform the ceremony. Many Japanese dignitaries appeared and made speeches. Among them, were the Police Chiefs, Military General, Court Judge, and a Japanese Methodist preacher. During the four-day celebration, many Methodist preachers were forced to take the "misogi" which is the purification ceremony or Shinto "baptism."

In June 1945, the Vice Governor-General invited fifty-five leaders from different denominations and suggested that the three major denominations (Presbyterian, Methodist, and Salvation Army) unite into the "Korean Christian Church." A Union Committee of twenty was appointed at this meeting to affect the Union. In July following, a General Conference was called and the number of delegates was arbitrarily fixed by the Union Committee. At the "General Conference" the "Regulations of the Korean Christian Church of the Japanese Christianity" called for the chief officers. Instead of regular elections, a representative of the Bureau of Education announced the officers. These officers were instructed to take their offices on August 1, 1945. Before an official announcement that had been carried to the local churches the Japanese Emperor made a formal announcement that he had accepted the Potsdam Declaration and the Japanese Army surrendered to the Allies. Immediately thereafter, the Presbyterian Church in the North organized their thirteen presbyteries and the preachers and laymen of the Methodist Churches in the north reorganized the West Annual Conference.

On April 6-7, 1946, a group representing the Central and East Annual Conferences of the Methodist Church met in Seoul and reorganized those two conferences.

After six weeks of the most sympathetic examination of the situation in Korea, after hearing everybody and reading all I could lay my hands on, I came away with certain overwhelming impressions and deep convictions.

The Church in Korea has been hurt, desperately wounded by its enemies within and its foes without. Seldom in history has a church, especially a young church, been called upon to withstand such "trials of cruel mockings and scourging, yea of bonds and imprisonments." One need not be surprised in the light of these facts to discover that there has been some falling away and some loss of "face" before the outside world.

If one looked only at this side of the picture and failed to remember that innumerable company of faithful witnesses who have emerged from the fires of affliction without the smell of fire upon their garment, he might yield to despair and skepticism concerning the future. The church in Korea is still in the hands of men whose Christian convictions have not only sustained them but made them courageous in the presence of danger. They face their tomorrows not with fear, not with resignation, but with boisterous hope. They are ready to move the way Christ leads, for they have proven Him to be the Divine Friend whose faithfulness has been tested in the supreme ordeals of life, in the dark but unprevailing bitterness of persecution.

The Methodist Church of Korea is autonomous and to it, we look for self-government and a major share in the propagation of the faith among its people. But this must not blind us to the fact that this young church is not strong enough to accomplish its task without continued help from the Mother Church in America. The preaching of the gospel to a nation of nearly thirty million souls: the social reconstruction of the national life; the cleansing of the cities; the building and maintenance of essential institutions; the training of the young – these are tasks of unspeakable urgency and cannot be accomplished without the friendly assistance of fellow Methodist in America.

Ours will become a pallid and nervous Christianity unless it experiences some desperate ventures with Christ. It is a poor faith that has no debt to pay in sympathy and goodwill to others. Our brothers and sisters at the ends of the earth must not be hard-driven with paralyzing possibilities before them and with inadequate resources both in personnel and money with which to meet these opportunities. To fail them now would convict us of treachery to the divine intention and bring disintegration to the brave, loyal, and needy young church. We must teach our people once more the joy of loving and saving the world.

We must take our appointed way in the quietness of spirit, chastened indeed, but confident we are not alone, that we can never be alone, because He, the Great Sustainer, has said "Lo, I am with you even to the end of the age."

World Outlook, October 1946, p. 31

Bishop Moore was awarded the National Medal of Korea, a civilian cultural award, by Young Han Choo, Korean Consul General at San Francisco. On the right is Bishop Hungki J. Lew of Korea, who holds the citation accompanying the award. Bishop Moore spent four months in Korea after World War II helping to reorganize the Methodist Church after the Japanese occupation of Korea.

CHAPTER SEVEN

A Post-War Mission to Korea
February 23-April 14, 1946

At Sea,
Saturday, February 23, 1946

Since the middle of last December, I have been engaged in completing the details of this trip to Korea and other countries in the Far East. Little did I dream, when the Council of Bishops met in special session at Buck Hill Falls, Pennsylvania, that this extra labor would be required of me. It seems that the Methodist Church of Korea is in peculiar need of someone to come out representing the Mother Church, to advise them as they face the unparallel problems brought about by nine years of war.

While there has been little actual fighting on Korean soil, the Japanese government has drawn heavily upon their men and materials. Now the Japanese are beaten and the forty years of Japanese domination and oppression are ended. Korea desperately needs help and cooperation in working out her future course.

Perhaps my six years of service for, and fellowship with, Korean Methodists accounts for my being chosen for this special mission. The trip will most certainly not be luxury travel. There are many difficulties, some real hardships, and the glorious opportunity to contribute to the unity and strength of the Christian Church in Korea, and that in turn will contribute to peace and the spread of world Christianity. For such a mission, I am not worthy, but to do my best will be a genuine delight.

The innumerable inoculations against possible diseases are behind me. The long series of conferences with government and military leaders concerning the importance and necessity of my going at this time has ended in the granting of my passport, military permission to enter Korea, and the assignment by the War Shipping Administration of space on an outgoing ship. It has been hard to decide what to take in the matter of clothing and supplies. Some of my travel will be by air and thus I am limited to quantity. The country to which I go has been stripped bare of available food supplies. The first part of my journey will be in winter, but before it ends the heat of summer will be upon me. Only experience can tell whether I plan wisely.

Mr. Asa Candler, Jr., of Atlanta, a dear friend and devoted Methodist layman, was gracious enough to see me from Atlanta to the West Coast in his new twin-motor Beechcraft plane. It is modern and swift. From Atlanta to San Antonio required only five and a half hours and from there to San Francisco another eight hours. In safety, comfort, and swiftness we finished that part of the journey within the United States.

This afternoon we boarded the USNS *Marine Phoenix* and sailed from Seattle at 6:30 p.m. The ship is a regular Army transport and has onboard approximately 3000 officers and men going out for duty with the Army of Occupation. By courtesy of the Department of State and the military authorities: approximately one hundred civilians have been allowed to have passage. These civilians represent many interests. They are a party of thirty-six United Nations Relief and Rehabilitation Administration workers going out to help feed the starving peoples of the world. They are in trim uniform and represent high intelligence and sacrificial spirit. America cannot close its eyes and shut its ears to the distressed people of the world and keep its place in world leadership.

The Department of State has onboard a group of its highly trained young men who are spreading out all over the Orient to reestablish our consular service. I am sharing the same cabin with some of these men and they make you feel proud to be an American. The rest of the civilian company is composed of war correspondents, a few businessmen and a small group of the advance guard of the Christian missionary army.

The three thousand soldiers represent a cross-section of American life. Already I have met men from practically every state in the union. They seem very young and I cannot help from feeling that it is a pity they are not at home in high school and college. They are good-humored and a fine lot to go with anywhere.

Sunday, February 24, 1946

Soon after coming aboard last night, Chaplain Robinson, who is the transport chaplain, came insisting that I preach this morning. It was a service I shall not soon forget. The sea was rough, the ship pitching, with many a lad from America experiencing his first case of seasickness. But, the lounge was filled with worshipers. When the chaplain asked for a volunteer to play the little organ, a handsome young lieutenant stepped forward. When the service was over, he introduced himself as Lieutenant Adams from Butler, Georgia. He said the Atlanta papers had announced my trip to Korea and he hoped I would be on this ship.

The chaplain is a fine fellow, a minister of the Nazarene Church, and is certainly busy serving all of the men. Today he provided a Roman Catholic, Jewish and Protestant service and had a service of hymn singing at 8:00 p.m., all of this while himself in the grip of seasickness. During the Protestant service, he felt compelled to make a hasty retreat but returned in time to hear me conclude my sermon and announce the hymn, "On Christ the Solid Rock I Stand."

Saturday, March 2, 1946

It was exactly a week ago today we came on board the ship. To say that the voyage thus far has been normal would not be exact. The ship is an Army transport built by Kaiser Shipyards in Vancouver, Washington. It is all steel with three decks. Its overall length is five hundred feet. It is seventy-one feet wide and has a cruising speed of sixteen knots or approximately eighteen miles per hour. It was built for one purpose – transporting men in large numbers to the war areas. There is no thought of comfort, it is spotlessly clean and is kept that way.

The enlisted men numbering nearly three thousand are quartered below. Yesterday I went on a tour of inspection and found them crowded. They have little deck space and if they should all come on deck at one time there would not be room. The officers and a few civilians aboard have a small lounge and here it is possible to sometimes find a chair. Here in a small space of one ship are enough people to make up a good-sized town.

There is of necessity crowding and a general lack of comfort. No one thinks to complain and thus far everyone has been cheerful and cooperative. The food is typically Army. Plenty of it but heavy. For me, it is another enriching experience to be allowed companionship with these officers and men for a couple of weeks.

My cabin mates are interesting fellows. Mr. Glenn Bruner, once a Methodist missionary in Japan, now with the Department of State, went out to Japan to fill a place on General MacArthur's staff. Mr. R. M. Shaplen is a war correspondent with a brilliant record. He represents *Newsweek* and will be a roving reporter throughout the Pacific area. Mr. Li Shu Hua, a distinguished Chinese who is the vice president of the National Academy of Peking, is returning to his native country after representing China at an important educational conference in London. Mr. Fanson Kuo is a young Chinese banker who after a long stay in America is to take up his work in Kunming. He is a sample of a well-trained China. Mr. William Van Buskirk, a spry gentleman of 82 years, who was a prisoner of the Japanese in China, is headed back to Shanghai which is the place he calls home. Despite our crowded conditions, we find time for long and animated conversations on the shape of things to come.

Sunday, March 3, 1946

Today's weather, while not sunny, is much better than what we have had since sailing from Seattle. As a result, the Protestant worship service was well attended this morning. The congregation was composed principally of soldiers, officers, and enlisted men. Civilians made up about one-third of the audience. We had a good sermon by the Reverend Paul Aspach, a Lutheran missionary returning to his station in China.

After the sermon, I administered the Holy Communion. It was a most impressive sight to behold the entire congregation on their knees while the boat rocked to and fro with the heavy waves. After the benediction, I spent a half-hour in conversation with those who are Methodists or who for some reason knew of me. Not soon can I forget a strong clear-eyed young soldier who marched down to a front seat bringing with him his own Bible with which he seemed perfectly familiar. Talk about a lily growing in impossible surroundings, it is not more beautiful than the sight of this lad clinging to his faith and ideals while surrounded by many who seem to have forgotten. While there I thought of his mother and dad and of how proud they must be to have a son like this. He was only one of a goodly company who seemed glad to "go into the house of the Lord."

Friday, March 8, 1946

This is the 12th time I have crossed the Pacific. Frequently I have found it true to its name but certainly not on this voyage. We left Seattle thirteen days ago in a rainstorm and bad weather in some form has been our lot. Only for two days have we been able to enjoy any sunshine. As I have already stated, the ship is crowded beyond description, and the fact that rain and rough weather have prevented much time on deck is added to our congestion. While these lines are being written the waves are running so high that the speed of the ship has been [reduced], otherwise the waves would break over the ship.

Two things happened today to break the monotony of the trip. The medical officer in charge announced that I must be inoculated against tetanus. So, I was. That makes the eighth inoculation I have had for this one trip. Nearly all of them have made me sick; maybe this one will prove to be the exception.

Also, today I was invited by the officers of the ship to make an address over the loudspeaker system on China. Many of these troops are to be stationed there and they are anxious to learn everything possible about the people and customs of this new land to which they are being sent. I prepared the best address I could and for 30 minutes the entire company seemed to listen with rapt attention. Who am I to pose as an authority on these marvelous and mysterious people who have made such an enormous contribution to human welfare? *(This letter was continued in the next issue.)*

Wesleyan Christian Advocate, April 12, 1946, p. 13

We are now about three days out of Korea. We are skirting the edge of Japan but not near enough to see land. What memories it brings back to me! For six years as I move to and fro in the Orient I watched Japan mobilize all her resources of men and materials that fit her imperialistic ambitions. How brutal and unwarranted were her aggressions in China and elsewhere! Now in bitterness and disillusionment are people who stand amid the ruins of folly tragedy did not seek her expansion by peaceful means. When will the nations of the earth learn to say to guns and bombs, "Make way for understanding, arbitration, and peace?"

Sunday, March 10, 1946

For the last two days, we have been at the mercy of a real storm. For some days we seem to play around its edges but Friday and Saturday are found at its center. It was a trying experience. When one remembers that ships like this one were constructed in a week we can but wonder how seaworthy they made them. The high waves have swept over us in all their fury. At times one hardly dared to leave his bed. But at last, the storm has subsided and today has been a lovely Sabbath at sea.

The worship service was well attended this morning. I suppose everyone felt some degree of thanksgiving to Almighty God for His protection of the ship and passengers from the perils of the sea.

We are now off the coast of southern Japan. If all goes well we should drop anchor at Jinsen [Incheon] Korea sometime Wednesday. This morning the captain of the vessel called us together for a lecture on the danger of floating mines. From here to our destination, we must face the peril of these deadly mines placed in these waters by the Japanese as protection against the American Navy. Naturally, they have not all been recovered, and floating around constitutes a real menace. We are compelled to keep our life preservers close at hand at all times. One is not allowed to go on deck without this preparation against a possible disaster. Such a danger helps to introduce a more serious atmosphere among the passengers. In this, as in all other things, it is good to put one's trust in Him who rules the seas.

Wednesday, March 13, 1946

At long last, we have sighted the land toward which we have been sailing seventeen days. The eagerness of the fine American lads crowding the rail and catching sight of their first foreign land moves me tremendously. The voyage is almost ended. Tonight we drop anchor in the harbor at Jinsen [Incheon] Korea and early tomorrow morning we disembark.

It was the spring of 1940 when I said goodbye to our Methodist people in Korea. We had finished the first Mission Conference following the union of the churches in America. How glad we were to be the representatives of the great church to the fine people of this land. But above our heads were the clouds of Japanese oppression. On every hand one saw truth being violated, justice mocked, and brute force triumphant. The church was under heavy pressure while the soiled hands of totalitarianism clutched at the beautiful garments of the Bride of Christ.

What a thrill for me to be in this first "landing party" of the army of returning missionaries. Tomorrow I shall greet, with a deep stirring of my emotions, those with whom I lived and labored in the gathering darkness of war, and together we shall build for a larger and better day.

Seoul Korea
Thursday, March 14, 1946

After seventeen days at sea, we caught sight of the Korean shoreline early this morning. The three-thousand soldiers who are en route to this country crowded the decks to catch their first sight of a foreign land. The Bay of Inchon into which we sailed was crowded with American vessels of every kind. We were greeted with the news that there was an epidemic of smallpox onshore and thus prepared for another vaccination.

This afternoon I came ashore in an army landing craft with the first contingent of troops to be greeted by Chaplin Peters. The news of my coming had reached here but no one knew exactly when or how. The chaplain placed me in an Army Jeep and over terrible roads, we started for Seoul, the capital city forty miles away. Upon arrival in Seoul, Chaplain V. P. Jaeger, who is the chief of the chaplains, took me in charge. Through the courtesy of the Commanding General, I was given a room and food. If I was strictly military, I would say I was billeted at the Chosun Hotel and assigned to the officers' mess. This particular hotel has been commandeered by the U. S. Army and houses the General and his staff officers. In other days it was Seoul's best and usually crowded with high-ranking Japanese. The American officers who are here are all soldiers of distinction, having fought their way up from the South Pacific. They are also courageous gentlemen as anxious for news from home as the humblest private. I am one of the very few Americans in Korea in civilian dress. There are as yet no missionaries except a handful here with the military in some capacity.

Friday, March 15, 1946

Today has been devoted to contracts with the military authorities. Early in the morning, I was received by Lieutenant General John Hodge, The Supreme Commander of all American troops in Korea. I found him to be gracious and typical American. After we had greeted each other, the General said, "Bishop, what do you want to do out here?" I replied, "I would like to survey the situation as it relates to the present state and plans of the Christian Churches, and especially my own communion, The Methodist Church." He promptly assured me I had his permission to go wherever I desire and that he would provide transportation as train and taxi services cannot be had at present. My next call was at the office of Major General Archer J. Lerch who is in command of the Military Government. Under his direction are all the forces and institutions which govern and direct the life and activities of the Korean people. There is naturally no government at present except that provided by the occupation forces. The general kept me for a long while and seemed genuinely interested in the return of missionaries. It now appears that those who have formerly served here will be able to return and resume their labors at an early date.

From the American side of affairs, I turned to the Korean. The Ewha High School was giving a reception to Dr. Henry Appenzeller, one of our missionaries whose father was the first Methodist missionary to Korea. Dr. Appenzeller was born here and has been devoted to these people. Like the other missionaries he was forced out by the Japanese. He has returned for a special mission with the Department of State.

For two hours we were entertained by more than a thousand girls who compose the student body. Never have I heard better choral music. Then, with the faculty, trustees, and distinguished guests, we went to a typical Korean feast. Food is scarce and prices are very high but one could not have discovered it around those tables. It was my privilege to assure these Christian leaders that the church in America was bound to the church in Korea with bonds that war could not sever. It was a high privilege to serve as a symbol at least of a band of missionaries who had been forced out by the Japanese but who would soon be returning.

Sunday, March 17, 1946

"Rejoice, give thanks, and sing" it is a line from a poem but it is also the language of my heart at the close of this wonderful day. Promptly at 9:00 a.m. this morning I was in the Chung Dong Methodist Church for a worship service with our American troops. This is the first Methodist Church built in Korea and is now being used by Chaplain Jaeger of the 24th Army Corp. It is a large brick building accommodating some eight hundred worshipers. Officers and enlisted men almost filled it for the service this morning.

The friends at home would have been thrilled to hear their men sing the hymns. The sermon was the best I can do on "Jesus, The Answer to the Soul's Quest." Following the service, I had a half-hour visit with the men. They were there from practically every state in the Union. It was a source of great comfort to have a Colonel say that more than twenty-five years ago he was converted under my poor ministry.

But my day had just begun. The eleven o'clock hour found me in another strange but moving service. The Japanese, while occupying Korea, built in this city as magnificent a capitol building as can be found anywhere. At the very heart of the building was the Throne Room. Here His Imperial Majesty, the Emperor, sat upon his throne and condescended to receive the favorite few who were granted that "sacred privilege." The room, which accommodates several hundred, is furnished in Oriental splendor. Here they exhibited, in other days, the head of a dynasty that is supposed to have endured for twenty-five hundred years and aspired to world domination.

The capital is now the seat of the American Military Government. The Throne Room has been set apart for divine worship. When I arrived for the service the place was so crowded that even the Commanding General had difficulty finding a seat. Chaplain Cleland was in charge. The audience sang heartily "O Come, All Ye Faithful", "Jesus Calls Us", and "Faith of Our Fathers."

My sermon dealt with "The Unchanging Christ and the Everlasting Gospel." It was an exaltation of Christ above men and movements that have their little day and are gone. Nations rise and fall. Like the mad imperialism of him who reigned as emperor in this very place they end in decline and dust. One banner triumphs over the wrecks of time. The tinseled pomp and glory of evil men fade but the name and glory of Jesus and his church endures through war, paganism, and death. "Unshaken as eternal hills, and immovable she stands." so the day closed with my heart saying, "Rejoice, give thanks, and sing."

Tuesday, March 20th, 1946

So much significance is happening out here one finds it difficult to decide what is most important. For example, one of the largest movements of its kind in history was the repatriation of Koreans and the evacuation of the Japanese. The problems associated with such large-scale movements are many and complicated. At the time these lines are written practically all of the Japanese living in Korea South of the 38th parallel have been evacuated. What is happening in the zone of Russian occupation is another story to be told later. Of the 600,000 Japanese in Korea, only 3000 remain and they must be out by April 1st. Each returning Japanese was limited to 1000 yen or approximately six dollars. All other property must be left behind. Millions of Koreans are returning from Japan, Manchuria, and Formosa. How happy they must be to return to a land free of the invader! How unhappy these Japanese who are compelled to leave houses and businesses to return to a homeland filled with the desolation of war.

For several reasons, Korea has become one of the nerve centers of the world. What happens here runs like an electric current around the whole earth and brings hope or despair to other small nations. Korea's future is absolutely in the hands of the so-called Big Powers.

This week witnessed the formal opening of the sessions of the joint Soviet-United States Commission which has been organized to solve the political, economic, and administrative problems of Korea and to prepare the way for independent self-government. This Soviet Commission numbers more than one hundred. Several of them are living in the hotel where I am staying and you may be sure I have been studying them. Here are Generals toughened in battle, experts on every conceivable subject. In the group are several ladies in uniform whose duties vary.

Korea at present is divided at the 38th Parallel. Thus, the Russians hold the industrial north and the Americans the agricultural South, including Seoul, the capital city. All transportation and communication between the two sections are prohibited. There is no mail service; newspapers are not allowed to circulate across the border. The boundary is carefully guarded and a Korean endangers his life while attempting to leave the Russian Zone. However, southern Korea is crowded with refugees from the north.

Naturally, the Koreans have looked forward with great hope to the coming of this Commission. Can two powerful nations cooperate sufficiently to create a united and independent Korea? The peace of the world, as well as the future of Korea, is at stake!

Seoul, Korea
Wednesday, March 20, 1946

One does not need to turn do the Acts of the Apostles to define those who have had "trials of cruel mockings and scourgings, yea, moreover of bonds and imprisonments." Korea is full of such, and like the writer of the Epistle to the Hebrews, "time would fail me" to tell of their afflictions. For three hours last night, I sat with seven Methodist pastors who have suffered unbelievable torture for no reason except that they are leaders of the Christian Church. The Japanese said they held "dangerous thoughts." For that reason alone they were snatched away from their loved ones, held for a long time in prison, and subjected to punishment which one might expect in the Dark Ages but certainly not now. Some day the full story of this "reign of terror" will be known and the church universal brought to a fuller appreciation these have suffered so much.

Friday, March 22, 1946

Last night I was the guest of honor at a Korean feast given by the Methodist people. Such gatherings were strictly forbidden while the Japanese were here, so this was a sort of celebration of their deliverance. The young layman, a doctor, who delivered the address of welcome said, "If during recent years we even dreamed of missionaries, we were considered traitors. Now that you are here with us it seems a dream too good to be true."

Whether or not I can help these friends remains to be seen but they have certainly helped me. To see how they have met life's trials courageously, how they have lived patiently when hope was deferred and dreams were unrealized, shames one's comfortable standards. I shall try a little harder to be faithful.

It was only sixty-two years ago when the first Protestant missionaries came to Korea. In this short term the church has grown to be a vigorous and self-propagating branch of the universal church. In 1939 there were more than three hundred thousand church members with an influence far greater than these numbers would suggest. The church had brought not only individual salvation to multiply thousands but it had also introduced democratic ideals, and improved life generally through schools, hospitals, and social service agencies. The servants of Christ had gone all about Korea teaching and preaching the gospel and healing all manner of diseases.

Within fifty years after the first Methodist missionary set foot upon these shores, an independent Methodist Church was set up with its Korean bishop. With devoted ministers, sacrificial laymen, and loyal missionaries, this church faced what to the human eye looked like a bright future. Then began an aggravated scourge of Christianity by the Japanese. The Korean National Council, the Sunday School Association, the Young Men's Christian Association, and other organizations linking Korea to the worldwide church were all abolished. In September 1940, more than three hundred pastors and laymen representing Protestantism were thrown into prison. By 1941, it was apparent that the presence of American missionaries made the Koreans suspect in the eyes of the police, and for this and other reasons all missionaries were withdrawn. With the police dictating, the General Conference of the Methodist Church was compelled to meet and changes in discipline were made, under compulsion. In one Methodist Church, a Shinto Shrine was erected and several leaders went through certain acts of purification. These are only a few facts lifted out of a long list of the activities of a totalitarian government that sought to make the Bride of Christ the mistress of a wicked government.

The most prominent of those Koreans who will probably take over the authority of government when the military forces withdraw is Dr. Sigmund Rhee. Many believe he will be the first President of the new independent nation. It was my privilege to spend more than an hour with him this morning. He is married to a lady who was reared in one of the European nations, Austria I believe. She is a charming and gifted woman. Dr. Rhee was, as a young man, Secretary of the Young Men's Christian Association. He went to America more than thirty years ago as a delegate to a General Conference of the Methodist Church. There he remained to carry on the long struggle for Korean independence. As soon as the American Army entered Korea he returned. He is Chairman of the Korean Democratic Council which is composed of the leaders of several political parties. It is this group that the Military Government turns to for guidance on matters related to the establishment of a sovereign nation.

This leads one to say that at present there are too many political parties. They are compelled to register with it and at present the number is fantastic. Some divisions and rivalries become arguments upon the lips of the Russians for a trusteeship rather than complete independence. Lt. Gen. Hodge, Commander of the American Forces, has gone on record favoring complete and speedy independence. Certainly, the division of the country between two Armies of Occupation is unfortunate and contributes to the spirit of unrest and disunity. Here we see a race between Communism and Democracy which leaves the main body of the Korean people floundering in a sea of uncertainty. To me it seems a tragedy that all of the country was not put in the American Zone. That would undoubtedly have produced a sovereign and united nation far quicker than the present division between two opposing forms of government.

Saturday, March 23, 1946

Since my arrival, I have devoted from twelve to fourteen hours daily to conferences with those Korean leaders who are trying to bring order out of chaos. This situation is hard to analyze and no general statement adequately describes it. The deliberate attempt of the Japanese to destroy organized Christianity has left "whirlpools" of confusion, charges, and countercharges. I am not referring to the fidelity and devotion of the individual Christians but to the results of the action of leaders which for the most part were forced by the police.

Wesleyan Christian Advocate, April 19, 1946, p. 10.

Editor's Note: This letter was continued in the next issue of the *Wesleyan Christian Advocate*

Some few, I must confess, seemed to have been "puppet leaders" who were completely subservient to Japanese domination. The main body of Christians was such outward conformity as was necessary to save their lives but remain true to Jesus Christ. Now that freedom has come, the difficulty is at the level of constructing the church organizations.

In July 1945 the police compelled the leaders of the Methodist and Presbyterian churches (the two largest in Korea) to declare these churches dissolved. Some of these leaders accepted an appointment as officers in the "Korean Christian Church of Japanese Christianity." It will be hard for Americans who have always enjoyed religious freedom to understand such action. Keeping in mind that the dissolution of these churches and the formation of the new organization was done under the rulers of the government against which no Korean dared complain. Within a month following this action, the Japanese army surrendered. In October, a small group of Presbyterian and Methodist pastors met and organized a United Church. They say there has long been a demand for a United Christian front and now that the nation is to be free and united, the churches should set the pattern. Thus, a good thing seems to have been done the wrong way and at an inopportune time. No one denies that the original Union Church was brought about by the force of the Japanese and did not represent the action or desire of the people involved. While it is true that the original union has been dissolved and another formed, the leaders are the same and thus may object because it is tainted by Japanese origin. There has never been a Plan of Union formulated and submitted to the Conferences and Presbyteries. No doctrinal statement has been prepared. It looks like the union by declaration and not by constitutional processes. Meanwhile, the Annual Conferences and Presbyteries are being reorganized and are confronted with the possibility of having a Methodist, Presbyterian, and a United Church. If ever wise and patient leadership was needed it is here and now.

Sunday, March 24, 1946

Once again, I was invited to preach in the Throne Room at the national capital. The congregation was even larger than the one of the previous Sunday. I was delighted to see several young ladies representing the American Red Cross and the Army Nurses Corps. These young girls are rendering splendid service. They represent American womanhood and have the respect of every man out here. My sermon was just what I would have preached in a church in America. Too many think soldiers to be unlike other men but they represent the average American and care not for frills. When I finished preaching about "That strange man of the cross" they sang with intent "I Take, O Cross, Thy Shadow."

This afternoon I spoke over Korea's most powerful radio station. After I had finished, a Korean pastor gave a translation for those who cannot understand English. I tried to say the spiritual made secure the secular and that they who build a nation would do well to give attention to spiritual ideals. The Christian teaching concerning the worth and dignity of human life is the fountain of democracy and that if this disappears from the spiritual realm, democracy will not long survive in the political realm.

Monday, March 25, 1946

Today has been given over to the two Christian colleges here in Seoul, Ewha College for Women, and Chosum Christian College for Men. They stand side by side just outside the city. Buildings, campus, faculty, and student body compare favorably with our best American colleges.

These institutions have, like other Christian institutions, suffered at the hands of the Japanese. Many of their buildings were seized for military purposes. Ewha, under the skillful leadership of Dr. Helen Kim, who is now in America, was kept going but with many difficulties. Chosun was closed entirely. They are again open with nearly one thousand students in each institution. The buildings require repair, but they are structurally sound. Korea would be poor indeed without these centers of Christian influence.

At the close of my address at Ewha, it was my happy privilege to present to the college a beautiful silk Christian flag which was placed in my hands by the Methodists of Jacksonville, Florida. The eight hundred seventy-two young ladies accepted it with a gracious Oriental bow and gave it a position of honor. It speaks of the fellowship of Christian believers in all lands.

Tuesday, March 26, 1946

These notes are being sent to America as a daily chronicle of events, sights, and impressions. They do not reflect my final judgment or conclusions on the many matters here mentioned. That will be done in another type of report when my mission is completed. My aim is to preserve for myself and others who are interested a record of my day-by-day experiences in a distant land in an exciting new day.

This seems to be a good place to mention my gratitude to Korean friends were making my visit pleasant and profitable. They are surrounding me with such kindness and hospitality the days are slipping by like hours. Many who knew him, in other days, will rejoice to learn that Dr. J. S. Ryang is well and has been faithful to every trust.

Wednesday, March 27, 1946

Under a Commission from the General Commission on Army and Navy Chaplains, the Methodist Commission on Chaplains, and Major General Miller, the Chief of Army Chaplains, I am giving some of my time to the chaplains. There are approximately seventy-five chaplains stationed throughout Korea with the troops. Today the Protestant Chaplains, numbering about fifty, assembled in Seoul for one of these conferences. I found many old friends in the group. Following the address, we had an hour for questions and answers. How eager they were to know about the church back home. Some of them confessed to a touch of homesickness, but they are carrying on magnificently. I owe a debt that can never be paid to Senior Chaplain V. P. Yoeger and his associates who have graciously assisted me in many ways. Without their help, I do not know what I would have done.

Seoul, Korea
March 31, 1946

Anyone who is seriously interested in the world of the mission of Christianity will find in Korea abundant proofs of the success of those of have labored here in the past, and strong grounds for hope that even greater progress may be seen soon. Despite all the persecution of recent years, it is altogether clear that the labors of the missionaries have gained a wonderful measure of success. Beyond the tragedy and turmoil of war, the eye of faith can see what may yet be accomplished by a virile church.

The Korean people have been for forty years the slaves of foreign despotism. They have seen many of their cherished customs uprooted, well-nigh all their liberties destroyed, while habits and laws that were utterly strange and abhorrent have been forced upon them. It is not surprising that such brutal and unwarranted oppression should result in the loss of faith in some. When the Japanese Army was forced to capitulate on August 15, 1945, many Korean leaders were expecting even greater disaster for their country. It is currently reported here that at least thirty-thousand leaders have been marked for slaughter. Whether that report is true or false I do not know but it is unmistakably clear that the Japanese Government had deliberately handed over the Christian Church to a heartless police system. Christians had their goods plundered and their spirits are broken.

During the past week, I spent two days in the ancient city of Songdo. Travel is a most difficult undertaking at present. Railroad equipment has so deteriorated that there are but few trains, running on irregular schedules, and they are so crowded that one abandons all hope of even getting aboard. It is a common sight to see hundreds clinging to the top of the few trains that are running. For some reason which I do not know these trains all move without any light whatsoever and thus constitute a danger to those who are out by night. Fortunately, for me, General Hope has provided military transportation. Sometimes it is an Army sedan, but often it is an Army Jeep. Riding in a Jeep over good roads is an experience but on unimproved Korean roads, it is an adventure! But if one wants to go bad enough and will endure long enough the Jeep will get him there.

Songdo is an ancient city built some 600 years before Columbus discovered America. The remnants of high stone walls and beautiful gates all speak of exquisite palaces and proud civilization. Within the last twelve months three different armies, none of them Korean, have marched through its streets. Until August 15 the arrogant Japanese filled the place. Then for a brief time, the Russian armies were in power. With the arrival of the Americans, the 38th parallel was fixed as the boundary between the Soviet and American Zones of occupation, and the American army took over. The line is only a short distance away and from my window, the Russian sentries can be seen on their posts. One day I sat at lunch with one of these Soviet officers and wished for a knowledge of his language to better understand the philosophy and policy of these people who have suddenly grown so powerful.

The Russian and American armies follow entirely different methods in their dealings with the Koreans. The Russians maintain no commissary and live entirely off the land. All supplies are requisitioned, and the people are compelled to surrender their scanty food reserves. The stories of far worse treatment that the natives are receiving at the hands of their "liberators" in the north can hardly be told here. Multiple thousands of people from the north have deserted their homes and at the risk of death have slipped through the mountain passes into the American Zone. The Americans import all their supplies from the United States and if any local produce is needed it is paid for at the prevailing market price. While on every hand I hear stories of rough treatment at the hands of the Russians, the people in the American Zone fraternize with and respect the American soldiers. The streets are crowded with little children who try out their few words of English on friendly G. I.s and beg for chocolates.

Prior to the Methodist Union, Songdo was the capital of the work of the Southern Church. Here were built a high school for boys, a high school for girls, a social evangelistic center, several primary schools and kindergartens, and a fine hospital, with a dozen missionary residences. There are five Methodist churches. None of these properties have been damaged but all have suffered from military occupation and greatly need repairing and refurbishing. The schools are open and crowded with students, but one fear is that much of the distinctive Christian contribution is lacking. The Japanese squeezed out the last bit of Christian idealism, and while the Koreans are again in charge it will require time to restore Christianity to its rightful place.

The above statement would apply more or less to every Christian institution in Korea. Not only is there the task of physical rehabilitation ahead but this longer and more difficult task of rebuilding a thoroughly Christian faculty and enthroning again those intangibles but imperishable values for which the Christian church exists. It is been my lot to be the first of the missionary group to return to Songdo. The gratitude and hospitality of the people simply overwhelms one and keeps his emotions upset.

Wesleyan Christian Advocate, April 26, 1946, p. 13

Editor's Note: Songdo is today known as Kaesong. The 1953 Korean Armistice Agreement left the city under North Korean control. Due to the city's proximity to the border with South

Korea, Kaesong has hosted cross-border economic exchanges between the two countries as well as the jointly run Kaesong Industrial Region.

Sunday, March 31, 1946

This has been a busy Sabbath. At nine-thirty this morning I was preaching to three hundred American soldiers. The service was held in one of our Korean churches. These American men amazed me with their church attendance. Of course, not all of them rise on Sunday to attend church services but many of them do. There must be something like twenty church services in this city alone each Sunday for the troops. It has been my privilege to preach in many of these services and everywhere I have found large attendance, inspiring music, and an atmosphere of devout worship.

The eleven o'clock hour brought me to a large congregation of Korean Methodists. The service was well arranged and dignified. My text was from Exodus, "Speak to the children of Israel that they go forward." These people desperately need and desire a message of good cheer, courage, and progress. Around them is tumult, bringing along with their deliverance many trials and burdens; ahead of them staggering responsibilities. They demand and must have a gospel that proclaims supernatural powers and offers abundant living.

Wednesday, April 3, 1946

Last night I watched a church come to new life. In other installments of these letters, I have mentioned the fiery ordeal through which Methodism and the other churches in Korea had been passing for many years. These institutions have been mastered by paganism, its pastors imprisoned and tortured, and their churches closed until one at least became a Shinto Shrine. Finally, under police pressure, the denomination was declared abolished. Since liberation, the Christian leaders have been trying to bring some order out of this chaos.

The meeting last evening was composed of Methodist ministers and laymen. They were not all of one mind as to the best way ahead. Some believe that now is the time to form the Christian Church of Korea and thus merge all former denominations. Others feel that however desirable church union may be that it is necessary to reconstruct the denominational structures before a union can be brought about by legal methods. They discussed their problems in an atmosphere of complete freedom which was a privilege they have not enjoyed in a long while. They voted to reorganize the Annual Conferences and then proceed from there toward the larger union. It was more than just another church meeting. It was a group of free men who felt they had lived through a horrible nightmare to greet the dawn of a lovely morning.

Friday, April 5, 1946

A considerable portion of my time has been devoted to the problem of human relief. The Military Government has set up a Department of Welfare. It is staffed with competent army officers and well-trained Koreans. A vital part of this relief program concerns what is to be done through the voluntary agencies in the States. Perhaps a few words here will help to interpret the problem in methods.

Let me say there is a great need. Rice is the one indispensable food out here. There was a good crop grown last year but much of it has been consumed. Everybody admits that the next six months will present a crisis. From my window, during this week I have witnessed "rice demonstrations." Rice is now selling for 320 yen per mal. This is roughly 18 pounds. The legal exchange rate is 15 yen for one American dollar which makes it worth approximately seven cents. Thus, one can see that a mal of rice costing 320 yen and weighing only 18 pounds costs more than $20. There is of course a vigorous black market. The leaders tell me that [the cost of living has] increased more than three hundred percent. I see no way to avoid suffering except by importing sufficient food to last until the next rice harvest.

The U.S. Military Government is working heroically to prevent famine. All available foodstuff is rationed but the Koreans have had their crops confiscated so often by the Japanese that it is difficult for them to distinguish between the wise methods of the present government and the confiscation of other days. The United Nations Relief and Rehabilitation

Association has only one representative here. She is a competent person but as yet no supplies have arrived.

The Church Committee for Relief in Asia is the agency through which all voluntary relief must be sent. Goods cannot be earmarked for a specific group. All goods come to the Department of Welfare and will be distributed to several Provinces.

The supplies most needed are these and in this order

1 – clothing, especially for women and children. Men have some available supplies from surplus Japanese army goods.

2 –footwear; shoes, boots, anything to cover the feet.

3 – food, especially for babies, such as Klim (powdered milk), etc.

4 – school supplies, notebooks, pencils. Textbooks will be furnished.

5 – hospital supplies, especially of the type contained in basic Army medical units.

The Church Committee for Relief in Asia has its general offices in New York and will give specific instructions to any group interested in sending relief to Korea. Shipping is still a major problem and only this committee is able to expedite the shipment of goods.

Saturday, April 6, 1946

This is an exciting new day in an ancient land. The Japanese are gone, and the Russians and the Americans say they too will soon depart, but the day has not been named. Thrills of excitement run up and down every street. This is the day of new patriotism, new government, new methods, yea of a new age! But the Koreans face it all with complacency. They have seen empires rise and fall and conquerors come and depart. Some of the cynics among them can but wonder if this new civilization is but a shadow passing over the sun. Meanwhile, to the young and hopeful, spring is here bringing not only green countryside and the planting of another harvest but new life and hope to the soul of the nation. So on he goes, unresisting yet un-surrendering, puzzled and a little sad that he is not left alone, but withal single-hearted, gentle and hopeful. God blessed him!

Frequently have I used the expression "A nation born in a day" but I am not sure that much thought was given to the pains and problems which always accompany infancy. August 15, 1945, will always be written in red letters by the Koreans. It was on that day the Japanese Army surrendered and soon thereafter the Americans marched in. That day ended forty years of bondage for the liberty-loving people. Long has their land been known as the "Land of Morning Calm" but these recent years have seen instead conquest and confusion but little calm. Today the nation is alive and healthy, but this does not mean the need for care and counsel is passed. Like most infants, this one cries, sometimes for the thing it does not need, and sometimes because it does not want what is best for its welfare.

So much depends upon the leaders who are to take charge when the armies of occupation move out. The Korean people are quick to detect disinterestedness, and if those who come to power truly have the welfare of the people at heart much can and will be accomplished in a short while. If they come with the greed of many old-time officials, there will inevitably follow a period of tumult and change.

The young people of Korea are on the march. They have lots of speed but only the future can tell how much inner discipline they have acquired for this day of liberation. On every hand, they are resisting the old order of privilege and demanding new ways, and new methods in the place of obsolete traditions and customs. In the northern part of the country, they have resorted to strikes and open conflict with the Russians. It is reported that many schools have been closed and several students have been exiled to Siberia.

Never have I placed a higher value upon Christian education. Unless man's faculties are put to school on the spiritual side, idealism wanes and selfish greed thrives. Much of the credit for the present-day leaders in Korea must be given to our church schools. I scarcely met an outstanding leader in the affairs of government who was not trained in one of our church institutions. Let it be said that the schools largely staffed by missionaries have blazed new paths in the field of education and caused the youth of the nation to desire and demand higher learning.

Speaking of youth, I must say a word of the mothers. On my journeys to the country places never do I pass through a village and catch sight of the mothers sitting on low stools in narrow streets patching clothes or fondling their children but I thank God for these Korean mothers with their hopes, their children, and like mothers everywhere, their sacrifices.

April 10, 1946

Since writing the above, my eyes have looked upon a scene that will not be easy to forget. Northern Korea like the south had many thousands of Japanese citizens. The American government has evacuated more than one million from its section. This has been done in a humane and business-like manner. The Russians have not as yet worked out any plan for the return of the many thousands who live in their zone of occupation. Now that spring has come with warmer weather, thousands of men, women, and children are slipping across the boundary and walking toward southern Korea where they expect to be sent by the Americans to Japan. These poor tired refugees are arriving here at the rate of a thousand per day. They are penniless, hungry, footsore, and unspeakably weary. I was reliably informed that eighty percent of the children under ten years of age who have undertaken this hazardous journey have died en route. It is pathetic to see these tired little mothers holding to their small children lest they be separated in the crowd and lost to each other.

This is part of the closing scene of the history of a mad-imperialism. Japan's warlords went forth in 1937 to destroy cities and wreak havoc upon women and children. Now the harvest of desolation must be gathered. At one time in 1942, Japan held nearly six hundred million people as slaves. Human life was cheap. Now the nation sits in anguish while its own come home broken and bleeding. Let him who would glorify war as a grand spectacle look again upon these sad people stumbling along strange roads, among their former enemies wondering where the next meal will be found. That too is a part of the war. In the end, it deceives those who put their trust in it.

In a quiet Chinese restaurant on a side street heavily guarded by police, I spent two hours with another one of the prominent leaders of Korean political life. His name is Kim Gu and he may be the first president of Korea. Certainly, he is one of the three well-known leaders from whom the choice will be made. Mr. Kim was a fighter for independence while yet a young man. After the 1919 insurrection, he was compelled to flee the country and has lived in China from then until last October. He spoke tenderly of the influence of his Christian mother and confessed his faith. His manner is that of a born fighter who appreciates what it has cost to produce a sovereign nation free from Japanese domination. It is not at all likely that Russia will ever give its blessings to this man because of his outspoken criticism of communism.

Wesleyan Christian Advocate, May 3, 1946, p. 10.

April 11, 1946

It is now two months since I took off from the airport in Atlanta with Mr. Asa G. Candler, Jr., in his luxurious twin motored plane. The experiences which have been crowded into these days are enough for an average lifetime. As these lines are written certain unforgettable experiences and impressions come to mind. Let me list only a few – a night in San Antonio during a storm wondering if bad weather would cause me to miss my boat – flying round and round over beautifully lighted Los Angeles while searching for the right airport – enveloped in fog and rain between Los Angeles and San Francisco and how beautiful the Navy airfield looked to us when searching for a safe landing – sailing out of the harbor at Seattle with three-thousand G. I.s in their irrepressible good humor despite our crowded conditions – Sunday morning service on a rough sea while a fine young Lieutenant from Butler, Georgia played the hymns – a room crowded with soldiers on a dark and stormy night in mid-ocean while we sang "Fairest Lord Jesus" – a service on board ship for a young lad who had committed suicide back in the states and asked that his body be cremated and his ashes scattered upon the sea – that strange feeling one has while carrying a life preserver every hour knowing full well you are in danger of floating mines – the severe adjustments one must make to live with three-thousand others on a boat and eight of them in the same small cabin with you – the thrill of sighting land after seventeen stormy days at sea – the exceeding great kindness of Army chaplains as they provided food and shelter for me – three hours of conference with Korean pastors who have suffered cruel torture for their faith – the feeling of helplessness one has when trying to salvage a church from the wreckage of a totalitarian government – eight hundred seventy-two Korean girls in a beautiful Oriental bow while I presented a Christian flag to their school from friends in America – and numb were my feet and legs after two hours on the floor while partaking of the feast in a Korean home – the fierce look of Russian soldiers and the evident fright of Koreans out in the villages when the Russians appear – an innumerable company of Korean children following American G. I.s through the streets shouting "hello" and begging for chocolate and chewing gum – the eagerness of Korean Christians to provide a feast and a gift even though the cost of living has increased three hundred percent and while many of them are on the verge of starvation. These and a thousand other memories that bless and burn come to one who has eyes to see and a heart to feel.

Sunday, April 14, 1946

Once again it was my privilege to preach to a large congregation of soldiers. Today is Palm Sunday and the men crowded the large church. This will be my last preaching service in Korea on this trip. In another two days, I am scheduled to go to Japan where I will have a short stay and then sail home. If all goes well, at an early date I should be at some port on the Pacific coast and with my loved ones soon thereafter. A more formal report will be written for the Council of Bishops and the Board of Missions. Meanwhile, I have enjoyed jotting down for my friends these day-by-day on-the-spot experiences.

Wesleyan Christian Advocate, May 24, 1946, p. 7

Editor's Note:
For further information I recommend:

Haga, Kai Yin Allison, "An overlooked dimension of the Korean War: The role of Christianity and American missionaries in the rise of Korean nationalism, anti-colonialism, and eventual civil war, 1884-1953" (2007). *Dissertations, Theses, and Masters Projects*. William & Mary. Paper 1539623326.

CHAPTER EIGHT

A Post-War Mission to Europe

July-October 1948

These lines are being written on Monday, July 12, and will likely appear in print about the time I take a boat for certain important duties in Europe. So many letters and telegrams have come bidding us "welcome" since our assignment to Georgia for another four years. The North Georgia Conference is in session this week and time for correspondence is limited. I am therefore using the columns of the *Wesleyan Christian Advocate* to chat with you about several matters of interest and importance.

If there are Methodists anywhere in the world who surpass those in Georgia in an intelligent consecration and sacrificial support of the church, I have not known them. To be reappointed to work with you and for you is as great an honor as can come to any man. No bishop could enjoy the finer or happy relationship that I have had with you during the past eight years. From the devoted ministers and the excellent laymen – men and women – have come unnumbered evidence of courteous consideration. All this is helping to make these years a season of happy and rewarding fellowship. As I begin my new assignment it is my desire and purpose to be a better minister and a more faithful servant of the church.

When the Council of Bishops assigned me to certain duties this summer, I placed a notice in the *Wesley Christian Advocate* stating that it would be my joy to take any funds placed in my hands and use them for the relief of the distress of our Methodist people in war-torn countries. Little did I dream so many would be moved to respond in such a liberal fashion. As I write this letter a total of $14,442.06 has been received. This magnificent sum has come from churches, Sunday School classes, Vacation Bible Schools, Societies of Christian Service, and a host of consecrated ministers and individual Methodists.

It will be my sacred duty to administer it most wisely and constructively. A complete list of all donors has or will appear in the *Wesleyan*. To one and all I say, "thank you" and "God bless you." It will be my purpose to report in some of my letters from overseas some of the purposes to which the sacred gifts were put.

On Wednesday, July 21, with a small company of Methodist preachers, I will sail from New York on the RMS *Mauritania* for England. While there I do hope to find a little rest for a tired body but shall have many pressing duties in the service of the church. We hope to visit England, France, Czechoslovakia, Switzerland, Belgium, Holland, Norway, and Germany. My official duties will be as follows:

1. Assembly of the World Council of Churches, Amsterdam, Holland, August 21 - September 4.
2. Preside over the Belgium Annual Conference, Brussels, Belgium, September 15-20.
3. Fraternal delegate to the Central Conference of Northern Europe, Bergen, Norway, September 21-27.
4. Fraternal delegate to the Central Conference of Germany, Frankfurt, Germany, October 5-11.

In addition to the above duties, I have agreed to assist in a conference for Methodist chaplains who were stationed in Europe. The time and place for this conference are yet to be chosen.

While I am overseas it will be my purpose to put down from day to day my experiences, impressions, and duties. These will be put in the form of a letter and sent to the *Wesleyan Christian Advocate*. I trust they will be of interest to our friends in Georgia.

Because this is an intimate letter to dear friends it will not be amiss for me to gratefully record that Mrs. Moore has made a marvelous recovery from her recent illness. She is now at home, and we feel confident that after a quiet summer she will be ready for her usual participation in the work of the church. She would want me on her behalf to say "thank you" to that very large company of friends who in so many ways have helped while she was in the hospital.

While away I shall follow all the preachers and people with day-to-day interest and prayers. We have some matters of far-reaching importance ahead of us this autumn and winter. As soon as I return it will be my joy to give myself with patient continuance and faithfulness to every duty. May God richly bless and keep you, one and all.

Wesleyan Christian Advocate, July 29, 1948, p. 8.

At Sea

Monday, July 26, 1948

We have now been at sea five full days. For me, they have been spent in quiet rest. Since April 15 I have been continuously in conferences. Never have I known so many pressing duties crowded into so few weeks. The result was a body completely fatigued and eager for a long period of complete relaxation. These days at sea have already worked their miracle of renewal, and I am beginning to feel like myself once more.

The North Georgia Conference closed Sunday afternoon, July 18. At 5 a.m. Tuesday, July 20, we left Atlanta by plane from New York. Once more I was the guest of Mr. and Mrs. Asa Candler, Jr., and their modern and very comfortable airplane. With Mr. and Mrs. Candler, their granddaughter, Nancy, Mr. Charles Candler of Madison, Mr. and Mrs. Andy Smith of Atlanta, the Reverend Leonard Cochran of Valdosta, and the Reverend Claire Cotton of Tallahassee, we left Atlanta just at dawn.

The weather was ideal for flying and we were in New York by noon. A stop of one hour was made in Washington while I hurried to the War Department for my military permit to enter the American military zone in Germany. Modern air travel soon makes one inpatient with slower transportation, but it also serves to increase the tempo of one's life which for most of us is already too fast.

Immediately upon reaching New York, I hurried to 150 Fifth Avenue for some pressing duties in connection with the Board of Missions and the Methodist Committee on Overseas Relief. Wednesday was devoted to some last-minute shopping. I was especially eager to take with me some articles of food which dear friends in England cannot find in their stores. When at the close of the day I went on board ship, I was heavily laden. In my possession, I now have two large Georgia hams, one for General Clay in Germany and one for Dr. Sangster in London. For Dr. Edward McLellan, who was our guest for much of last winter, I have a large food package containing many items which are unobtainable at present in England. The doctor is a great smoker, and you would be surprised to see me with so much smoking tobacco. For the ladies, Mrs. Moore has insisted upon my bringing over a reasonable supply of nylon stockings.

Perhaps a word should be said concerning the good ship *Mauritania* on which we are making this voyage. It is a very large ship but not quite in a class with the RMS *Queen Elizabeth* and RMS *Queen Mary*. We have approximately 1200 passengers on board, and everyone is quite comfortable. Our immediate party is composed of six Methodist preachers. They are Bishop Paul B. Kern of Nashville, Tennessee, Reverend Leonard Cochran of Valdosta, Reverend Claire Cotton of Tallahassee, Florida, Reverend J. Loy Scott of Savannah, and Reverend R. B. Hays of Buford, and your humble servant. Some of us are seasoned travelers while some are being initiated into the mysteries of ocean travel. It is a jolly party and as we gather three times daily about a large circular table in the spacious dining room much food is consumed, and some tall tales are told.

Yesterday was the Sabbath. For me, it was a busy day. On Saturday, a fellow traveler from Ohio died suddenly of a heart attack. His companions requested me to hold the service at 10:00 a.m. It was most impressive. From that service, I went immediately to the regular Sunday morning service where the commander of the ship read the Church of England service. The balance of the day was devoted to some books which I have waited a long time.

Early Tuesday morning we are to dock at Cobh, Ireland. Then onward for a few hours to Cherbourg, France, and early Wednesday we should be alongside the dock at Southampton, England. The more I see and know of this beautiful country and these great people the more eager I am to claim kinship with them. Nature has been bountifully kind to most localities in England; romance has been spread over nearly every foot of English soil; man has wrought marvels of architecture and everywhere one turns, lovely gardens and exciting history greet the eye and engages one's attention. For example, Southampton, where we leave this ship, is the very spot from which the *Mayflower* sailed with the Pilgrim fathers who, under God, brought our beloved nation into existence. Although it has been my happy privilege to visit England many times, I returned eager for more about English history, English beauty, and English life. In a subsequent letter, I hope to jot down some of my impressions of England as she emerges from the devastation of war. Meanwhile, "so long."

Wesleyan Christian Advocate, August 19, 1948, p. 16.

RMS *Mauritania*

London

August 3, 1948

We have now been in England for a week. Tomorrow, we cross the channel for a similar visit to France. In his *Home Thoughts from Abroad*, Robert Browning sings:

"Oh, to be in England
Now that April's there,
And whoever wakes in England
Sees, some morning, unaware,
That the lowest boughs in the brushwood sheaf
Round the elm-tree bole are in tiny leaf,
While the chaffinch sings on the orchard bough
In England – now!"

This of course is early August and not April; but had Browning been living on earth today, he would have rejoiced at the sunshine and flowers and been proud of the evergreen loveliness of this land. Early July, they tell us, brought rain and cool weather but when we arrived it was as warm as Georgia and almost as beautiful.

When RMS *Mauritania* put in at Southampton, we were delayed in going ashore, waiting for a royal party aboard the RMS *Queen Elizabeth* to come to an end. The King and Queen had come to be special guests onboard that mighty ship. We had already touched and disembarked passengers at Cobh [*pronounced cove*], Ireland, and Cherbourg, France. It was my first sight of the green hills of Ireland from which my great great grandfather sailed to America. Its beauty charmed me and we sailed away resolving to come again someday for a more extended visit. I shall not mention France just now as we are to write about our visit there in another article.

One is always puzzled to know how to spend his time in England if he has only a few days in which to attempt to visit so many historic places. Naturally, a group of Methodist preachers such as we would turn immediately to these places which are so important in the life story of Methodism. Today there comes to London from every part of the world men and women who owe, under God, their supreme joy in life and their hope of heaven, to the teaching of the Methodist Church. And what do they want to see in London? Many people and places, of course, but a large number of these from overseas do not think they have seen London that they have paid a visit to the historic shrines of Methodism.

We devoted almost an entire day to City Road Chapel. Here is where John Wesley lived, preached, and died. You can hardly imagine how moved we were together in the little room where every morning for many years John Wesley went for prayer. Bishop Paul Kern offered a special prayer for us all.

Bishop Moore and Bishop Paul Kern

It was in the Foundry, situated not far from the present Wesley's Chapel, that Methodism had its center and where Mr. Wesley had his abode until in 1778 the new chapel (as it was then called) was opened, and the present Wesley's house built in the following year. These are sacred spots to the Methodist Pilgrim from overseas. They want to see the chapel in which Wesley preached, the house in which John Wesley lived and where he died and the grave wherein he is buried. Because of the German bombing, there is much devastation all around. Though some incendiaries fell on the building, they caused no damage to the chapel itself.

The damage that the sacred edifice has suffered is almost entirely due to the blast. The late Dr. Luke Wiseman said more than once that he was sure that the providence of God was over Wesley's Chapel and Wesley's house; they had been miraculously preserved because their work was not over, their day not yet done. As visitors come to the chapel, they find as they enter there is a sacred aura in the place that speaks of God. The memorials are not flamboyant works of sculpture that glorify man, the tablets in busts proclaim how God has been served. In its essentials, the message of Methodism is still the same, and how best to maintain and proclaim that message in the present generation is the problem that is facing us now. It seems difficult, but prayer and supplication will surely bring the inspiration from God that will make the way clear.

The busy crowds that go up and down City Road every day of the week are not there on Sunday. It must have been as difficult in the early days to reach the Foundry and Wesley's Chapel (for they were literally in the fields) as it is now for any suburbanite to reach the place. God has spared Wesley's Chapel for his purposes, and it is an obligation on us today by prayer and sacrifice to discover that purpose and by God's help to fulfill it.

Reverend Dr. Edward McLellan

Our party has been most fortunate to have as its guide a distinguished Methodist preacher, Dr. Edward McLellan. He was in America for six months last year. Mrs. Moore and I will never cease to be thankful that we had him as our houseguest. He and his lovely family have almost suspended their personal affairs to conduct this group of Americans about their lovely country. One entire day was spent at the country estate of the Doctor's son, Dr. Edward McLellan, Jr. He lives in a wonderful country place situated on the Thames River about 65 miles from London. The glorious house was constructed during the reign of Queen Elizabeth and is, therefore, more than three-hundred years old. One is at a loss for words to describe the beauty of the place and the abounding hospitality of the McLellan family.

There is still much austerity in England. Food is carefully rationed, and certain articles simply cannot be had. No restaurant is allowed to serve more than three courses at any one meal or charge more than five shillings which are approximately $1.25 in American money. Only one towel is given to a guest in the hotel, and it serves for both, the face and the bath. No napkins are given to guests at the table.

On almost every hand there are signs of the terrible damage caused by the German bombings. In some sections, whole blocks are destroyed. We stood last Friday in the ruins of the lovely old church, St. Giles of Cripplegate, in which Cromwell was married and where John Milton, who wrote, *Paradise Lost*, was a regular worshiper. Today, with thousands of other priceless buildings and sacred shrines, it is only a pile of rubble. When one walks through these bombed-out areas one is made to wonder if our civilization can stand another war.

The most marvelous thing in England is the indomitable courage of the people. After nine years of war and its terrible aftermath, they carried on with the spirit which cannot be described. The men wear old clothes for the most part and not many of the ladies have yet been able to put on the "new look," but all of them are proud of their long and glorious history and face the future with confidence and hope. My hat is off to England and I am one American proud to call her "The Mother Country."

Wesleyan Christian Advocate, September 2, 1948, p. 15

The nave of the Church of
St. Giles at Cripplegate, London.

Lucerne, Switzerland
August 12, 1948

Henry Van Dyke, while away from the United States, wrote a wonderful poem, "Home Again." In it are some lines that run something like this:

> "London is a man's town with power in the air.
> Paris is a woman's town with flowers in her hair."

We have just completed five days of sight-seeing in Paris. Like the typical American, we dashed breathlessly from one historic spot to another. The Cathedral of Notre Dame, Napoleon's tomb, the Palace of Versailles, the Eiffel Tower – we took them all in our stride. However, there were times for more orderly and serious observation when we earnestly sought to see and study France and understand some of the problems confronting this nation which has been so sorely tried. Here, as in England, we were impressed with the fortitude of the people.

There is more food in France than in England and the people as a whole are better dressed. This does not mean, however, that France is back to its pre-war days. Far from it. A lovely mother, the devoted wife of a French pastor told me almost accidentally that there had been no milk of any kind on her table for ten long years. The American tourists with their magical American dollars can find food including meat and milk but when you leave the boulevards and get amongst the plain people you find austerity and real privation.

Paris is a city that still has its charm. It is mentioned first in Caesar's commentaries under the name of Lutetia. It was an important city of northern Gaul when it was conquered by the Romans. Clovis settled down in Paris in 497 AD and the city was almost destroyed in the Norman invasions in 887 AD. One has the feeling that the centuries look down upon him as he goes from one historic place to another.

Paris, unlike London., was not severely bombed in the late war. Hitler expected to use it in his plans for world conquest and so it was spared physical destruction. However, the Army took complete possession and the entire population was under unspeakable tyranny of the Gestapo and the stories of their arrogance and cruelty seem like a page out of the Dark Ages.

No serious-minded visitor to Paris can afford to forgo a visit to Versailles which is just outside the city of Paris. The town of Versailles has a population of one hundred fifty thousand but no one gives any attention to the town. It is the magnificent Palace to which all eyes turn. It began as a mere hunting lodge for Louis XIII and was promoted to the dignity of a royal court residence under Louis XIV. The amount expended on the cost of its erection staggers the imagination. Louis XIV died here on September 1, 1715, and immediately his successor Louis XV called in the great architects of that day to design and construct additional wings.

The French Revolution drove Louis XVI and his beautiful queen from the Palace and brought them to their execution at the hands of an enraged people. Napoleon attempted to restore the Palace to its former glory but it was Louis Philippe who gave back its bygone splendor and made it into the national museum dedicated to the glory of France.

It was in the magnificent Hall of Mirrors in this Palace that the Treaty of Versailles which formally closed World War I was signed. When Germany defeated France in the war of 1870 Bismarck, the German Chancellor, forced France to sign the terms of surrender in the same room. It seemed fitting therefore that France with her victorious allies should bring Germany back to the same place for the hour of Germany's national humiliation. Alas! What a grand opportunity was afforded the statesman of the world to use that occasion to build a peaceful world, rather than leaving one in which every nation seems ready to take advantage of another's weakness.

There is too much grandeur, significance, and beauty here for a Georgian who goes wandering about the earth to describe. For example, we stood in one room of the Palace in which 19 kings were born. It was in this little room that poor little frightened Marie Antoinette met in terror on the night of October 6, 1789, the mob that came to drag her to death. The gardens on the Palace grounds are until this day the most original and magnificent display of flowers I have ever seen. One cannot soon forget a day spent amid such splendor and a visit to the scene of much of the most exciting history of the French people.

On Sunday, August 8, our party attended services at the American Church in Paris. The preacher was Dr. Leber, Foreign Secretary of the Board of Missions of the Presbyterian Church. It was good to worship in the house of God and especially helpful to hear a sermon in your language. I should add that our party has been diligent in church attendance. On our first Sunday in London, we went several miles to worship in a Methodist Church and were rewarded by hearing the good straight Methodist sermon. At 3:00 p.m., we went to Westminster Abbey to hear an Anglican bishop from Scotland and at 6:30 the same evening we were all hearing Dr. Leslie Weatherhead.

These lines are being written from Lucerne, Switzerland, the land of majestic mountains, innumerable lakes and a great wonderful people. But that story must wait.

Wesleyan Christian Advocate, September 9, 1948, p. 11.

Geneva, Switzerland
August 20, 1948

Tomorrow, we take a train for Holland after an unforgettable week in glorious Switzerland. We were two days in Lucerne, three days at Interlaken, and two in this famous city, to which so many travelers and international organizations come. Here one comes immediately under the spell of a marvellous civilization that is gone on continuously since 44 BC. Other nations offer one antiquity, massive buildings, and proud histories; but Switzerland has something plus. To describe its beauty is beyond me. Mark Twain was here once and had this to say about the majestic mountains, lovely valleys, and wonderful people of Switzerland:

> "I had a finer and grander site where I was. This was the mighty dome of the Jungfrau softly outlined against the sky and faintly silvered by the starlight. There was something subduing in the influence of that silent and solemn and awful presence; one seemed to meet the immutable, the indestructible, the eternal face-to-face, the trivial and fleeting nature of his existence the more sharply by the contrast. One has the sense of being under the brooding contemplation of the spirit, not an inert mass of rocks and ice –a spirit that had looked down through the slow drift of the ages, upon a million vanished races of men, and judge them; and would judge a million more and still be there, watching, unchanged and unchangeable."

Only a people of industrious habits and strong bodies could have conquered this part of the earth. The total land area is forty-one thousand acres, and only thirty-two thousand of this is capable of producing any crops. The rest is mountainous and therefore, unproductive. Many of these hearty people have emigrated to other lands as this eternal struggle to live will not support all the people who are born here. Here he has the same rights and privileges as all other men. Surrounded by nations where there are monarchies and ruling classes of genuine democracy. Here is a nation of slightly more than four million inhabitants, each of them a free citizen and having equal rights.

One of our most interesting experiences was a motorcoach trip from Lucerne to Interlaken. With a party of twenty others in a bus built especially for rugged mountain climbing, we made this difficult and some of us thought perilous trip.

We climbed to the top of Furka Pass which has an altitude of eight-thousand feet. The road was very narrow and getting our large bus around those narrow corners was a most exciting experience. When we reached the top, we were in a heavy snowstorm.

Bob Hayes of Beaufort has made the entire trip thus far with his Georgia straw hat. Bishop Kern and I tried to auction off Bob's hat during the snowstorm but no one seemed to need a straw hat with the temperature a little above zero.

Here in Geneva, we have carefully inspected the buildings which were used to house the League of Nations. There are no finer buildings anywhere. The nations of the earth, cherishing their dream of peace and committed to the principle of collective security, organized the League of Nations and erected splendid buildings to house its Secretariat. Woodrow Wilson was the prophet who dared to tell the world that there was a better way than that of war. Alas, it was our own America who refused to follow its leader and thus put to death the organization that under God might have prevented World War II.

I confess that these buildings depressed me. There is some activity in them and certain international organizations continue to meet here. But it reminded me of holding a kindergarten in a cathedral. These buildings echoed the footfall of mighty leaders of the nations of the world. Instead of comradeship and peace, the world turned again to suspicion, arrogance, hate, and destruction. Today whole cities are in rubble, and millions of people are so bewildered and oppressed that they know not what they do or why they do it. The church of the Living God must protest against the effort to rebuild the world upon the old decaying foundations of materialism. The helping hand must supplant the mailed fist. The national rivalries which have drenched the world with blood twice in a generation must give way to some organization that is determined to find a way to overcome these seemingly insufferable difficulties of readjustment.

Tomorrow, we are going to Holland where in Amsterdam practically all the churches of the world have sent their chosen representatives to study how the church can play a more worthy part in reshaping the world. The Roman Catholic Church has not seen fit to send representatives. Russia would not allow the Orthodox Church to send its messengers. It should be a rich and rewarding experience to sit down with Christian leaders from forty of the nations of the earth. But, that is another story.

My vacation days are finished. The rest of my story in Europe will be crowded with exacting duties. I follow with love, interest, and prayers to all.

Wesleyan Christian Advocate, September 16, 1948, p. 11.

Amsterdam, Holland
August 28, 1948

This quaint city of eight hundred thousand is reported to have a million visitors as these lines are written. The beloved Queen Wilhelmina is relinquishing her throne after a half-century reign. She is greatly beloved. During this last week of her reign she has come out of semi-retirement and is making a tour of Holland. The entire countryside is in holiday attire it seems that the entire population is on parade. Lights are burning everywhere, children's choruses are singing in the streets, and many people dressed in colorful Dutch costumes give the place a rare and interesting beauty.

Next Monday, September 6, Princess Juliana will be crowned the new Queen of the Netherlands. She is thirty-nine years of age and the proud mother of three lovely children. One afternoon this week she spent the entire afternoon at our Church World Council and impressed us all with her charm and beauty.

In addition to all the Dutch people who have flocked to Amsterdam for the coronation of the new Queen, delegates from nearly fifty of the nations of the world are here for the First Assembly of the World Council of Churches. Churchmen representing practically all the Protestant churches of the world are here. Last Sunday afternoon, as we assembled in the great and beautiful Cathedral, it was a most colorful and impressive service. This is indeed a World Council.

Holland owes its special position in the world church primarily to its geographical position. For centuries Northwestern Europe was the center of European culture and the leader of the world. In this setting, the Netherlands protects the mouths of the great rivers in the middle of the great cultural countries of Germany, France, and England. Moreover, it is a predominantly maritime country; not only is it situated on the seacoast, but it is through a constant struggle with the sea that the Dutch have become great.

The inhabitants of the Netherlands, especially those in Holland and Zeeland, became the seafarers of Europe. In the seventeenth century, their merchant fleet was twice as large as those of all the other countries put together. Especially after the discovery of America and the Eighty Years' War of Liberation, owing to its important hinterland, its connection with England, and its coastal trade, the Netherlands in the seventeenth century occupied a central position not only among the neighboring countries but in the whole of the known world.

Although this central position might have been exclusively economic in character, it was true also of religious and cultural life. As far back as the sixteenth century, the Netherlands was, to an outstanding extent, the place where the three great cultural forces of humanism, Catholicism, and Protestantism met and where the struggle between them took place.

In May 1940, the German army invaded this country. In five days the war was lost and for five years the people had to suffer from the Nazi occupation and its tyranny. National Socialism was not satisfied with a merely military occupation of the Netherlands. On the contrary, they wanted to "educate" according to their ideas. The conqueror made many mistakes. He did not realize their desire for independence and freedom.

Each measure evoked fresh resistance. It was obvious that the churches had been asleep, but that they had not died. They found themselves involved in spiritual resistance. It was a time of much change and uncertainty, but gradually the resistance became stronger.

The churches had to withstand many assaults. The conqueror attempted to seize parish funds so that people in distress might be dependent upon him. The churches refused.

The Germans wanted to combine the youth organizations of the church with those of national socialism, which had very few supporters. Here again, the churches refused to cooperate, and it was again proven that right is greater than military might.

Now that liberation has come, there is a spirit of hopefulness and industry everywhere. Here, as in England, practically all of the best-manufactured goods are shipped abroad to bring in money with which to rebuild the economic life of the nation. The people seem to accept austerity with a smile.

Although there are hundreds of thousands of cattle grazing in the lowlands, it is practically impossible to obtain butter and cheese. These are all for export. Prices are high and the people of very moderate income, which includes practically all of them, are having a hard time financially.

I shall not at this time attempt an evaluation of the work of the World Council of Churches. We are now only at the halfway mark and the final results are not yet in evidence. My own humble opinion at this moment is that we are spending too much time discussing the world's disorder and too little time discovering our spiritual assets. Maybe that will come later. The great church leaders of the world are all here and undoubtedly a strong Christian pronouncement will be forthcoming.

Our little party was saddened today when Leonard Cochran of Valdosta was called to Germany to be with the widow of a young Army captain who had been killed flying the lift into Berlin. Captain and Mrs. Howard were with us recently in Switzerland. Early Sunday morning, August 15, in the English church in Interlaken. Cochran assisted by Bishops Garber and Kern and I baptized the beautiful baby of this fine young couple who were members of our church in Valdosta. How tragic to think that in less than a week this proud young father and a fine soldier had gone down in flaming death. Brother Cochran, had a plane put at his disposal by our American Government; and as these lines are being written, he is flying back to America with this devoted young wife and baby who have been plunged into such sorrow.

The rest of our little party, Bishop Kern, Loy Scott of Savannah, and Claire Cotten of Tallahassee will sail on RMS *Mauretania* next week for home. Bob Hayes of Beaufort is remaining to visit some German prisoners of war which he served so faithfully when they were at Monticello in prison during the war. As for me, I have another six weeks of strenuous work ahead. Belgium, Germany, Austria, and Norway are busy with the task of helping to make Methodism and Christianity victorious and effective in an hour of unparalleled need.

Wesleyan Christian Advocate, September 23, 1948, p. 11

Garmisch, Germany
September 14, 1948

These lines are being written at Garmisch, a most picturesque German city, situated in the Bavarian Alps right close to the border of Austria. A short auto trip yesterday took us across the border into Austria. It would be impossible to describe the majesty of these mountains. From my window here in this little hotel, I can see the pinnacle of Mount Zugspitze which lifts its head nearly nine thousand feet. It is only one of the magnificent, breathtaking mountain peaks from which may be seen, an unequalled panoramic view of the Bavarian, Tyrolean, and Italian Alps.

Perhaps this opening paragraph would give one the impression that I am here on holiday. Such is not the case. For nearly a week I have been in Germany as a guest of the United States Army and as the special representative of the Methodist Commission on Chaplains. The Army authorities have provided me with transportation both by air and auto and thus I have had a most extraordinary opportunity to see the country, meet our Army personnel, and to view the German countryside close up. My particular duty in this place is a two-day conference with our Methodist chaplains stationed in Germany.

It would be impossible to exaggerate the importance of the ministry of these faithful chaplains. They are serving our soldiers with skill and fidelity. I discover that so many of our soldiers over here are mere boys. They are far from home and the influences of the church. These chaplains watch over them with the care and kindness of a true shepherd of the sheep. Let us not get the false idea that now that the shooting war is over we need not be concerned about the work of the chaplains. If anything, it is more important now than ever before. We must stand by these men with our prayers, understanding, and support.

Oberammergau, the home of the justly famous Passion Play, is very nearby. I have been told that all the characters in that mighty presentation as it was last given become members of Hitler's party except for the village blacksmith that played the part of Judas Iscariot in the play. I had no way of checking on this story.

I did discover that it was in a great underground factory near Oberammergau that the German army first manufactured the rocket bombs which were turned loose with such disastrous results in English towns. Once again, the lovely village is at peace. Just now they are busy and competition by which the men and women who were to play the leading role in the Passion Play when it is again presented are to be chosen. 1950 has been fixed as the time for the next performance.

Two days ago I visited Berchtesgaden, another lovely mountain village which will forever be famous because it was there Adolf Hitler built his mountain home. On a high mountainside Hitler, Göring, and Bormann, who were the three architects of that iniquitous thing we now know as Hitlerism, built their palatial homes. The three houses were connected with underground tunnels, and I am told the houses were luxuriously furnished. Alas, they are now in complete ruins. The American and British Air Forces bombed these houses again and again until only a pile of rubble was left. I climbed up through the debris and stood at last in what was left of the room where Hitler slept and saw the room in which Eva Braun, his famous and faithful mistress spent her time. Still higher up the mountain, Hitler built his "Eagles Nest" which is reached by a most difficult climb and then an elevator lift of four hundred feet.

There at the very pinnacle, he built a house from which he could look one way into his native Austria and the other to duped Germany which he was leading toward doom and destruction. I cannot describe my emotions as I stood in this place of arrogance, intrigue, and war and observed that it had all ended in dust and ashes.

Hitler boasted he would build a Germany that would last forever, but over and over again, as I stood there, the phrase "the abomination of desolation" kept coming into my mind. All around me was unbelievable chaos, cities reduced to rubble, a nation bankrupt, and millions of German people disillusioned. In another article, I should deal with general conditions in Germany and try to evaluate the present situation.

Berchtesgaden

Last Sunday I preached in the ancient city of Heidelberg. Here across the centuries has stood the famous University of Heidelberg. There is no more lovely city anywhere than this one. Fortunately, it escaped much heavy bombing and is, therefore, intact. That cannot be said for many large cities in Germany. When I was last here in 1939, I preached for several days to a Methodist Conference in the beautiful city of Heilbronn on the Neckar. It was a city with the population of more than one hundred thousand. Last week I was there to discover the entire city had been totally destroyed. I rode and walked mile on mile through what had once been a proud and ancient city. Not a building is standing. They are all, including churches, libraries, and public buildings, in total ruin. Where I had once witnessed the hurrying life of a great city, I beheld miles of ghostly ruins, dust, and ashes. Out of these ruins, some lovely flowers were growing as if God would hide the scars of man's hatred.

In Heidelberg, these two cities are about seventy-five miles apart. I preached in a large German church to a congregation of approximately five hundred. Most of them were Americans, military and civilian. Our Army headquarters are located here. There are hundreds of Americans here and civilians employed by our government. It was a joy to preach to them. There were soldiers of all ranks present from generals to privates. Imagine my surprise and delight to discover in the congregation my grandson who has been a soldier over here for almost three years.

Tomorrow I hurry back to Belgium where from September 16-20, I preside over the Annual Conference of Belgium. Then I go up to Bergen, Norway, for the Central Conference of our Methodism in Norway, Sweden, Denmark, and Finland. I shall be there from September 21 to October 1. Then I return to Germany where it is to be my pleasure to have a conference with

General Lucius Clay, our Supreme Commander, who is doing such wise and constructive work for the entire German nation as well as our own.

It is to be my privilege to fly the airlift into Berlin and to see firsthand some of the significant things which are happening there at present. October 5 through the 10th finds me in the Central Methodist Conference for Germany which meets in Frankfurt on Main. Bishop J. W. E. Sommer is the beloved Methodist Bishop for Germany. What a privilege it will be to spend nearly a week with my fellow Methodists who have suffered so much. What a joy it is to place the funds so generously given me for relief in so many places where there is such acute need. It will require another article to describe my second visit to Germany. Meanwhile, I confess to a bit of homesickness, and it will be with joy that I board the RMS *Queen Elizabeth* October 18 bound for America and home.

Wesleyan Christian Advocate, September 30, 1948, p. 5.

Bishop J.W.E. Sommer

Oslo, Norway
September 19, 1948

The Annual Conference in Belgium came to a happy conclusion Sunday, September 19. Early next morning I took an airplane for Oslo, Norway. This flight was made over the KLM Airlines which happens to be owned by the government of Holland. Whatever the Dutch undertake, they do well. The day was clear and from my plane window, I saw the harvested fields of Belgium disappear in the lowlands of Holland with the dikes holding back the sea. A brief time was spent in Amsterdam and soon we were on our way to Norway. This flight required nearly three hours over the North Sea. Flying over the mountains and looking down in clear sunlight upon the beautiful villages surrounding the innumerable inlets of the sea, which are called fjords, was a never to be forgotten experience. Night found me in the capital city of Oslo, and at 8:00 p.m. I was greeted by a very large congregation of Methodist people in our large Central Church.

From Oslo, I went with a large company of delegates to Bergen where the Central Conference for all our Methodism in Northern Europe was scheduled to meet. It required twelve hours for our train to climb over the tall Norwegian mountains and across the country from east to west. One could easily imagine he was traveling in either Switzerland or Japan. The scenery compares with any I have seen anywhere, and the people are clean, devout, and industrious. Their homes are spotless, and while some houses need paint after the scourge of war, you feel that everything has been scrubbed and made as clean as a dinner plate.

Lofty mountains shut Bergen in on all sides, only seaward, to the west, there is open space towards the world. The people of Bergen have ever since the days of the Vikings been a roving people. It was a simpler matter for them to reach England, Scotland, Germany or Holland, than the interior of their land. Many came sailing to Bergen from other countries, settled, married, and became good citizens. Bergen is a self-centered town, that for centuries had to live its own life. A roving people that looked out toward the sea for its means of existence. This brought about an attachment to home. It bred local culture, and independence in business, possibly also a certain amount of self-overestimation. But, at the same time, it created a distinctive people, who were capable of giving their town character. Nature bestowed on it is beautiful situation and surroundings, but the citizens have built up the city in the course of nine hundred years of faithful affection.

When the traveler arrives at Bergen, he finds a modern city with some hundred forty thousand inhabitants. It is distinctly a shipping and commercial town but possesses great cultural interests. A tour of the town tells the history of centuries in its old churches and buildings, in picturesque town borders, and in museums and art galleries. Here, two hundred fifty years ago, the poet Ludvig Holberg first saw the light of day; in this town stood the cradle of Professor I. C. Dahl, the founder of modern Norwegian painting. It was from Bergen that Ole Bull set out with his violin to capture the world. In this city lived Edward Grieg and here, also, he composed most of his music which is today the world's common property.

The city was founded in the year 1075 by King Olav Kyree. Its excellent situation quickly made it one of the most important harbors along the treacherous and exposed coast. Shipping and commerce always have been its existence. In the Middle Ages, it was the biggest town in the North, the greatest and most important center of commerce. The town is dependent on its harbor, around which the city has sprung up.

The Central Conference corresponds to our Jurisdictional Conference which met this past summer in Columbia, South Carolina. The main difference here is that separate nations are represented, Sweden, Norway, Denmark, and Finland all come together to form the Central Conference of Northern Europe. Bishop Theodore Arvidson of Sweden was elected Bishop four years ago. He is greatly beloved and trusted by the Methodist people of all the Scandinavian countries.

Our church in all these countries was planted something like a hundred years ago by natives who had gone to America as sailors and soundly converted at Methodist altars. With their new experience of Christ, they returned home to tell their families and friends. As a result, the movement spread, and soon there was a Methodist Church established. The people are deeply pious and take their profession as a serious business. To date, we have a well-trained ministry, good church buildings and the congregations are all self-supporting. In addition, they have sent out and supported thirty missionaries to Africa, China, and Sumatra. Nowhere have I found a people more worthy of the Methodist tradition than those with whom I have been associated in this Conference.

The organization and activities of the Deaconess work are most praiseworthy. There is something like three hundred sisters who have dedicated themselves to lifetime service for Christ and his church. They are all graduate nurses and, as a result of their service, our church owns and operates most successfully three great hospitals. The work of these consecrated women is a remarkable feature of Methodism's life in Germany, Switzerland, as well as in Scandinavian countries.

Norway was taken by Hitler's army early in the last war. The king and most of his army found refuge in England. The Germans ruled with a rod of iron and the hardships of the people can hardly be described. Practically all of their foodstuff was taken by the German soldiers and the native population was reduced to complete dependence on the sustenance of the fish they could take from the sea. Even now one scarcely sees any meat upon the tables. It is fish, usually cold, for breakfast, dinner, and supper. They do have some excellent cheese, and in a short time, I have learned how to have breakfast from cold bread, cheese, and coffee. An egg is something you greet about once a week and as a long-lost friend.

The noonday meal comes at 2:00 p.m. and when guests are around it becomes quite formal. Between courses, songs and speeches are made. Several times I have remained at the dinner table from two to five. We have grace at the table before eating and a prayer of Thanksgiving when we finish. These are God-fearing people who specialize in the essentials of life. America would certainly be helped by some more of the religious devotion which characterizes these people and certainly, our digestion would be better if we would take more time for our meals.

Following the Central Conferences, I went with Bishop Arvidson on a preaching mission to several of the Norwegian towns. We traveled by boat up and down their enchanting coastline. In every place, we found nice church buildings and large and appreciative congregations. Tomorrow, I have my last service in Oslo, the capital city, and take a plane for Gothenburg, Sweden. My days in Sweden will be devoted to preaching in our Methodist Seminary at Gothenburg and some of our Swedish churches. Methodism in Sweden are the strongest we have in northern Europe. If time can be found I may write a brief article on my experiences there.

As I write, the Norwegian radio is telling of the tension in Paris at the United Nations Conference over the situation in Berlin. My schedule puts me in Berlin for next Sunday, October 3, where I am to preach to a German congregation. I am also to have the privilege of a conference with General Lucius Clay who commands all of our American forces in Germany. All are tense over the possibility of another war. I cannot believe the statesman of the world are willing that we should have another open conflict. However, our whole position is bound up with what happens in Berlin. I am quite sure that if we yield to the Russians at that focal point, they will spread out all over Western Europe. A world dominated by Stalin would be as bad as one dominated by Hitler. At any rate, I hope to look upon Berlin with my own eyes. My last official duty on this trip will be the Methodist Central Conference in Frankfurt, Germany, October 5 to the 10th. Then to Cherbourg, France, to go onboard the RMS *Queen Elizabeth* on October 16 which will take me to dear old America.

Wesleyan Christian Advocate, October 21, 1948, p. 15.

General Lucius D. Clay

Brussels, Belgium
September 20, 1948

After an absence of nine years, I have just spent the last few days in beautiful little Belgium. The past five days have been devoted to the presidency of the Annual Conference. My last sight of this company of wonderful Methodists was in July 1939. At the close of the Annual Conference that year I took a boat for my duties in the Belgian Congo far down in Africa. While I was in Africa, war was declared and the only way I could get from Africa to China was by a long detour through South America and then to the United States and across the Pacific Ocean to Shanghai. One can imagine the joy that was mine to greet once more old friends with whom I labored from 1934 to 1939. What eventful years have passed, and what heavy sorrow as I followed up on these people since last we were together.

Belgium, like Poland, is so situated on the continent of Europe that every great war comes to their territory. The first world war made Belgium the scene of fierce fighting and the second world war repeated that experience. The Germans soon conquered Belgium and for five years these liberty-loving people were under the heel of an Army of Occupation. Naturally, there were some who during those years found it to their selfish advantage to collaborate with the Germans and now they are reaping the reward of their treason. Even the King, Leopold III, was thought of as being under German influence, and not until now has he been allowed to return to his throne. The question of his return is just about the hottest political question in Belgium's political life just now.

The country, due to enormous riches in the Belgian Congo, has regained more economic stability and prosperity than the average European country. The Congo is rich in rubber and copper and the abundance of these colonial supplies has proven a lifesaver for the mother country.

Prices are sky-high and inflation is working a severe hardship upon the people. While the stores are full of goods the average person has no income with which to pay these high prices. I found our Methodist pastors suffering terribly from the mounting high prices and with income altogether insufficient for such living costs.

Methodism in Belgium is not very old. At the close of World War I the Methodist Episcopal Church, South, opened work in Belgium, Czechoslovakia, and Poland. Under the blessings of Almighty God, the work has grown and prospered in all these nations. Among all the younger churches I have observed around the world none is more evangelical and aggressive than our church in Belgium. We are blessed by the ministry of well-trained and consecrated men. Dr. William G. Thonger, who preached at both the Florida and South Georgia Conferences last summer, is the beloved and wise Superintendent of the work in Belgium.

The Annual Conference which closed last night was a time of rejoicing. The hindrances imposed by war conditions are slowly disappearing. Several of our church buildings which were destroyed by bombs had been rebuilt. A splendid country house has been secured as a camp for our young people. In many ways, the year has brought spiritual triumphs. The pastors and lay delegates gathered to sing with new enthusiasm, "A Mighty Fortress is Our God." If the Methodist Church in Belgium could enlist the active and intelligent support of our churches in America it could make phenomenal gains in the years just ahead. There are some opportunities here for expansion I would like to lay upon the hearts of American Methodists.

One of the most active laymen in the Conference was a man whose life the redeeming power of Christ has been so wonderfully illustrated. He came out of World War I with the highest military decorations the government could bestow upon its heroes; with the decoration and with a pension. Strong drink wrecked the life and home of this brave soldier. So wicked did he become that the government took from him its decoration and his pension. It was then that the Methodist Church entered the picture. Some twenty years ago this hopeless drunkard was brought to Christ. He became a new man in Christ Jesus. His life was transformed, his home was reestablished, and the town had a new citizen. He lived such a beautiful Christian life that a few years ago the Belgian government, by a special act that required the signature of the King, restored the military decoration and the pension. Today he is loved and honored by everyone. What a privilege to know and work with such a man. His great interest just now is the enlargement of the public school for Protestant children for which he is largely responsible. The day of miracles has not passed.

Although my days in Belgium have been crowded, I did take time to drive to Dunkirk which is just over the Belgian border in France. It was from the beaches of Dunkirk that the entire British Army had its miraculous deliverance. When the lines broke in the early months of the war the English army was pressed back until it stood in apparent helplessness on the beaches of Dunkirk. The German Army was pressing hard and only a miracle could save them. A miracle was practically England's one hope of survival. Then the miracle happened. The English people put out across the nearly always turbulent English Channel which is sixty miles wide in almost every sort of boat imaginable to rescue their soldiers. God stilled these troubled waters and for history-making days these English boys went home in these improvised boats.

What might have been the greatest tragedy in English history was turned into a miracle of deliverance. Standing there I could certainly not understand it all except by simple belief that God willed it so, and that he delivered this army so that in a few short years it could return with our American troops to deliver Europe from one of the worst tyrants the world has ever known. By the way, the Methodist pastor, the Reverend Edouard Smith, I appointed there in 1938. Through all the agony of war he stood by and although he and his wife and lovely young daughter were compelled to live in the trenches for several weeks, they never left their post of duty. What an experience to sit at their table and drink tea and eat cakes that they have received from the Methodist Committee on Overseas Relief from friends in America.

In two hours, I shall take a plane from Brussels to Amsterdam, Holland, and on to Oslo, Norway, where I preach tonight. Oslo is more than a thousand miles from Brussels but if all goes well I will across the lowlands of Holland, the wide waters of the North Sea, and the tall mountains of Norway, and will be at home in the presence of a company of Norwegian Methodists before I sleep tonight.

Wesleyan Christian Advocate, October 14, 1948, p. 15.

Editor's Note*:* The two preceding letters were published out of sequence. The events in the letter written in Brussels predate the events in the letter written in Oslo, Norway. A decision was made to retain the order as originally published.

Berlin, Germany
October 5, 1948

The famous American writer, Irving Cobb, once tried in an article to describe the Grand Canyon and gave it up with the remark, "One can no more describe this spectacle than he could the final Judgment Day." That is exactly how I feel about all I have seen in Germany in this capital city of Berlin in particular. But, let me begin where my last article ended.

Friday, October 1, found me flying from Gothenburg, Sweden to Copenhagen, Denmark, and on to Frankfurt, Germany, which is in effect the present capital of the American Zone. Our plane tarried for a while in the city of Hamburg which is in the British Zone. That was the last city I saw in Germany when I was here in 1939. Well, do I recall how the giant bombers of Hitler's Air Force stood row on row that August day nine years ago. What a change has been wrought. Much of the city is in ruins and all the evidence of Hitler might have gone with the wind.

Sunday, October 3, found me preaching to a large company of Americans in one of our Army chapels in Frankfurt. The Commanding General in Frankfurt is General Robinson Duff. He and his wife were faithful members of my congregation in San Antonio twenty-six years ago. They have kept their keen interest in the church and their enthusiastic commendation even before I arrived was responsible for a packed house. There are hundreds of American civilians over here and they with the soldiers gave me a fine hearing. Incidentally, I have met four army colonels over here whose marriage ceremony I performed while they were young officers stationed in San Antonio. Some of them have requested that I baptize their children on this trip and it has been a great joy.

Gen. Lucius Clay and Gen. Duff had graciously arranged for me to see Berlin. That once proud city is now a small section of Germany completely surrounded by Russians. The city itself is divided into American, British, French, and Russian sectors but all surrounding territory is held by the Russians. It now appears a stupid arrangement, but I suppose at the time the agreement was made our leaders supposed Russia would act like a civilized nation. Alas, they have become as belligerent and dangerous as ever was Hitler.

The only way to reach Berlin is by air as the Russians have blockaded all train and auto travel. The American and British armies are attempting to feed the millions of Germans who live in their zone by air transport. It is called by the Americans Operation Vittles. These enormous motor transport planes loaded with the most essential articles such as food, coal, medicines, etc., take off from Frankfurt every four minutes. My transportation had been arranged on one of these planes. We left Frankfurt by night. The pilot was good enough to invite me up front where I could look out on the lights of German towns while we passed over them at a height of approximately six thousand feet.

We had to be sure that we were exactly on schedule and at the exact altitude as there were scores of other such planes in the air before and behind us. I shall not soon forget when the captain pointed out the lights of the last town in friendly territory. From there on we were over Russian territory, and I was told that only "by the grace of God and the faithfulness of our giant engines will we make it." In due time we were down on the great Tempelhof airfield in Berlin. Later that night as I tried to sleep the everlasting drone of those planes going and coming on an errand of mercy, plus the fact that I was emotionally upset over all I had seen kept me from sleep.

Sgt. Don Weldon of the U. S. Air Force has written the following poem describing the airlift. He calls it "Thou Great Swan."

> Take to thy wings as the West wind sings,
> rise to the heavens, thou great Swan;

surge through the sky while clouds go rushing by,
  thy mission, of charity, has begun.

Night and day, an endless array,
accepting the challenge of lightning and rain;
except for a "sacred few," thy cargoes keep
coming through to sustain life amongst want and pain.

So, hum to the moon thy engines vibrant tune,
sweeter music has never been sung;
far behind thy silvery nose,
ten tons of Good Faith repose,
  thrust forward, roar onward, Thou Great Swan.

Early on the morning of October 4, I was ushered into the office of General Clay. He is a Georgian and a Methodist. He greeted me with what is known as true Southern hospitality. Soon we were busy discussing not the problems of war but about persons and things "down in Georgia." The general has kept in close touch with happenings in his old state. Together we discussed Methodist pastors who had preached to him as a boy and one of my neighbors who had coached him in high school athletics. It was hard for me to realize that I was in the presence of a four-star general and one of the great soldiers of the world. He looks and talks more like a college professor. He has a keen mind, an exceedingly kind and gracious manner, and seems to possess complete physical and mental poise. Here was the man upon whose decisions rest the fate of the German people and the peace of the world. He was gracious enough to make me his guest both in Berlin and in Frankfurt and I am deeply indebted to him for a hundred kindnesses.

Berlin, I knew very well from 1934 to 1939. It is now seventy percent destroyed by bombs. Most of its former magnificent splendor is gone and one walks endlessly it seems the streets of debris and dust. It is so changed by all that I have had great difficulty finding the places I once knew. However, it should be said that the German people despite these indescribable conditions are "digging out" and there are signs of recovery. I see thousands of German women hauling away the mountains of debris and on a few streets some shops are open. The currency reform instituted only a few months ago seems to have worked magic and there is every reason to believe the German people are cooperating in their greatly needed economic recovery. Much of today has been spent visiting our Methodist churches, hospitals, and people. What stories of suffering and hardships have I heard, yet not one word of complaint. Food is still short, electric power is available for only two hours each night. The Russians control a vast section of the city and the people live in fear of them. But hope and courage still live in these Germans Christians who only want a chance to live in peace.

Tonight, I go onboard another transport and will ride Operations Vittles out of the strange scene where allies who fought a war together now carry great burdens all because one of their wartime partners will not play the game according to the rules.

The Central Conference of German Methodism opens tomorrow in Frankfurt, and I must write at least one other article in which something will be said about Methodism in Germany.

Wesleyan Christian Advocate, October 28, 1948, p. 11

Airplanes ready to airlift food and supplies
to Berlin in Operation Vittles.

Airplanes ready to airlift food and supplies
to Berlin in Operation Vittles.

Somewhere at Sea
October 19, 1948

In previous articles, I have tried to describe the rubbled streets, gutted buildings, and ragged walls of the bombed cities of Germany. When one walks through the ruins of what were once proud cities, down street after street lined with blasted homes or destroyed factories, gazes at open roofs and fallen floors gutted by fire, he comes to see as never before that this thing we call civilization is a fragile thing. Twice within the short space of a quarter-century, the entire world has been plunged into total war. In these two struggles uncounted millions of men, women, and children have died, vast quantities of wealth have been destroyed, the economic systems of mankind almost wrecked, international relations so poisoned that today all around the world we find a harvest of hunger, hopelessness, and hate. It is impossible to understand or describe the present plight of the human family but one cannot easily escape the conviction that it is all the inevitable result of withdrawing the restraint and idealism of Christianity from the life of our world. We have put too much faith in our secular civilization and left too little room for overmastering faith in the God of righteousness.

However, amid all these shadows we find God and His Church building away at a new world. This may be a day of divine judgment, but it is also a day of deliverance. Beyond all this angry inferno of man's wickedness, one can discover the faint outline of the city of God being built in the earth if he only has the eyes of faith to behold it. The church may not at this hour be sweeping the world with great spiritual triumphs such as we have known in other days but has not capitulated to the forces of evil. It is still the one organization that seems to be able to bridge these chasms of hate and to carry all men in its love. Of all the forces now at work for the healing and redemption of the world, the church more than all others is purifying the life of human society and redeeming human character. I found this to be especially true in Germany. The church is easily the most creative and redemptive force at work in this divided and needy nation. In holy boldness, the Methodists of Germany are at the very front of the Christian forces which are apt to produce a better nation and to grow a people worthy of that nation. They have a staggering task before them in the physical rehabilitation of their destroyed properties, but even greater is their task of holding their youth in a time of great national bewilderment and of bringing to bear upon the disillusioned people of Germany the claims of Christ and of making known His power to redeem men and nations.

The Central Conference of Germany met in Frankfurt on October 5-10. It was my high honor to be there as the Representative of the Council of Bishops. The delegates came from the Americans, British, French, and even the Russian Zones of Germany. We were pleasantly surprised and grateful that the Soviet government after long negotiations finally agreed for the sixteen delegates representing Methodist churches situated in the territory now under Russian control to participate in the conference.

It has long been a tradition that Methodist conferences should open with the familiar hymn, "And are we yet alive and see each other's face." But, never before in my experience did those words mean quite so much. There they were living in desperately hard situations, twenty-six of their members had fallen in battle as conscripted soldiers in their nation's army. Nearly all of their cities bombed, many of their people hungry, their entire nation under the complete mastery of victorious foreign armies but still they were singing, "And are we yet alive?" It greatly moved me.

Bishop J. W. E. Sommer is the trusted and beloved leader of this church. He was always opposed to Hitlerism and its pagan philosophy of life. He is a gifted, wise, and deeply consecrated leader of his people, and they are most fortunate to have him in these trying after-the-war years. He was elected bishop three years ago for a limited term. This conference unanimously and enthusiastically elected him as bishop for life. For five wonderful days, I sat with German Methodists and watched them lay plans for a new thrust forward in the work of Christ and His church.

They may be sorely tried but they are not cast down. They know all too well that a formal fainthearted, self-indulgent Christianity will not suffice for a crisis such as is now upon them. They are determined that there shall be no faltering in the face of present-day difficulties. They interpret all that has happened to them and the world as a call from God to His church for aggressive action.

It would hardly be fair for me to bring this article to a close without some word concerning the American Army of Occupation in Germany. To begin with, I think that all Southerners are naturally skeptical about the good accomplished by armies that remain in a country after the actual fighting is done. The deep resentments which linger in the Southland until this day are not there because our fathers surrendered at Appomattox in 1865, but because of the "Tragic Era" which followed. Naturally, therefore, I was most anxious to see if our Army of Occupation was doing its work in a wise, humane and constructive fashion. I sincerely believe we are. From General Clay down to the private soldier, I found the desire to assist the German people to purge from their nation's life those pagan influences which we associate with Hitlerism and to promote and defend those Christian standards and democratic ideals which will eventually give Germany a rightful place once more in the Family of Nations. To say no mistakes have been made or that every individual is always pursued these high aims would be an exaggeration. But, our work thus far has been so constructive and our love for liberty, justice, and equality so manifest that doubtful Germans have no hesitancy in affirming that no greater tragedy could come to Germany just now than for the Americans to withdraw. Ours is a delicate and difficult task. It requires time, men, and money but it also demands brains, skill, patience, and understanding on a scale and in such amounts as we have scarcely ever imagined. As these lines are written the United Nations is debating "The Berlin Situation." Russia by her arrogance and unreasonableness has become as great a threat to the peace of the world as Hitler ever was. A single act of aggression on their part could easily become a bomb that would set the world ablaze again.

Here these articles must be brought to an end. They have not been written as studied and thoughtful conclusions on the affairs of the world but only as day-by-day impressions as I have moved from place to place. They have covered my travels and experiences for a little more than three months. Curiously enough now that I am about to conclude this last article it is not yet been my privilege to see any of the earlier ones in print. It may appear, possibly, that there is a lack of consistency in my viewpoint. If so it is because with additional information I altered my viewpoint.

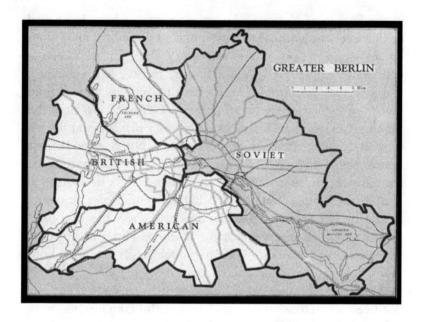

The Methodist Church has highly honored me by sending me as its messenger on this "special mission." By land, sea, and air I have traveled since July to England, France, Switzerland, Germany, Belgium, Austria, Holland, Norway, Sweden, and Denmark. In every place, I have sought to encourage our Methodist people and to help defend, preserve, and promote all those imperishable values for which Methodism stands. I come back greatly concerned because of the black and threatening forces which hang like a cloud over the heads of men, but absolutely confident that Christ has illimitable resources at His command and that alone guarantee the ultimate supremacy of righteousness in the world. This is a time for us who call ourselves Christian to live and act like men and women who believe in God.

To all the ministers and members of our church in the North and South Georgia Conferences to whom I owe my first duty, I am grateful for their generous sharing of my time and strength with our fellow Methodists on the other side of the Atlantic. To a brave and gracious wife who throughout the long years of my incessant world travels has always supported and encouraged me by her prayers and affection, I render my grateful praise. If, at the end of my earthly way the Heavenly Father has any praise or reward to bestow, to her will certainly go the greater part.

This proud ship RMS *Queen Elizabeth* on which these lines are written is now somewhere at sea. The ocean upon which we sail is shrouded in dense fog, but if all goes well, we shall find our way in two more days to the land "where the air is full of sunlight and the flag is full of stars." It is the best nation in all of the earth. As I draw nearer, I find the attraction stronger and stronger. I want no higher honor and could have no more sacred duty than to spend and be spent in the service of these dear ones who love and serve our Savior in the fellowship of the Methodist Church. Thanks and may God bless everyone.

Wesleyan Christian Advocate, November 4, 1948, p. 5

The RMS *Queen Elizabeth*

CHAPTER NINE

An Emergency Mission to Asia
October 1949- March 1950

Decatur, Georgia
October, 6, 1949

Under the orders of the Council of Bishops, I must sail on November 4th on the SS *President Monroe* from San Francisco for an emergency mission for our Church. My assignment will take me to Malaya, Borneo, Sumatra, Java, and Burma. Mrs. Moore will accompany me. We will arrive in Singapore on December 9th and plunge at once into a round of Annual Conferences which will require all our time until February 10th, when we take a ship returning home. We are expected to arrive in San Francisco on March 5th.

Bishop Edwin F. Lee, who was for several years the Presiding Bishop of the Methodist Church in the above-named nations, retired in 1948 and died shortly thereafter. The General Conference meeting in Boston in 1948 gave authorization to the Conferences in that area to organize themselves into a Central Conference and to elect a bishop as is provided in our Church *Book of Discipline*. However, there has been so much disturbance in that section of the world and especially in Burma that bringing people together for conferences has been difficult, if not impossible. Conditions have now quieted somewhat, and it seems possible to proceed with the several Annual Conferences, and we hope the Central Conference. We will establish a home base in Singapore and go from there by plane to the other countries. The first Annual Conference will be in Medan, Sumatra, December 14-18. The second will be in Penang from December 29-January 1. We will then return to Singapore and hold the Annual Conference in Malaya on January 4-8.

Immediately thereafter I hope to fly to Borneo for a two-week visit to that interesting country. While I am there the Annual Conference will be held. Then back to Singapore where in the last week of January the Methodist representatives from these several nations will come together for their Central Conference, and it is hoped that a bishop will be chosen at that time.

This mission will require approximately four months to complete. The countries to which I am being sent are halfway around the world from Georgia. Traveling there and back by boat will require sixty days, and I hope to remain on the field for at least two months. It will be a long and strenuous trip, requiring days and weeks of prolonged and arduous labor. The war has left innumerable problems in that part of the world and the Christian Church is not outside this Zone of disturbance.

I have made two emergency missions to disturbed areas for our Church since the war ended. In 1946, I spent two months in Korea, and in 1948, two months were given to some perplexing problems in Europe. This third mission is perhaps the most difficult of them all, and we shall need the prayers and support of all our dear friends here in the homeland. In the days and weeks between now and November 4 when we must sail, there is much I would like to accomplish in the work of the Church in Georgia. October and November have been designated as the time when all our congregations will be asked to go "the second mile" by assuming the support of some additional missionary special. Then, in December we will be thinking of that great sacrificial offering for our worn-out preachers to be made on December 18. "Life is not resting in the clover, it's up to the walls and over!"

Wesleyan Christian Advocate, October 6, 1949, p. 1

At Sea
November 7, 1949

My first crossing of the Pacific Ocean was in September 1934. The ship was the RMS *Empress of Canada*. My cabin was below decks and crowded with three other men. Since that day aoI have crossed the Pacific fifteen times and am now far out at sea on my sixteenth crossing. What memories came trooping back. Proud ships that were once my home for days have disappeared. The SS *President Coolidge*, the SS *President Hoover*, the RMS *Empress of Japan*, and the RMS *Empress of Canada*, all those lovely ships were Japanese owned and operated. The last war swept them from the sea. So much is changed, but the blue Pacific remains the same. Sometimes pacific according to its name but at other times lashing in furious waves like an enraged lion.

When I landed in New York in October 1943, from another one of these emergency missions for the church I thought surely that would be my last of such missions. For fifteen years the service of Christ and his church has carried me to faraway places. It seems only fair that others should assume these responsibilities, but the Council of Bishops thought otherwise.

So here I am on my way to nations half-way around the world. But I do not complain. No greater honor has come to me than having had a small part in the missionary work of the church during this time of world convulsion. There are millions of men and women who are better and happier because the church in America has taken seriously the command of our Lord to preach the gospel to the ends of the earth. So, with a new determination to evade no peril, to seek no discharge from duty, and with cheerful confidence to serve as best I can I am again on my way.

The last three months have been hectic with preparation. There were so many things to do, churches to be dedicated, and plans for great movements of Georgia Methodism to be set in motion. All these added to the details of travel preparation, the inoculations against disease and strange lands, etc., made life strenuous. At last, the day of departure arrived and on Monday morning, October 31, Mrs. Moore and I say goodbye to our children and friends and started on a journey that will take us to ten nations and keep us away from home until March of next year.

Mr. and Mrs. Asa G. Candler, Jr., of Atlanta, graciously agreed to take us from Atlanta to San Francisco in their lovely private plane. How grateful I am for this consecrated layman and his equally consecrated and gracious wife. We took off from the Atlanta airport at 9:00 a.m. The weather was cloudy and did not appear to be good for flying.

Pretty soon, however, we were up to an altitude of eleven thousand feet in the sunshine with the cloud banks far below. By 2:30 p.m. we were in San Antonio, Texas, with our daughter, Evelyn, and her lovely little family. There we spent the night and enjoyed the fellowship of good people whom we served while pastoring Travis Park Church many years ago. Early on the morning of November 1, we were on our way to California. Bishop and Mrs. Paul E. Martin of Little Rock, Arkansas, joined us in San Antonio. They are on board a ship with us en route to India.

We had breakfast at El Paso, lunch at Phoenix, Arizona, and having flown seventeen hundred miles we were on the field in San Francisco at 4:00 p.m. We had three days in San Francisco for shopping and last-minute preparations. While there we were quartered at Hotel California – one of the best – which is the property of the Methodist Church.

Noon Friday, November 4, found us on board the SS *President Monroe* on which we shall remain until we reach Singapore, Malaya, December 9. We sailed out under the Golden Gate Bridge and took a last long look at the shoreline of our homeland. It will be four and a half months before we will sail back into that harbor and greet those we love best. This ship will be our home for thirty-five days. Through wind and weather, it will carry us on our way. Our cabin is quite comfortable with twin beds and a private bath. The dining room service is exceptionally good. Counting the books I purchased and those sent to the ship by kind friends I have twenty-three volumes in our stateroom. Surely this is a fine chance to catch up on one's reading. This is not a large ship as modern vessels go. It is four hundred ninety feet long and has a capacity for approximately one hundred passengers. It began its voyage in New York, went down the Atlantic coast, passing through the Panama Canal, and then up the Pacific coast to San Francisco. Many of the passengers are on an around-the-world cruise and will stay on board until they reach New York next February. We will disembark at Singapore and return across the Pacific on another vessel.

Yesterday was the Sabbath Day and the Captain asked me to take the service. We had a good congregation and a splendid service. I noticed in the congregation Mr. and Mrs. Baxter Maddox, Jr., who are members of the First Methodist Church in Atlanta. They will disembark at Honolulu.

Today we will put in at Honolulu, Hawaii, and have a part of two days there. Already words come from our missionaries there telling of a reception which they have planned for us. The same is true in Tokyo, Colby, Hong Kong, and Manila. More and more I am grateful for the fellowship of the Christian church. There is hardly a city in the world where I could not find friends and hospitality. All of this is a result of being a part of the church.

We have been advised that while in Japan, General and Mrs. Douglas MacArthur will entertain a luncheon for Bishop and Mrs. Martin and Mrs. Moore and me. Our boat is to call at a port on the island of Formosa. We have some hope of seeing General and Madame Chiang Kai-shek if they are there when we call. We had hoped to see Shanghai but on account of the disturbance in China that is now impossible. We will call in Formosa and Hong Kong.

This letter will be sent back from Honolulu. The next one will be two or three weeks later as it is several days by sea from Honolulu to Yokohama, Japan, which will be our next stop. Our friends, our churches and all that Methodism seeks to accomplish are always in our love and prayers.

Wesleyan Christian Advocate, December 1, 1949, p. 15

General and Mrs. Douglas MacArthur

At Sea, Between Hawaii and Japan
November 11, 1949

This is Armistice Day in the United States. We are some five hundred miles west of Honolulu bound for Japan so there is little chance for a celebration for us. My mind turns naturally to that day of victory in 1918. I was at Camp Wheeler near Macon where I put in almost two years with fine soldier lads from Georgia, Florida, and Alabama who made up the old 31st Division. It was for us that day a time of great rejoicing. So many momentous and world-shaking events have followed that it is difficult to recall the full significance of that day. At least we are in the spirit of the day as our boat pushes on through wind and weather toward Yokohama, Japan, which will be our next port of call.

We arrived in Honolulu, Hawaii, at 2:00 p.m. on November 9 and had twenty-four never-to-be-forgotten hours on that lovely island. Perhaps a few facts concerning this group of islands that are an essential part of our nation will be of interest to the readers of the *Wesleyan Christian Advocate*.

Mark Twain called Hawaii "the loveliest fleet of islands anchored in any ocean." Another admirer of these paradise islands said: "To leave Hawaii is to die a little." For those who have experienced the thrill of arriving at these beautiful islands, and later, the sadness of departure, know and appreciate the truth of these poetic quotations. A visit there is a memorable experience, treasured through a lifetime.

The territory of Hawaii is a group of islands totalling six thousand four hundred thirty-five square miles and extending three hundred-fifty miles from Kauai in the north to Hawaii, the largest of the group, to the extreme south. Too many people mistakenly believe that Hawaii is a single island – the one island of Oahu, the locale of Honolulu, the largest city, and the famed Waikiki Beach. Nothing could be further from the truth. The various islands which neighbor Oahu are equally as interesting, as those who visit them by plane or ship will testify. Hawaii, a volcanic-coral group of islands, combines eight main islands and covers an area of approximately three hundred ninety miles. It grows ninety percent of the world's pineapple.

Hawaii's temperature is made especially for those islands, so they say, and is mild as the soil is fertile for tropical fruits and vegetables. Cane sugar is its chief product and its other products consist of coffee, rice, cotton, nuts, bananas, and potatoes. Some livestock is raised. In normal times, the tourist business is Hawaii's third-biggest source of income. At least eighty-six percent of the islands' population, although racially heterogeneous, are native-born.

Hawaii's governor is appointed by the President to a four-year term and there is a locally elected two-house legislature. Hawaii's delegate to the House of Representatives in Washington has all floor privileges, but no vote. Legislation is now on the floor of Congress to make Hawaii a state.

Methodism is quite strong on these islands. We have in our church membership Americans from the States, Chinese, Japanese, Koreans, and, of course, Hawaiians. For many years, Dr. W. H. Fry was the beloved and able superintendent. He is now retired and has been succeeded by Dr. Leonard Oechali, who came out from California. Travelers to and from the Orient have come to appreciate the hospitality of our Methodist people on the island. Our boat was hardly alongside the wharf before we were greeted by the hearty welcome from a group who had come to meet us. The newspapers with the always alert photographers were there. Honolulu always welcomes the guest by placing about their neck lovely wreaths of fragrant flowers which they call leis. They present you not with one, but many. These were placed about our shoulders until soon Bishop and Mrs. Martin, our traveling companions, Mrs. Moore, and I were almost hidden. We were quickly off on a grand sightseeing tour of the island. We had the opportunity to see many of our churches and the young people's assembly ground down near the sea.

The dinner hour found us in the lovely dining room of the Army Y.M.C.A. seated with a group of some sixty friends. What friends! What fellowship! It is a great privilege to be a member of a church that stretches around the whole world and makes one a member of a worldwide fellowship.

Our boat was not scheduled to sail until noon, so we were up early for another tour of inspection. This time we were the guests of a group of Methodist Chaplains. They gave us the privilege of meeting some of the high-ranking officers in both the army and the navy.

Not soon shall I forget two of the places which we visited. First, we were taken to the Punch Bowl National Cemetery. This is a new burial place opened by our government as a final resting place for our men who die out in the Pacific area. It has been converted into a place of rare beauty. Already more than twenty thousand of our boys are sleeping here. As I read the names on the headstones, I noticed that they represented many branches of our Armed Forces. The grave of that gallant correspondent who made the common soldier famous attracted my attention. I refer to Ernie Pyle. He followed the troops on almost every battlefield and finally was killed on Okinawa. It seems altogether fitting that he should sleep with the boys whose hardships he shared and whose deeds he immortalized in his writings. His grave along with many others is properly marked. There are many, however, with the single word "Unknown." Let us be thankful that their names are all known to God.

We were privileged to see Pearl Harbor as close range. This is a naval installation of great magnitude. Some 30,000 navel men and civil employees with their families live and labor here. What sensations are created by the very name, Pearl Harbor. Here one quiet Sunday morning the bombers of Japan without any Declaration of War sneaked into the harbor to rain death upon thousands of unsuspecting men. We look carefully at the ruins of the battleship USS *Arizona* which has never been raised. A part of its superstructure is above water. It is said that the bodies of some nine hundred men have never been removed from those ruins.

Noon found us back on our ship– the band was playing some typical Hawaiian tunes and, as we sailed away a group of native singers sent us on our way by singing their lovely and justly famous song *Aloha Oi* which in English is "Farewell to Thee." We cast our beautiful flowers into the sea which was our way of saying "We will come again soon." Truly "these are the loveliest fleet of islands anchored in any ocean."

From Honolulu to Japan is nearly four thousand miles and we hope to arrive there on November 20. There again we will be greeted by fellow Methodists with an added privilege – General and Mrs. Douglas MacArthur have invited us to be their guests at a luncheon. But Japan is another chapter.

Wesleyan Christian Advocate, December 15, 1949, p. 8.

The Territory of Hawaii

Kobe, Japan
November 25, 1949

Is not easy to describe one's deepest emotions. The last five days have been spent in Japan. Here I labored from 1934 to 1940. Those were days of staggering responsibility and anxiety. The militarists were in complete control and the nation was being driven to its doom. As one looked upon the brutal and unwarranted invasion of China and later read of the bombing of Pearl Harbor, he wondered how a peaceful people such as the Japanese could be caught up by such madness. Well, they sold the wind and at last, the harvest was a whirlwind. When I sailed away in the spring of 1940, the entire nation was at war. What has followed in the nine intervening years is too well-known to be recited here. What changes have been wrought! What transformations in the total outlook in life of the people!

Upon our arrival in Yokohama early Sunday morning, November 20, we were greeted by friends. There in the early morning mist stood Japanese friends that we had loved and trusted through all the war years. Alongside them, some of our American missionaries would come to welcome us. With them, were Army chaplains who brought transportation (something very difficult to find just now) and a carefully worked out schedule of things to be done and the places to be visited.

As soon as we could pass through the usual passport inspection, we were on our way to Tokyo thirty miles away, where at 10:30 a.m. I preached in one of the Japanese churches. The pastor is the Rev. Zenouke Hinohara. For twelve years he was the president of our famous school for women in Hiroshima. This wonderful school was destroyed by the atomic bomb and many of the students were killed.

Brother Hinohara has built, since the end of the war, a most attractive church and parsonage in one of the best residential sections of Tokyo. His congregation is made up largely of young people. The entire property is out of debt except for $750.00. I hope some consecrated person in America will give me that sum to free this promising new church entirely of debt. My sermon was delivered through an interpreter but was not difficult. The experience of other years proved valuable. From this Japanese service, we were driven immediately to the American Embassy where we had the high privilege of being entertained by General and Mrs. Douglas MacArthur. We were received with the greatest cordiality. Mrs. MacArthur is from Tennessee and is a most gracious and lovely lady. She even gave us biscuits to be buttered and eaten in true Southern style.

There were only four guests, Bishop and Mrs. Paul Martin of Little Rock, Arkansas, who are traveling companions, and Mrs. Moore and I. For more than two hours we sat and talked with General MacArthur about the great task confronting us in Japan and the problems of the whole world. He is a man of wide learning and great courage. America does not yet fully appreciate the magnitude of the problems he has faced as Supreme Commander of the American Forces in Japan or the great wisdom and courage he has exhibited in his handling of these complex problems. The Japanese people almost worship him on every hand. I heard the most extravagant praise of his treatment of the conquered people.

It was a dramatic hour when General MacArthur stood on the USS *Missouri* in Tokyo Bay on September 2, 1945, to receive the formal surrender of Emperor Hirohito's army and navy. The man who dominated that scene has remained to guide the destinies of eighty million Japanese people as they struggle to rebuild their nation after one of the most overwhelming defeats recorded in history.

Perhaps it is well that we repeat some of the wise words he spoke that day.

"It is my earnest hope and indeed the hope of all mankind that from this solemn occasion a better world shall emerge out of the blood and carnage of the past. – A world founded upon faith and understanding – a world dedicated to the dignity of man and the fulfillment of his most cherished wish – freedom, tolerance, and justice."

More than four years have passed but General MacArthur has remained at his posted duty. He is now sixty-five years of age. He rises early and works long hours every day. By his foresight and wise handling of innumerable problems affecting every phase of the nation's life, he has transformed Japan from a beaten, floundering country into an American beachhead against Soviet Russia. On every hand, the visitor to Japan can observe the final results of the American initiative. There is still much to be done but it is surprising how much has been accomplished in four years. The Japanese respected General MacArthur for his power and his benevolence. He has been both just and kind. He has not only uprooted the military dictatorship, but he has planted in the Japanese mentality the will and energy for their rehabilitation. Undoubtedly here is one of history's most humane and sensible treatment of the defeated aggressor.

The average person moving hurriedly through the bombed-out areas or looking at the beautiful countryside would never see or feel the anguish of this defeated nation. But if one has eyes to see and heart to feel the hunger, the physical, and moral collapse, he comes to understand what war brings to the people. Here one finds humiliation, the result of the defeat which has left them helpless among the nations of the world. Here is confusion as they seek to adjust themselves to concepts and standards which were until recently utterly foreign to their traditions. Here is appreciation as they face the future stripped of their former power and prestige. But here also one finds courage and hope, and above all else, one sees the greatest opportunity the Christian church ever was given to win a whole nation to the side of Christ.

Although this letter is already too long I feel that I must record another moving experience. While seated at the table with General MacArthur, I expressed a desire to see a former Japanese General who is now serving a life sentence in the famous Sugamo Prison where so many war prisoners are serving their sentences. The General immediately made it possible for me to visit this famous prison and have a memorable visit with General Jiro Minami. The average reader in America will hardly recall the name but if one had any experience in either Japan or Korea between 1934 at the beginning of hostilities between America and Japan they will recognize the man. He was a famous General in the Japanese army. He was the man who led the invasion into China in 1931 when Manchuria was taken from China and made an important part of the Japanese Empire. I knew him as the Governor-General of Korea. There he lived like an Oriental Potentate and was Lord of life and death over the conquered Korean people.

In those dark years, the Christian church was under terrific pressure from the Japanese both in Japan and Korea. As the Methodist Bishop, I went from place to place trying to prevent the church from being made an agent of Japanese imperialism. These duties brought me into contact with General Minami. We had many long discussions about freedom of the individual conscience but apparently, I was always unsuccessful in my efforts. However, I came to have a sort of secret admiration for the old general and I think he respected me. Always, following our long and sometimes heated discussions, he would invite me to his palace for a meal. Well, when Japan was defeated, and a certain number of leaders were placed on trial as war criminals, my old-time opponent was among those to be tried. He was found guilty and given a life sentence. This is the man whom I visited at the Sugamo Prison.

When he was brought into the room where I waited, I beheld a man grown old and gray. He now wears a long white beard. He was dressed not in the splendor of the Japanese General, but the garb of a prisoner of war. I confess it pained me. We talked about those other days when I told him that often he was in my prayers he arose and embraced me; tears were in his eyes. He is, I suppose, a Buddhist and I am sure a sinner, but Christ died for him and I wanted to tell them so.

From Tokyo, we were given space on the Allied Limited which is a special military train operated to serve the American Forces. For two days now we have visited our Methodist missionaries, schools, and churches in Kobe and Osaka. This area was the scene of the missionary efforts of the Methodist Episcopal Church, South. Yesterday morning I preached in Kwanai Gukain, which is a Methodist University founded by Bishop Walter R Lambuth, and where there are now enrolled more than five thousand students. Yes, Christian missions go on and our labor for Christ is not in vain.

The last thing we did before coming back to our ship, which will eventually bring us to Malaya, was to visit a quiet little hidden cemetery in downtown Kobe. There we stood at the grave of Dr. J. W. Lambuth, the father of Bishop Lambuth, and the founder of the work of the Southern Methodist Church in Japan. What God has wrought since that brave man came to this land as the Messenger of Christ has not and cannot be told. Only eternity will reveal it. Inscribed upon his tomb were his last words, "I died at my post." We need hundreds of brave and consecrated young Christian missionaries who will come over in the name of the Savior and live at this post.

Wesleyan Christian Advocate, January 5, 1950, p. 12

Japanese General Jiro Minami

Taipei, Taiwan (Formosa)
November 30, 1949

My first glimpse of China came as the RMS *Empress of China* steamed up the Whangpoo River for Shanghai in September 1934. I was convinced immediately that China had an important part to play in world affairs, but little did I know how dramatic its part would be. I was hardly ashore before my heart was given to the Chinese people and my interest absorbed in the struggles of the nation. From that day until now, through good and ill, I have been committed to this wonderful people.

It was, therefore, with unusual interest that I set foot again two days ago on Chinese soil. Our ship had been prevented from going to Shanghai as originally planned. The Communists are in charge there, and it was impossible for this American vessel to enter Shanghai harbor. We were sent to Keelung which is the principal port of Formosa.

Formosa, which is now called Taiwan, is an island about one hundred miles off the mainland of China. After a war between Japan and China in 1895, this lovely island was taken from the Chinese and made a part of Japan. At the end of World War II, it was given back to China. It is now one of the nerve centers of the world for here the China Nationalist Government, led by Generalissimo Chiang Kai-shek has its headquarters. The port is crowded with vessels, all of them bringing supplies to Chiang's government. There are more than seven million inhabitants living on the island.

The Japanese during their fifty-year occupation made some great developments here. A modern railway spanning the length of the entire island was built. Hundreds of miles of paved roads were constructed and many modern buildings were erected. The mountains which rise at one peak of fourteen thousand feet are as magnificent as those in Switzerland.

In the lovely valleys and along the seashore, fertile and well cultivated fields yield to rice and tea crops each year. The principal exports are tea, bamboo, fruit of several varieties and two rice and tea crops each year. The capital city is Taipei and has a very large population. At the very center of the city stands a magnificent statue of Chiang Kai-shek done in bronze. They honor him here for many reasons but especially because he recovered Formosa from the Japanese. The congestion at Keelung, the port, is unbelievable. Vessels of every description are pouring cargo and passengers onto the island as fast as possible. I have some very good ideas concerning the kind of cargo we unloaded during our two days stay, but this is not the place to state those ideas.

Knowing that Generalissimo Chiang Kai-shek now has his headquarters here, I made bold to send him a radiogram announcing that we would be in port for two days. I had no way of knowing whether the General would be on the island or at Chung-King in West China where his armies are fighting to stop the advance of the Communist armies. Based upon his kindness at other times, I felt sure he would grant us an interview if possible.

As soon as our ship was at the dock, Mr. Hallington Tong, who is the Minister of Public Information, and Mr. Liu, who is the Director of Public Relations for Governor Chen Cheng came on board to give us a hearty welcome and advise that plans been made for our reception and entertainment. The Generalissimo was away but his office had placed at our disposal two very modern American automobiles, and Mr. Tong was to be our guide and interpreter for the day.

Generalissimo and Madam Chiang Kai-shek

All Americans who have been in China within recent years will recall Dr. Hallington Tong. He has been and is one of the closest advisors of General Chiang and since 1937 has been the Minister of Public Information. He is a Christian and attended Park College and Missouri State University and holds a Ph. D. Degree from Columbia University. I saw him last at Macon when Madame Chiang made her visit to Wesleyan College. We spent some time talking about Georgia and he asked especially about Ralph McGill of the *Atlanta Constitution*. We were driven at once to the Governor's Palace in Taipei which is about twenty-five miles from the harbor.

There we had two memorable hours with the Governor and Mrs. Chen Cheng. He is not only the governor of the province of Taiwan but is a general in Generalissimo Chiang's army. For many years he has been one of the trusted advisors and one of the most successful generals.

He is perhaps the second man in position in all affairs of Nationalist China. To talk intimately with him about present-day conditions and problems was a rare privilege indeed. Mrs. Chen is a graduate of a Christian college and speaks some English.

At the noon hour we were the guests of the Governor and his wife and had a real Chinese feast. Bishop and Mrs. Martin and Mrs. Moore and I proved to be lovers not only of Chinese beauty but of Chinese food as well. None of us will soon forget that stimulating fellowship of interest as well as the feast of fine food.

Immediately after lunch we were on our way to the guesthouse of Generalissimo Chiang. It is some ten miles from the city up in the mountains. Here is scenery as wonderful as one could desire. Hot sulfur springs with hotels attracted the leading Japanese when they were here. Now the entire mountain village is given over to the residence and headquarters of General Chiang.

The guesthouse was of Japanese design and had exquisite workmanship. The beauty of the garden with its varied plants and flowers will long remain with us. While the ladies were being entertained at a tea, Bishop Martin and I availed ourselves of the invitation to take a hot sulfur bath at the home of the

Generalissimo. The natural temperature of the water was too hot for the comfort of one unaccustomed to such hot baths, but we endured and enjoyed it, even if we did emerge as red as lobsters.

After another round of tea, we drove back to the capital where he paused at the statue of the Generalissimo. He stands at the top of a high stone column looking out over the city and the people for whom he has done so much.

Why America would fail to support his struggles against atheistic communism and thus allow the Soviets to overrun all of China is a question to which I have no answer. To fight Communism in Europe and give it no opposition in Asia looks to me like stupidity. Democracy and Christianity will have to fight for their very existence if Russia is allowed to consolidate or get into China.

I came back to our boat wishing desperately that even yet England and America might be more realistic about affairs in China.

Tomorrow we are due in Hong Kong and there we wish to see more of China. We have been at sea almost a month. In ten more days we are due in Malaya where five conferences and many perplexing problems will confront me. These lines may appear in the *Wesleyan Christian Advocate* before Christmas. Whenever they appear, I would like to extend to all of our Methodist people – and they are my people – our best wishes for a Merry Christmas and a Happy New Year.

Wesleyan Christian Advocate, January 12, 1950, p. 6

At Sea
December 10, 1949

These lines are being written one day out of Malaya. Tomorrow we are due in Singapore and as soon as we are ashore work will begin. Already our schedule of engagements has been sent to us, and literally every hour is pledged to some kind of service.

The Methodists in Singapore have secured the city auditorium and planned two mass meetings at which I am to preach. All of the Methodist people including Malaya, Chinese, American and British friends are to be present there. The sermons will have to be given through an interpreter. On Monday, December 12, I am to lay the cornerstone of a school building which, when completed, will cost $400,000, most of which has been contributed by the Methodists of Malaya.

Tuesday, December 13, will find us busy with preliminary committee meetings which must be held before the Malaya Annual Conference opens the next day. Following the adjournment of this conference and the opening of the Malaya Chinese Conference in Penang, some four hundred miles to the north on December 28, we are to make a tour by automobile of the entire Malaya Peninsula. We are to visit our church, greet our native Christians, spend some time with our missionaries in their homes, and, of course, preach one or more times, and we shall have a wonderful opportunity to see the dense jungles, as well as the thriving towns of Malaya.

Bishop Moore laying a cornerstone at the Anglo-Chinese School in Singapore, 1949

The first two weeks of January will be spent in Sumatra and the last two weeks in Borneo. Mrs. Moore will remain in Singapore while I go down below the Equator to hold these conferences and preach in our churches. I hope to give in subsequent letters a full account of life and conditions in these far-away lands. There is a good deal of political tension in both countries, but I anticipate no serious trouble.

The SS *President Monroe*

It has now been thirty-five days since we came on board our ship, the SS *President Monroe*. Except for two small typhoons which gave us a bit of rough weather, we have had a good crossing of the Pacific Ocean. I confess that I shall be glad to disembark tomorrow and to sleep again in a bed that does not rise and fall with the waves of the sea. However, I must record that of the sixteen times I have crossed the Pacific this has been by far the most comfortable voyage of them all.

Since my last letter, we have had two days in Hong Kong and three in Manila. It is not easy to describe the life of these two great cities. Hong Kong, with a million inhabitants, is easily the busiest and most prosperous city we have seen since leaving America. The harbor is crowded with ships and the streets packed with new and expensive American automobiles. Magnificent apartment houses have been built upon the mountains which rise above this beautiful harbor.

Life in Hong Kong would appear to the eye to be calm but one senses an undertone of uneasiness. The Chinese Communists are only a few miles away. We were told that in the city itself, which is a British Colony, there were many Communists. The British Government has rushed out heavy navy, air, and army forces to protect the colony in any emergency. We counted nearly twenty fighting ships in the harbor, and soldiers from England and Australia could be seen everywhere. Although there seemed to be no danger of an immediate Communist attack on Hong Kong because of possible recognition of the Red Regime by Britain, one could not escape the feeling that there is a powder keg that could explode any day.

In both Europe and Asia I have seen the terrible effects of the bombing which took place in the last year. In London, Berlin, Frankfurt, and other places I have looked upon vast stretches of rubble. As we passed through Japan and saw what damage had been wrought in Tokyo, Osaka, and Kobe I thought certainly this was war's most frightful result. However, Manila is worse than any of these. I am told that the two cities in the world which suffered most from bombs are Warsaw, Poland, and Manila and I am prepared to believe it. Everywhere one turns in Manila he is confronted with acres of gaunt ruins. The city was practically destroyed. In the harbor, as our boat made its way to the docks, could be seen the wrecks of proud ships that were sunk in the attack. A citizen of Manila told me there were one hundred and eighty such wrecks.

Our Methodist property did not escape this avalanche of destruction. The lovely Central Church which stood near the great National University was destroyed. The same was true of our May Johnson Hospital, which was the pride of our Women's Society of Christian Service. Both are being rebuilt and I am to have the great joy of assisting in their reopening as we return to America in late February.

We who live in the sheltered cities of America cannot appreciate the almost destruction war brought to other lands, nor do we yet understand the terrible sufferings through which our missionaries and native Christians passed. One night, while in Manila we sat at supper with a company of missionaries, every one of whom had spent more than three years as the prisoners of the Japanese. It has cost a great deal for some of our comrades to keep the flag of Christ floating above the terrible struggles of war.

We have had but little mail from home since sailing, but we hope to have more when we arrive in Singapore. Although we are far away our thoughts and prayers are to a large extent with the churches and people back home. Tomorrow, December 11, our pastors will be presenting the appeal for our worn-out preachers, and the next Sunday, the offering will be received. No greater cause has ever been before us, and I feel sure our people will respond cheerfully and generously. These lines will appear in the *Wesleyan Christian Advocate* at a much later date but from way down near the Equator where the temperature even in December is nearly a hundred, I send my thanks to all who have shared in this Christ-like enterprise.

Wesleyan Christian Advocate, January 19, 1950, p. 8.

Singapore, Malaya
December 20, 1949

After thirty-five days at sea and having traveled exactly halfway around the world we set foot on shore in Malaya, on December 12. Due to heavy freight shipments for Formosa where we spent two days, we arrived here behind schedule. This is a strange and beautiful part of the world with a strange and wonderful mixture of people. Malaysia – that part of Asia which is the land of the Malayans – is an island world, for it is composed of thousands of islands which we call the Dutch East Indies and the almost island peninsula which is known as Malaya. Included in the term Malaysia would be the Malay Peninsula, Borneo, Java, and Sumatra. The general territory sprawls over the equator and is a land of perpetual summer where nature has let her fancy run riot. Here are towering mountains and smoking volcanoes, dense jungles, and terraced rice fields.

In 1453, when Turkey took Constantinople and cut off the spice trade from these islands it became necessary to find a new route. That is what Christopher Columbus was attempting to do when he discovered America in 1492. As early as 1511, the Portuguese rounded Africa and arrived in Malacca where I am to preach tomorrow night. The population of Malaya is made up of Malays, Chinese, Indians, and English. The original Malays are small brown people. They dress in bright colors and live generally near the sea or on the banks of streams. They are great fishermen and rice growers. In recent years the great rubber plantations and mines where tin ore is found have lured many of them into an industrial civilization.

Hundreds of years ago the Chinese came down to trade with the Malays and gradually established themselves as the merchants and traders of the land. During the last century, hundreds of thousands of Chinese have come here until today more than half of the population is Chinese.

From overcrowded India, which is not far away, many thousands have found this is a land of promise. So many Chinese and Indians now live here that they outnumber the Malays. In the sixteenth and seventeenth centuries, a great struggle for trade supremacy went on in this part of the world between the Portuguese, the Dutch, and the English. The Malay Peninsula is under the British flag but much of the actual government is in the hands of the Sultans. This is not a full historical statement but does give a broad outline for the readers of the *Wesleyan Christian Advocate* a general sketch that I trust will enable them to have a speaking acquaintance with the peoples and the lands where I am now at work. In a few days, I will be over in Sumatra which is a part of the great new Indonesian nation which only this very month has secured its independence from the Dutch.

Singapore is a great city in this part of the world. It is quite British in its architecture but there are more than a million people representing many races. They say out here that should one go to a drug store to buy a patent medicine there you would find the directions given in ten languages. t is a modern city and compares favorably with the truly great cities of the world.

The climate is humid and the temperature uniform. There is very little change throughout the year. During the day the temperature ranges between ninety and one hundred degrees. The nights are a little cooler and occasionally a sudden squall known as a Sumatra brings a cooling breeze. The evenings and early mornings are usually fragrant and cool. It is bearable for foreigners provided they wear the right clothes and make use of the open verandas which are to be found at every house built by Europeans and Americans. The trouble is the monotony. The day we arrived I hurried to a tailor and bought four suits of white clothing which is worn by everyone.

It is almost Christmas time in America and I can imagine you are enjoying cool weather but here the electric fans are going. The slightest exertion means perspiration and fatigue, not to mention at least two complete changes of clothing daily. Words would fail me should I attempt to describe the wonderful green foliage, the gorgeous flowers – even orchids are plentiful and on every hand is beauty unsurpassed. This is the melting pot of races and the scene of political problems, on whose solution the peace of Asia and maybe the world depends.

This entire week has been spent at the Malaya Annual Conference. Our sessions have been held in the beautiful Wesley Church which would adorn any American city. The delegates have come from many places and a great distance. I have preached twice daily as they simply will not allow a visitor to rest. The appointments were read this morning. An entire volume could be written about the church and in this land, about heroic missionaries, a young but consecrated church, and a vast system of Methodist schools in which more than thirty thousand students are enrolled. Should I attempt to describe even a part of it this letter would monopolize more space than the *Wesleyan Christian Advocate* could afford.

Tomorrow Mrs. Moore and I begin a week's auto journey up the Peninsula. This will give us an unusual opportunity to see the interior, visit the missionaries in their stations and preach in the native churches. Travel is not altogether a luxury just now as some of the mountains are infested with guerilla bands who sometimes sweep down and molest travelers. We shall keep to the main roads and seek to avoid as much danger as possible. The missionaries live year in and year out in these remote places and we are eager to visit them and show our appreciation for their heroism and devotion.

Wesley Methodist Church, Singapore

On January 28, the Malaysian Chinese Conference will open in Penang which is five hundred miles north of Singapore. Meanwhile, Christmas and my birthday will have come and gone. It will seem strange to be so far from those we know and love best. We are to have the great joy of spending Christmas night with Reverend and Mrs. Paul Snead at Telok Anson. Mrs. Snead is the daughter of Brother and Sister Betts, our Methodist pastor at Adairsville, Georgia. It was my privilege to baptize their lovely baby, Elizabeth Ann, on Christmas Day.

After the Chinese Conference has ended in Penang, Mrs. Moore will return to Singapore and live with Reverend and Mrs. M. Dodsworth who have so graciously opened their home to us. I shall take a plane and fly to Sumatra. There is where the new Indonesian Republic is coming to birth. Another nation, another people struggling up to self-expression, another place where powerful forces contend, and ferment is felt everywhere. That is another story. We have both kept well and for that we are grateful.

Wesleyan Christian Advocate, January 26, 1950, p. 9.

Penang, Malaya
December 27, 1949

Five hundred miles by motorcar through strange, beautiful, old-new Malaya gives one an unforgettable experience. Like all other moving experiences, it is difficult to describe. Early on the morning of December 20 accompanied by Dr. Dodsworth, our missionary superintendent, and Dr. Raymond Archer, on of the secretaries of our Board of Missions, Mrs. Moore and I were on our way to visit the several Malayan mission stations.

We started in the city of Singapore and went straight north to Penang – a distance of five hundred miles. When names such as Malace, Kuala Lumpur, and Ipoh are read in America they will no doubt seem faraway places and mean but little to readers there. But, to us, they have been places of indescribable beauty, gracious hospitality, new friendships, and adventures in Kingdom building.

The roads over which we travel while narrow were paved. The everlasting forests of Malaya pressed hard upon us. To go even fifty feet from our car was to be swallowed up in the great plantation, a coconut grove, a field of banana trees, or just plain jungle. The nearness of this land to the equator, plus daily rains and the hot sun makes it perpetually a land of strange and wonderful beauty. In the jungles are found rare woods, ferns that grow as high as trees, exotic flowers – even orchids and strange air plants which flourish in the treetops.

For more than a year there has been a great tension in this land produced by a band of Communists or just plain bandits who have organized themselves into a guerilla army. They wear a green uniform with a red star on their caps. There was such an army during the Japanese Occupation supplied by the American and British forces with ammunition. But when the Japanese were driven out they continued their warfare and turned against businessmen of every kind. Locally, they are called terrorists. No one seems to know who furnishes the leadership or supplies ammunition. They have become a terror to the entire population.

England has brought in several thousands of troops to free the country of this unseen but dangerous enemy. Because they hide in the jungle fastness and strike at unexpected places, they are hard to deal with. The government is spending $300,000 daily to resist them. All foreigners are in constant danger. In a single day last week in four separate attacks, they murdered twenty-four soldiers and police. The roads are lined with blockades and many of the autos are armored. Soldiers constantly patrol the roads. One would not dare travel on side roads or at night. While we were assured that the main roads were relatively safe, we cannot help but wonder what sight would greet us when we turned the next curve or passed through the next mountain pass. But we were in safe and wise hands and although we were on the road for seven days we were not molested. However, it felt good to come to our destination safe and well. It was one of those thrilling experiences about which you are glad to speak but would not like to pass through again.

In Malacca, we stood reverently in the presence of old churches and other ruins that date back to 1511 when the Portuguese, having rounded Africa, arrived to capture the place and then build a walled and fortified city. Later it was taken by the Dutch who ruled until the English took over somewhere around 1795. Here live many rich Chinese who own and operate large rice plantations, tin mines, or grow rubber. We took time out to purchase a Malacca walking cane famous all over the world for our good and generous friend Mr. Asa G. Candler, Jr.

He furnishes the airplane for our long travels in America, it seems fair that I should at least keep him supplied with walking canes. Malacca is still one of the most picturesque towns in Malaya. Its ruined churches and fortresses remind one of the historic past. The narrow-crooked streets all speak of the past but when one moves into our magnificent schools for young people, one finds young people as modern as can be found anywhere on the earth.

These lines are being written from Penang. This city is located on a beautiful island separated from the mainland by the sparkling waters of the Strait of Malacca. Penang has long been a city of commercial importance because of its strategic position and wonderful harbors. From the open windows of the mission residence where we are being entertained, we look upon the green-clad hills of this island and on beyond the sea. Only sixty miles away is the border of Siam and only one hour by air to Sumatra where we go for our next conference.

This week I am presiding over the Malaysia Chinese Conference. It includes the work among the Chinese people who live here in such large numbers. All the work of the Conference, including my sermons, must be translated into two Chinese dialects.

Today, December 27, is an important day in their history. After three hundred years the Dutch government has granted independence to Indonesia. There is considerable concern out here as to whether the turn-over will be peaceful. Next week I will be in Sumatra, a part of the strange and troubled nation. More about it later.

The Methodist Mission in Malaya was opened in 1885. Those two great missionary leaders whose names are enshrined in Methodist history, Bishop James M. Thoburn and Bishop William F. Oldham, were the pioneers here. Dr. Thoburn came first to India and was soon followed by Oldham who was an Englishman, having been born in India. He served as a young man as a government surveyor but became convinced that he ought to become a missionary and help India's millions. He resigned his post and sailed to America with his bride to educate himself for missionary work. After studying at Allegheny College and Boston University he was on his way back to India ready to go wherever he might be sent. However, the need in Malaya was so urgent that this promising young recruit was sent not to India but fifteen hundred miles beyond to Singapore.

It is almost unbelievable what successes came to Methodist work in this part of the world between 1885 and 1949. From the beginning, the Methodist mission has been a pioneer and powerful factor in education. In many of the towns and cities as well as in remote country villages we have built schools. Today we have thirty-five thousand students enrolled in our church schools. I have visited practically all the schools and have been amazed at the splendid buildings in which the schools are housed.

Many of these buildings have been erected with the gifts of local donors. Here is an opportunity to train the youth of this nation and thus determine the future of these people. Seldom has such an opportunity been given to any church.

The larger percentage of our missionaries are occupied with running the schools. In addition to these heavy duties, they devote their time on weekends to preaching in our churches. Here as elsewhere, our missionaries are overworked. The highest government authorities whom I have contacted speak in the most enthusiastic terms of our Methodist schools.

The Malay people are practically all Mohammedans and very difficult to reach with the Christian message. The Chinese and Indians that make up the larger part of the population have been won in large numbers to Christ. As I visited these churches large congregations greeted us. It is refreshing to see Methodism take root in the soil of different nations and become part and parcel of their life and culture. It is my conviction that we need in Malaya a new evangelistic thrust, and that many new congregations should be organized. Millions of Chinese from wealthy merchants to those living in crowded slums challenge the church here. Another large group is the Tamils-people who come over in large numbers from India. Here indeed is a wonderful opportunity and a staggering responsibility. May God help us to present the Christian gospel to these Malay millions before Communism wins them to its fold.

It is easy to sing "the kingdom is coming," but when one gets close to the life of the great throbbing multitudes, he discovers that only sacrificial love and heroic endurance will get the job done.

Wesleyan Christian Advocate, February 2, 1950, p. 8

Medan, Sumatra
January 8, 1950

If one examines the map he will find Indonesia to be a crescent of verdant and fertile islands stretching two thousand miles on both sides of the equator. It has been my privilege to be here and watch the red and white flag of the United States of Indonesia flying for the first time above the seventy million people who are to live under this flag. For more than three hundred years this has been a part of the Dutch empire. For ten years the land has witnessed either struggle against Dutch troops or the ravages of Japanese occupation. Now a new nation has been brought into being. The formal transfer was made by Queen Juliana in Holland on December 27.

It has been an interesting experience to have a ring-side seat and to observe the dream of the passing of an empire and the birth of a new nation. For these people to arrive at this point has been a long and painful process. At the very least the Dutch government sought to appear in the role as a generous benefactor but until the last few months of negotiations reluctance and resistance have characterized the actions of the Dutch. Even the pressure of the United Nations was necessary to secure final action. However, one can hardly blame the Dutch as this has been a vital part of their economic lifeline and an important part of their colonial empire. With it gone, Holland seems destined to take its place in the ranks of small and inconsiderable nations of the world. They have, however, reconciled themselves to the loss of this rich part of their empire, and however long delayed they have demonstrated their good faith in the Indonesians.

The new nation comprises all the islands in the former Dutch East Indies with the present exception of Dutch New Guinea whose status is still in dispute. They have a total area of seven hundred fifty thousand square miles and a population of seventy-seven million. The United States of Indonesia will be an independent sovereign federal republic like the United States of

America. Its territory will be organized into sixteen states of which the largest will be the Indonesian Republic in the islands of Java and Sumatra. The other states – including East Java and Pasundan, East and South Sumatra, Madura, East, and West Borneo, and East Indonesia – now have their semi-autonomous governments.

The Republic will be governed by a President, a Senate, and a House of Representatives. Each state will have two members in the Senate, the house will be selected based on population. Relations between Indonesia and the Netherlands will be governed by a statute of a union under which they will be equal partners with the Queen of the Netherlands as the symbolic head. The Union resembles the British Commonwealth and should form the basis for enduring friendship between the two countries.

The Republic will recognize the primary Dutch commercial interest in Indonesia and will protect Dutch interest and investments in Indonesia. But the republican government will have final and complete authority over Indonesian economic and financial policies. It is evidently in the interest of both the Netherlands and the Indonesians that they should continue to cooperate very closely with each other. Indonesia needs Dutch capital and administrative experience as well as their assistance in the economic development of the country. The Netherlands, on the other hand, needs Indonesian raw materials and trade which will help her to be profitable and secure her investments. To secure this cooperation, the Dutch and Indonesian leaders will have to convince their people that it is essential for the welfare of their two countries.

The most difficult task facing the Indonesian government is the restoration of peace and order throughout the country. Guerilla warfare is still being waged by the Communists and the government must assume effective sovereignty without delay and take the firmest action to put down banditry and insurrection. Unless this is done it will make but little progress toward recovery. Much will depend upon the ability of the new nation to alleviate the people's distress and improve their living standards. Communism is to be kept in check.

Yesterday, I lunched with the Ephorus or Bishop of the Batak Church. This is a body of more than six hundred thousand Christian people who live up in the mountains of Sumatra. About 1890 the Rhenish Mission from Germany started work among these people back in the jungle. The last war forced all of these German missionaries to leave the country, but they left behind this wonderful Christian church which is entirely self-supporting. They need educational institutions and hospitals, but they have already demonstrated that once Christianity takes root in the hearts of the people it will live and grow.

Our Methodist work has been here only since 1904, yet, today I read the appointments at the closing session of an Annual Conference. We have here a devoted body of Methodists ably led by native pastors who are assisted by a small group of eight missionaries. We have fourteen schools with approximately five thousand students. There is much-unevangelized territory here; if we only had more leaders to preach the gospel and plant new churches.

The flight here across the Strait of Malacca was without incident. In three more days, I fly directly to Singapore, a distance of some hundreds of miles. After three days there I will fly to Borneo and once in that country take a river launch and go far back into the interior where Methodism is at work with the Dyaks. But that is another story.

The everlasting summer out here which goes on twelve months out of the year gets one's strength. There is no relief day or night from the heat unless it be a gentle breeze which sometimes dries up the perspiration on one's body. Today as I preached the church was beautifully decorated with gorgeous lilies. It was difficult to understand how one could have such beauty in January. It must be winter in Georgia but out here it is like mid-summer. However, we keep well. We have now been here one month and have presided over three annual conferences. During the next month I must preside over two additional conferences and on February 9th we will turn our faces toward those we know and love best.

Wesleyan Christian Advocate, February 9, 1950, p. 8.

Sibu, Sarawak, Borneo
January 25, 1950

Borneo is the third-largest island in the world. But, aside from its coasts and lower river valleys, is practically unknown. As a growing boy down at Brookfield in South Georgia, I read about Borneo and the "wild men" who came from there but never imagined it would ever be my privilege to see that "far-off" land. But, as the servant of the church, for nearly two weeks I traveled by plane, a small steamer, and native canoe up and down the country. We have gone far up the Rajang River which is more than six hundred miles in length and is one of the truly great rivers of the world. Quite recently this and the other numerous rivers of this beautifully strange land were traversed primarily by pagan tribesmen. Maybe with a few paragraphs, I can help my friends to see a little of this almost unknown country.

If one goes far enough inland as we did, he will discover some lofty mountain ranges from which the many rivers take rise. Most of the country is low and swampy, covered with tropical jungle so dense that one leaves the riverbank only with the greatest of difficulty. The rainfall is very heavy and, in some places, exceeds one hundred sixty inches each year. This keeps the rivers at high levels most of the year. The jungles are so dense that practically all the movements of the people are along with the watercourses. Game is abundant as the natives are not permitted to own firearms, and edible plants and fruits such as papaya, pineapple, coconuts, and bananas grow in abundance. The warm climate never varies very much. Natives have long since concluded that clothes are superfluous. Were it not for the debilitating effect of this constant tropical climate Borneo would be an ideal place in which to live. The total population is today less than three million.

Borneo is divided between the British and the Dutch. Sarawak is a province or state in British Borneo and Sibu from where I arrived, is one of the remote river towns with a population of about six thousand. Practically all these are Malays and Chinese. The Dyaks are up the river in the far interior. I doubt that there are twenty British to be found here and they are all in government service. The Methodist Mission accounts for all the Americans in Sarawak which amounts to three missionary couples. It has been a thrilling experience to visit these missionaries in their outpost stations and see them, by the power of the Christian message, bringing people from ruthless savagery to the decencies of civilization and the graces of the Christian life.

The whole story of Borneo reads like a fairytale. It will be difficult for those who live amid the refinements of our Western civilization to imagine a land, where less than a hundred years ago, headhunting was an accepted practice, and now giving way to Christianity and civilization. It is a dramatic story and one would need a book instead of an article in the *Wesleyan Christian Advocate* to tell it. Here is drama, struggle, tragedy, and victory played out on a large stage.

The story of James Brooke, an Englishman with idealism and courage, and what he did in Borneo, is one of the most amazing I have ever heard. Like so many of his countrymen, Brooke went early to India where his father was an officer in the British East India Company. While still in his youth, Brooke visited China and Burma, and only one of these voyages stopped at Singapore. While there he heard the strange tales of Borneo and of the bloodthirsty people who lived there.

In 1839, James Brooke came and was well received by these warlike people. At that time travel was unsafe, women and children were captured and carried away in tribal wars, and the law of the people was almost the only law. The Rajah, or native chief, received Brooke and soon sought his help in putting down the rebellion. Later the Rajah asked Brooke to become the chief or Rajah, which he did, and remained to rule this land wisely and well until he died in 1868. He was then succeeded by his nephew Charles Brooke who in turn was succeeded by his son, Sir Charles Vyner Brooke, who ruled until 1946 when he gave Sarawak to Great Britain and it was made a crown colony.

Nowhere in the administration of remote people and their lands do I find a story like this. From 1841 until 1946 these "White Rajas" spent their lives in this remote corner of Asia devoting their energies to the prosperity and happiness of their subjects. Although they were absolute rulers, they took from the country only a modest salary. The jungle is still here and there are sporadic outbursts of headhunting. Many of the people still go their native ways but these White Rajas started something which someday will make this no longer a jungle but a tropical paradise. All honor to them for their high and unselfish purpose.

In the very town from which I write, the British Governor-General was stabbed to death less than a month ago. He had just been appointed by the King in London and having arrived was making a tour of his territory. He came to Sibu and while receiving a group of students, one of them in a sneak attack stabbed him to death. It is said out here that certain revolutionary youth resent their country being taken over by the British and that they are fighting for the return of the White Rajah. Perhaps the truth is that some poor, misguided youth thought that by murdering a white man of high rank he would contribute to the freedom of his people. At any rate, many of the underprivileged people of the world are reacting violently against the very forms of government under which they have learned something about the rights of man. That sentiment would apply to much of this part of the world.

I thought while here it would be interesting and helpful if I could press far up the Rajang River and see our Methodist Mission to the Dyaks. By river launch and native canoe, we have just finished a five-day trip. It was all quite strenuous but interesting. These Dyak people are the tribes from which have come the most ferocious headhunters. I found those I visited peaceful and kind. They lived together in a sort of community house which is called a "long house." These huge structures range 200 to 400 feet in length and 30 to 60 feet in width. They are always built near the riverbank and stand some 30 feet above the ground on high posts.

In the Chief's house, where I sat down on the floor to eat rice, from the rafters were gongs and many ceremonial devices. In one large rope basket hanging nearby were not less than fifteen human heads. It was a gruesome sight and did not especially help me to enjoy my meal. My host, however, was a Christian and had given up the practice of "taking heads." His neighbors had not all accepted Christianity and they insisted upon keeping these heads hanging from their walls to ensure the fertility of their fields. These heads were elaborately decorated.

64

The latest head was that of a Japanese officer who made the mistake of straying far from his army. What an experience! If Christianity can convert these warlike people into being friendly toward Christians, we should see that the gospel is carried to them.

Tomorrow, I go back to the coast to the town of Kuching where, after a wait of three days, a plane will fly us back to Singapore. The Central Conference for Malaya, Burma, Sumatra, and Borneo will open in Singapore on February 1. I shall preside until a new bishop for this part of Methodism's worldwide church is elected and consecrated. On February 9, we fly to Manila and wait there until February 23 where we take the SS *President Cleveland* which is due in San Francisco on March 17.

February and March are not the best months to be at sea, but we shall be happy because whatever the wind and weather we will be "going home."

Wesleyan Christian Advocate, February 16, 1950, p. 11.

Bishop and Mrs. Moore sailed home on
the SS *President Cleveland*.

Manila, Philippines
February 22, 1950

My last travel letter was written from Borneo. The strange beauty of that lovely and undeveloped country is still about me. As long as I live the majestic mountains, wide and rapid rivers, the dense jungles, and primitive but very friendly people will live on in my memory. It was with the pain of regret that I said goodbye and flew from Kuching to Singapore.

To catch the plane which operated once each week, we traveled by motor launch for two days down the Rajang River and then went on board a Chinese riverboat which was but a little better, if any, than our launch. The flight across the China Sea was only a matter of a few hours and we were back in the great metropolitan city of Singapore.

On February 1, the Southeastern Asia Central Conference opened in Singapore. This was the chief reason for my coming on this emergency mission. The four Annual Conferences over which I have presided in Malaya, Sumatra, and Borneo all pointed toward the Central Conference. Delegates traveled from Burma and other countries mentioned above. There were at least a dozen languages and dialects spoken by these Methodists. There were Burmese, Indonesians, Chinese, Indians, and a few Americans. They had all passed through the indescribable horrors of war and some of them have spent nearly four years in prison under the heavy-handed treatment of the Japanese. In good Methodist fashion, the Conference opened with the traditional Conference hymn, "And are we yet alive, and see each other's face?"

Methodism in Southeastern Asia had as its bishop for more than 20 years the late Bishop Edwin F. Lee. He retired in 1944 and passed to his eternal home a short time later. The fruits of his wise and efficient labors are to be seen everywhere. The General Conference of 1944 authorized the Annual Conferences referred to above to organize themselves into a Central Conference and to elect their bishop.

The presidency of the Conference was a tedious and important task. We were making history and the entire structure of a Central Conference had to be built. The delegates worked hard and harmoniously, and everyone was pleased with the results. The election of a bishop claimed everyone's attention and there was much pre-conference speculation as to whom he would be. On the first ballot, Dr. Hobart B. Amstutz, Dr. Marmaduke Dodsworth, both of Singapore, and Dr. Raymond L. Archer longtime missionary but more recently one of the secretaries of the Board of Missions and Church Extension had about an equal number of votes. It was not until the eleventh ballot that the deadlock was broken. On that ballot, Dr. Archer received the necessary two-thirds of the votes cast and was declared elected. On Sunday, February 5, in our beautiful Wesley Church, Singapore, it was my high privilege, assisted by Bishop Clement D. Rockey of Lucknow, India, to consecrate the new bishop. Having served in Java, Sumatra, and Malaya as one of the missionaries, Bishop Archer is no stranger to the people with whom he is to labor. National leaders in both church and state hailed his election as a sign of Methodism's growing influence in this part of the world.

Following the Consecration of the new bishop, the Conference adjourned to the beautiful Victoria Hall, which is the City Auditorium of Singapore, where a congregation of more than fifteen hundred had gathered. A choir of nearly a hundred voices rendered excellent music and it was my privilege to preach the closing sermon of this historic conference. The four days remaining of our stay in beautiful Malaya were devoted to a series of entertainments. If there is more beautiful hospitality to be found anywhere I have not seen it.

February 9 found us on a Pan-American clipper for the long flight from Singapore to Manila. In this giant four motored plane we were soon above cloud and weather flying at an altitude of several thousand feet. We hardly saw the sea during the nine hours of our flight up to Manila. Upon our arrival, a company of missionaries greeted us with a typical Methodist welcome.

We have now been in the Philippine Islands for nearly two weeks. What I had hoped would be a quiet time has proven to be about the most strenuous two weeks of this journey. Bishop José Valencia is our Methodist Bishop here and it so happened that two of the three Annual Conferences we have in the Philippines met during our stay. At the Bishop's insistence, I have preached fourteen times since our arrival. One of these conferences was far back in the interior and we had a splendid opportunity to see the countryside.

Yesterday we dedicated the beautiful Central Church here in Manila. This lovely church was built some years ago to serve the students at the great National University which is nearby. It was destroyed by the shelling of Manila in the last war. With the help of funds received from the Crusade for Christ, it has been rebuilt. It is a lovely cathedral with a large congregation, which includes some of the high-ranking leaders of the government. It is easily the most outstanding Protestant church in this capital city.

Bishop and Mrs. Paul E. Martin, who traveled with us on the outward voyage, have now completed their two and one half months; visit to Methodism in India and have now rejoined us. Tomorrow, we go onboard the SS *President Cleveland* for the voyage home. We are all weary beyond any description. We have gone day and night in the service of the church. How grateful we are that we can have this time at sea to recuperate and prepare for our duties at home. We are due in San Francisco on March 17, and through the kindness of our good friend Mr. Asa Candler of Atlanta, we hope to reach home on his private plane on March 19. Only those who have been away from home and loved ones for a long time can understand what a joy that will be.

Wesleyan Christian Advocate, March 16, 1950, p. 12

Dyak children standing in front of a "longhouse' like the one where Bishop Moore had dinner with the chief, a former head hunter.

Dyak women

CHAPTER TEN

The Bishop Is On a Delicate, Difficult Mission to Korea

October-November 1951

Bishop Moore Is Called to Korea in an Emergency

In response to an urgent request from The Methodist Church in Korea, Bishop Arthur J. Moore has been appointed by the Council of Bishops to proceed there on an emergency mission. He will leave by air for Korea on October 16 and be away from Atlanta for approximately six weeks.

This is the fourth emergency postwar mission to which Bishop Moore has been sent since the end of World War II. In 1946 he was in Korea. In 1948 he was in the nations of Europe which were involved in the Second World War. In 1950 he was sent to Malaya, Burma, Borneo, and Indonesia on a similar mission. Now he returns to war-ridden Korea to give guidance to church affairs there.

Bishop Moore was for several years the Bishop of the Methodist Church with responsibilities in Asia, Europe, and Africa.

The Methodist Church in Korea has been practically destroyed by the fighting of recent months. Practically all Methodist people and pastors are in emergency centers in southern Korea. The Bishop of the Korea Methodist Church was taken away by the Communists more than a year ago and is presumed dead. The church is, therefore, leaderless and without an official body to deal with the tragic situation. Bishop Moore will preside over an emergency session of the General Conference at which a new bishop will be elected and consecrated.

Bishop Moore when interviewed said, "This is the call of duty. I hardly see how I can clear my schedule to be away for six weeks, but someone must go and that quickly. The church in Korea into which so much sacrifice and money have been poured is in danger of total extinction. If it ever needed sympathetic guidance and practical help it is now.

For eight years I labored there; I know all of the leaders who are left. The Council of Bishops appointed me to carry this extra responsibility. It is a delicate and difficult mission and I sincerely ask all my friends to follow me with their earnest prayers."

Wesleyan Christian Advocate, October 18, 1951, p.1

October 17, 1951

Tonight, at 7:00 p.m., I begin a six-thousand-mile air journey to Japan and Korea. I go on Eastern Airlines to Chicago, and Northwest Airlines from Chicago to Tokyo, Japan, and onto Pusan, Korea. From Wednesday night to Friday noon is a long time to be in the air, but it is the quickest way to get to the ends of the earth. This is another emergency mission to one of our younger churches. 1946 found me in Korea trying to help our Korean Methodist leaders to recover from the heavy hand of Japanese occupation and make ready for the enlarged opportunities that liberation has brought to them.

Since then, the juggernaut of war has moved not once, but several times over their countryside. The Korean people have been called upon to undergo one of the supreme ordeals of their long and bitter history. Buildings are in ruins, leaders are dead or in captivity, and normal life has been practically suspended while the civilian population finds some way to escape from the destruction of war. Homelessness and hunger have plunged these fine people into bitter agony. They need help and need it now.

In response to an urgent plea from the Korean Methodists and under instructions from our Council of Bishops, I go to render whatever service is possible. In Southern Korea, beyond the range of guns, we will convene a General Conference; elect and consecrate a bishop and seek to devise some plan to keep the church alive and creative in the presence of such overwhelming difficulties. My schedule puts me in Pusan, Korea, on October 20, and there I will remain for approximately three weeks. Then I shall return to Japan for one week of service and then return to the folks and the duties at home. If I have good luck, I will be back in Atlanta by November 25.

This is a delicate and difficult mission and I need the prayers of God's people. In troubled situations, there are times when the only thing to do is respond to what seems to be an overwhelming duty. To fail Korea now, would be treachery to a brave, loyal and needy church. So I go confident that I am not alone because the Savior of the world once said: "Lo, I am with you, even to the end of the world."

Wesleyan Christian Advocate, October 25, 1951, p. 1

Pusan, Korea
October 23, 1951

When the plane which had brought me six thousand miles over sea and land arrived here two days ago, there stood on the field to greet me a company of Korean Christian leaders and American missionaries. I was here only a few hours until once again I was admiring the easy way these missionaries keep company with hardships and dangers. Here are a courageous and gallant band in a land of war, poverty, disease, and hunger. They are without the comforts of living but cheerfully bring healing, enlightenment, and a sustaining faith to a people who walk in the shadow of death. Certainly, no weak or timid soul would leave family and country to sail the seas and undertake a mission that involves as much real sacrifice as serving in Korea does at present.

During the first night after the Communists had invaded South Korea, six of our fine missionaries who were in Kaesong were captured and taken away. Despite all our efforts through international agencies, we have never been able to establish contact with them. These three heroic American men and three American women of devotion and courage we can only commit to the care of the Heavenly Father and devoutly pray that He has preserved them and that one day they will be restored to us.

Those who welcomed me to Korea are of the same heroic mold and meet the demands of the trying situation with unflinching courage. If they knew I was describing them in this manner they would protest, but I must salute them for their gallant cheerfulness and courage. They may be unconscious of their magnificent contribution, but I am not. I want to pay my tribute to those who by faith and service make deserts blossom like a rose. To have a small part in their splendid work is a privilege I do not deserve.

Yesterday was Sunday and I was up early to preach to a large congregation of American soldiers. Chaplain Jaeger, who has served our Army with such distinction was in charge. A choir composed entirely of Korean young people sang two anthems and I have never heard sweeter music. The congregation numbered approximately four hundred equally divided between officers and enlisted men. It was my great joy to preach on the Cross of Christ and to insist that in the Savior one finds intellectual and spiritual satisfaction. After the benediction, practically everyone present came to greet me, and among them were men whom I had known in the States. They greeted me like a long-lost friend.

Pusan is a city of refugees. There are more than four million refugees in Korea, and when one rides about this port city, he is apt to feel that most of them are here. The hillsides are covered with temporary shacks thrown up out of cardboard or tin. Every old, dilapidated building is overflowing with homeless people. Entire families live in a single room and some wander about without any fixed abode. Today we discovered a beautiful Korean mother who taught in one of our mission schools living with her three children in a space not more than eight feet square – no heat, lights, or furniture, only a few grass mats on the cold floor. There are hundreds of thousands living in that fashion.

Before the invasion, we had only one Methodist church in Pusan, as this territory had been allocated to the Presbyterian Church. Now there are eleven Methodist churches with large congregations, composed entirely of Methodists who have been driven out of their native villages and away from their homes. They meet in tents, attics, under trees – anywhere there is room to meet, sing and pray. Everything else out here seems to have come tumbling down but the church, stripped of all earthly possessions, goes triumphantly on its way.

Several of our Methodist institutions which were driven from their original location are carrying on here in exile. Ewha University is a shining example. Its home is in Seoul where it has a beautiful campus, many beautiful stone buildings with excellent equipment, and well-trained faculty that make it the outstanding university for women in all of Korea.

When the Communists came in, faculty and students fled for safety leaving behind, of course, all their earthly possessions. But have they folded up? Certainly not. Here in Pusan, they have thrown up some small shacks and covered them with canvas and to my surprise, I found a college with a student body above seven hundred. In one tent a beautiful girl practiced her music on a battered piano; in another, a laboratory had been set up; in still another, some rain-soaked books did service as the college library. Doctor Helen Kim secured permission from the United Nations army authorities to make a trip to Seoul (now in our hands) and to transport enough equipment to carry on down here. There were the girls who stood singing in the rain about whom I wrote in another article.

The President of the Republic of Korea is Dr. Syngman Rhee. For thirty years he was compelled to live outside Korea to carry on the fight for Korean independence. With liberation, he returned and became the first president of the Republic of Korea. He was gracious enough to give us an hour of his valuable time this morning. Miss Margaret Billingsly, who is the Executive Secretary for Korea of the Women's Division of Christian Service, and I were received in his official residence which is an unpretentious house built in Japanese style.

President and Mrs. Rhee, who is a European lady, received us in the friendliest manner possible. Throughout the whole conference which lasted for nearly an hour, the President referred time and time again to his experience as a Methodist Layman and to the time when he went as a delegate to a General Conference in America.

He called by name many of the early missionaries and asked about them and their children. He was most insistent that additional missionaries be sent to Korea. I believe him to be a man of sincerity and marked ability to do a good job against overwhelming odds.

The President's Cabinet is composed of strong and proven leaders. They have had only five years' experience in the art of government and those years have been characterized by change and now with war. I feel, however, that they have done and are doing a good job against difficulties within and enemies without.

I have met practically every member of the President's Cabinet. Several of them are earnest Christian men and more than one is an active Methodist. They know that if atheistic communism is allowed to prevail in Korea or elsewhere in the world it will more deeply wound the human family than any economic or political system, however bad, possibly could. Without exception, they are opposed to any peace treaty which will leave Korea divided at the 38th parallel.

As these lines are written the radio is saying that the truce talks now going on near Kaesong are about to end in an agreement between the United Nations forces and the Communists of the North. Where the line will be drawn, I know not. The questions involved are too profound and the danger of involving the nations in another world war is too great for me to express an opinion. I think I know, however, that if Korea could be united and then helped to develop along the lines of a Christian democracy, that fact would not only save Korea but would give hope to teeming millions of Asians who are under the threat of communism.

Someday, please God, victory will come and for that day we must make the Korean church strong. Upon the ruins of war, a more enduring civilization must be built. Instead of the soldier must come the surveyor, and the hands that used a sword must take up the task of reconstruction. Korea is a land in which there has been material destruction on a wide scale. Dealing with this destruction and disaster will demand faith, skill, and money. But beyond the physical destruction is the even more difficult task of social, moral, and spiritual rebuilding. The gospel must be preached in a land where Christianity now claims only one million believers out of a total population of 30 million. The social reconstruction of the people, the building and maintenance of institutions of learning, and the training of young people in Christian service – are tasks of unspeakable urgency and cannot be accomplished without the friendly assistance of the Christian people of other lands.

Whatever others may do, the Christian church in America must see in all this bewildering change the need for a new venture with Christ in the building of a Kingdom which will endure.

Wesleyan Christian Advocate, November 29, 1951, p. 12.

Pusan, Korea
October 23, 1951

You can hardly imagine how full the days are out here. I rose at 6:00 a.m., had breakfast, and then went into conferences with missionaries, Koreans and church leaders, people in distress, and those I have known in other years. We have here in Pusan not only refugee individuals but refugee institutions as well. Ewha College, the Methodist seminary, Severance Hospital, and other institutions that once thrived elsewhere in Korea are trying to carry on here. I must add that they are doing exceptionally despite unbelievable difficulties.

Tomorrow, I speak to the Methodist seminary and try to find time for conferences with individual missionaries. We have in Korea about eight men missionaries. No women have yet been allowed to come – we hope for two nurses to arrive next week. Margaret Billingsley is attracting a great deal of attention because women are so few.

Before you receive this letter, I will of been up to Seoul and returned to Pusan. I will stay there for about three days inspecting Methodist properties and having conferences with the chaplains and then return to Pusan.

Monday, October 19, I will have an all-day conference with the chaplains who are stationed near Pusan. I will preach next Sunday in the chapel at one of our great airbases. From that point, our boys take off for bombing raids in North Korea. The chaplain at this camp is Chaplain Barnes, his brother married the daughter of Brother Dunaway.

The General Conference will formally open Thursday, November 1. There is so much to be done. Not only must we elect and consecrate a bishop, but we must provide for the continuing relief of the thousands who have been driven from their homes, and devise a plan to return both pastors and people to those places where there is no longer fighting and in general, rebuild the organizational life of the Methodist Church in Korea. I am enthusiastic about what they are now doing. Stern days are ahead and the church must not only survive but help rebuild the young nation. Pray for us.

Wesleyan Christian Advocate, November 8, 1951, p. 1

Seoul, Korea
October 25, 1951

As a military train brought me into Seoul, the capital city of Korea, early this morning, I was aware of its importance in ancient history as well as in what is happening while I write. Not far away vast armies are locked in deadly battle not waiting to see what results will come from the truce talks which are being carried on just outside the zone of battle.

The average American imagines he is too busy to read history, especially ancient history made in an obscure corner of the world, but what is happening here just now has significance for free men everywhere.

Korea has been thrust into the international limelight and the eyes of the world are focused on this little nation which was once known as the "Land of the Morning Calm". It is my conviction that what is now happening in Korea cannot be fully understood and evaluated unless viewed against the long and torturous history of these peace-loving people for whose independence and freedom so many are today fighting and dying. Let me condense in capsule form several centuries of exciting happenings. The history of Korea can be traced back as far as 1122 BC. In that year a man called Kija exiled himself with 5000 followers from the Chinese court and immigrated to what is today Korea. By the first century BC., there were three independent kingdoms. One who takes time to read history finds a story of continued struggle until the 10th century AD when these separate kingdoms were at last welded into a single nation and Korea of the present day was born.

As early as 1592, Japan found Korea ripe for invasion and entered it as a stopping place on the way to China. A seven years war followed which so weaken the country that it became easy prey for the Manchus who had seized the throne of China. As a result of these devastating invasions, the Korean people attempted a policy of complete isolation, and this continued more or less until 1833 when a treaty was signed with the United

States of America. Following this came the adoption of many Western customs and Korea began to turn its eyes away from the stagnant East toward the developments of Occidental civilization.

In 1894, Japan again cast greedy eyes toward Korea. China had her ambitions and as a result, a war between China and Japan followed, in which China was defeated. Then Russia entered the picture and in 1904-1905 the Russo-Japanese War was fought with Japan once more the victor. In 1905, the Treaty of Portsmouth gave Japan a protectorate over the bewildered Korean people. In 1910 outright annexation followed and Korea became a part of the Japanese Empire with her glorious past and pride buried in national slavery which continued until 1945. Then came the surrender of Japan to the Allied Armies and Korea was liberated.

One wishes he might record that this marked the beginning of a new life for a sovereign, independent, democratic Korea. Instead, it must be recorded that Korea was again divided, this time at the 38th parallel with the Russians in the north and the Americans in the south.

For purely military purposes this division was necessary but the Russians began immediately to remake the government and its institutions and oppress the people of North Korea with their Communistic ideology. In 1949, the American troops were withdrawn and all of Korea south of the 38th parallel was in the hands of the government of the Republic of Korea.

To have their country so divided and much of it under a Moscow plan for trusteeship was the "fruit of bitterness" for the Korean people. They accepted it temporarily as a matter of military expediency but knew all the while that it carried the danger of a permanent division of their beloved country into two weak states; that it left Korea as a hostage in international politics; and the scene of an inevitable war if and when the Russians decided to occupy the whole of the country.

The Americans, believing that an orderly government had been established, withdrew all military forces and left Korea to be master in its own house. But alas, we either forgot or ignored the new and brutal imperialism coming out of Moscow imposing its brutal reign over helpless people whenever possible. The rest of the story is very well known to all Americans. Our fathers and sons are encamped on Korean battlefields. Many suffer and die while America seeks once more to be a good Samaritan upon the broken roads of Korea.

The dawn that streaked Korean skies on June 25, 1950, was host to a disheartening sight. The air was filled with the rumble of Korean tanks and the bark of Korean guns as soldiers poured across the 38th parallel. The hope that the great war that ended five years before had crushed the forces of tyranny and ushered in a reign of peace was gone. The Soviet Union and its satellite, North Korea, placed the blame on South Korea, but the world now knows that this brutal and unwarranted act of aggression was initiated without warning and provocation by the Communist forces.

This ancient and proud capital, Seoul, was soon in the hands of the enemy and a population of more than a million souls lived under terror. Of course, many fled to the South for safety. Since then the city has been fought over more than once and is finally come again into American hands, but as I write this, it is a city of desolation.

Look where you will and there you see gaunt ruins, burned-out shells of buildings, twisted girders, and mountains of debris. It should be said, however, that our American troops have cleared the streets and despite the damage, one makes his way without too much difficulty. The civilian population is not supposed to be here, but many thousands have slipped through the lines to reoccupy or rebuild the only homes they ever knew. One could write at great length about what is happening here but much of it is of military importance and I must content myself with the word concerning: (a) my conference with the chaplains (b) my interview with General James A. Van Fleet (c) my inspection of a large evacuation hospital and (d) my visit to damaged Methodist churches and institutions.

Before leaving the United States, I was requested by the Methodist Commission on Chaplains to visit our Methodist chaplains wherever possible. That was for me a happy assignment because I hold in my heart the highest appreciation of these brave men who have left home, family, and Church to stand alongside our fighting men. Everywhere I have found them true to their mission as ministers of the gospel. They bring comfort and consolation to men who are in places of danger and death.

This afternoon was spent with thirty-two Army chaplains. All of them, with one exception, were Methodists. They had been summoned from the fighting front to give me a chance to confer with them. Never was I more impressed with an audience. Here were men who walked in dangerous places and kept company with death.

My sermon was based and built upon the story of the Good Shepherd whose concern was to bring the sheep out of the barrenness of the wilderness into green pastures and beside still waters.

Maybe this figure of speech was not the most appropriate, but certainly here were men who were forgetting their safety to carry on a Christ-like ministry of redemption and conservation. I take off my hat to these brave chaplains and salute them as good ministers of Christ serving in places of great danger. May God bless and preserve them.

Early today I called at the office of General Van Fleet to pay my respect. He was out at the airport receiving a very important military dignitary from Washington. This afternoon something like an alarm went out over the Military Police radio to "find Bishop Moore." While I was inspecting the bombed-out buildings of Severance Hospital a fine young chaplain found me and, in his Jeep, broke all speed laws while taking me to General Van Fleet's office.

The general while wearing four stars on his uniform is still a kind, considerate, and friendly gentleman. One easily understands how he has come to have such a high position and is entrusted with such heavy responsibilities. I would not presume to quote him on the important matters we discussed but I violate no confidence when I say that his interests are not limited to a speedy military victory. He carries in his mind the speedy restoration of the churches, schools, and all other institutions which work for the religious and cultural development of the Korean people. As much as I deplore the necessity of war, I must record before the close of this eventful day, my gratitude for the presence and leadership of a wise general and the healing ministry of these brave chaplains.

It was a happy surprise to find upon my arrival this morning that Rev. Harvey Hardin of the Florida Conference is the Protestant chaplain at the large evacuation hospital located near here. He was one of the fine young pastors in Florida when I was the bishop there. He entered the chaplaincy early in World War II and has remained in the military serving with fidelity and distinction. It was a joy to greet him and watch him work.

To this large evacuation hospital, the wounded are brought immediately after they receive first aid in the field hospitals. This hospital alone handled during September thousands of wounded. The doctors and nurses are all well trained and the equipment is of the best.

My visit to several of the wards where I had extended conversations with the wounded was a privilege that I prize but did not enjoy. As I went from bed to bed, we talk of the family back home, the promise of getting back home soon, etc. Some were in too much pain for conversation, so I breathed a prayer and reminded them that "underneath are the everlasting arms." Too much cannot be said for these doctors and nurses, and Americans simply cannot do enough for these lads who are paying such a price for a free world.

We have lost much valuable property in Seoul from bombing and looting. This was quite a Methodist Center. Before the war, we had forty-five Methodist churches in the city alone. Twelve of these have been destroyed and sixteen badly damaged. Here was Severance Hospital, Ehwa College, Chosum Christian University, Seoul Evangelistic Center, two Theological Seminaries (one for men and one for women), the Christian Literature Society Building, a magnificent YWCA building, a fine home for the Bible Society, and a score of missionary residences. Some of these were of course inter-denominational and Methodists had only a partnership. On the other hand, our Methodist property values reached a large figure. There has been damage at every place and destruction in many places.

All this destruction of property distresses me but the two things which keep sleep from my eyes although my body is weary and the hour is late are these: not very far from where I write

American lads are fighting up mountain slopes against unbelievable odds and some will suffer and die before morning comes; – in addition, sorely tired people of South Korea go homeless in their land without adequate food or shelter wondering if Korea will ever again be called "The Land of the Morning Calm."

Wesleyan Christian Advocate, December 6, 1951, p. 4

Seoul, Korea
October 26, 1951

No words of mine can describe the changes which have taken place since I was here in 1946. This lovely city has been fought over several times, and practically all of it is now in ruins. The fighting front is not far away, and that makes the atmosphere tense and electric.

Soldiers of many nations are in the streets, and planes roar overhead night and day, carrying the deadly instruments of war up to the enemy lines. I am here by courtesy of the military authorities and for security reasons must not go into detail. This much, however, can be told.

When I arrived in Pusan a week ago I asked at once for permission to go up to Seoul. The Methodist Church has a great deal of property here and I wanted to see what happened to it in the fighting of the last year. Then too I must confess to a desire to see what things were like where one of the decisive struggles of history was being fought. As you know, I brought with me a commission from the Methodist Commission on Chaplains to visit as many of the Methodist chaplains as possible. The military authorities were gracious enough to call them in together so that I might meet them and speak to them. Practically all of them came out of the front lines and I count it a high privilege to see them and bring them greetings from the church at home.

There were thirty-two present when we sat down together. They are men of genuine piety and wonderful courage, seriously devoted to serving God and country. Following the meeting with the chaplains, I turned my attention to the inspection of Methodist church properties.

We had forty-nine churches in the city, twelve of them have been destroyed and twenty-three partially destroyed. Only twelve of the forty-nine escaped some serious war damage. Thirteen of our pastors were arrested and taken away by the communist. In addition to these, the bishop of the church and many influential laymen suffered a similar fate.

This afternoon I was privileged to have a visit with General Van Fleet, who commands all the UN forces in Korea. He has a most pleasing personality and seems genuinely concerned about the religious and educational life of the Korean people. I shall not soon forget his kindness to me. All Koreans were evacuated from Seoul last spring but inspite of the fighting which is going on at their very doors, they are slipping back into the city. One finds it easy to understand why. They are homeless elsewhere and getting back home is an instinct of the human heart. I have been here two days and they will remain unforgettable days with me. In a few hours, I take a special military train back to Pusan.

Next Sunday I preach for our American flyers at a large airfield. On Monday I will have a three-hour conference with chaplains located in southern Korea. On Thursday, November 1, the General Conference of the Methodist Church will open. Thus, you get some idea of how very busy I am.

Wesleyan Christian Advocate, November 8, 1951, p.1.

October 23, 1951

On a muddy wind-swept piece of ground, seven hundred girls stood singing, "Out of My Bondage, Sorrow and Night, Jesus I come." The place was in southern Korea and the singers were lovely Korean girls who comprise the student body of Ewha University.

Driven by brutal and unwarranted invasion from their campus in Seoul, the capital city, there they stood in exile but still singing. Refugees, every one of them, bearing burdens that would crush a less heroic people, gallantly carry on their college classes in tents without floors and meet for chapel in the out-of-doors, because in the city of nearly a million refugees there is no building available.

Dr. Helen Kim the president of Ewha University one of the world's great women took my message and translated it into Korean. The students stood shoulder to shoulder in a light mist of rain, listened eagerly, and then sang triumphantly, "Jesus, I Come to Thee."

I have witnessed many moving sights as I have gone up and down the world, but the sight of these heroic girls singing in the rain will never fade from my heart and mind. You simply cannot defeat or dismiss the people of such heroic mold.

But I am getting ahead of my story. For forty years Korea has been tangled up with my life. As far back as 1909 in the early morning of my Christian life, I volunteered as a missionary to this land, but the committee thought me unfit for such service. But in 1934 I was sent as Bishop in China, Japan, and Korea until 1940. From then until now the struggling people of this tortured little country have had a large place in my life. In 1946 I was again sent to be with them in their hour of liberation, to help reconstruct the church and watch the new nation take its first awkward steps. After nearly a half-century under Japanese domination, liberation had come. There was hope in every Korean's heart and only one dark cloud still hung over them. The Russians were in North Korea.

In August 1945, the Japanese surrendered, and Korea was liberated by the Allied armies. To facilitate this disarming of the Japanese troops, Korea was divided by the American and Russian forces at the 38th parallel. This might have served a military purpose but at once Russia used it as a means of separating two interdependent sections of the new nation. In the American Zone, twenty million people were living in the nation's breadbasket, in the North, another ten million were to be found in the bulk of the industrial resources. Whatever the political and military expediency of this arbitrary division, it has served to make Korea not a united and happy people, but an unhappy nation, torn into parts with irreconcilable forms of government, and now the scene of bloodied conflict. Korea is being held as a hostage in the larger world struggle between the free nations on one hand and Russia and her satellites on the other.

It was not difficult to see. If American troops were withdrawn from South Korea the brutal imperialism which had occupied North Korea since 1946 would march in with heavy boots. That is exactly what happened and now brave young soldiers from Korea, America, and many other nations are fighting and dying to check the communist armies and to give these kind-hearted people, who love peace, a chance to achieve independence, freedom, and equality.

If Korea is surrendered to her greedy neighbors with their atheistic ideologies, then all of Asia, yea, the entire world is endangered. The people are not downhearted. In the same street with wounded Korean soldiers hobbling by on crutches and unnumbered children begging are well-dressed women, businessmen intent on business, soldiers and trucks carrying on the grim business of war, governmental officials hurrying from one conference to another; ships unloading the sinews of war, missionaries bending over stricken people like the good Samaritans they are, church bells ringing, people singing and praying, and bombers overhead on their way to drop death on the enemy.

How can one describe a country in which the total population is so driven by war? It all staggers the imagination, it sends you to your bed crying, "How long, O Lord, how long?" There are so many ugly realities that one cannot help being haunted and confused. Here the entire nation was once known as the "Land of the Morning Calm," now the scene of terrifying fighting. The people are besieged by fierce complexities, breaking hearts, and bewildered lives while a large section of their nation is in the hands of plunderers. Here democracy fights for its life as the nation pours out its treasure of life and funds to survive.

Wesleyan Christian Advocate, November 22, 1951, p. 12

At Sea, aboard SS *President Wilson*
November 12, 1951

For the privilege of having a small part in the Christian missionary movement, I am profoundly grateful. For twenty years my missionary duties have been my highest joy and my most sacred obligation. I will not say "I fought the good fight," and I would not like to think "I have finished my course," but I do claim to have "kept the faith." Whatever mistakes we have made and whatever reverses have come, it remains true that there are millions of men, women, and children in the world who are freer, happier, and better because we have taken seriously our Lord's command to preach His gospel to the whole creation.

This is the final article based on my experiences in Korea and Japan. Yesterday I came on board the SS *President Wilson* at Yokohama and began the fourteen-day voyage to America. I came out by air in forty hours, and the return voyage will require two weeks. I chose the ship to have a few days of rest after one of the most strenuous assignments of my life. The miseries of the Korean people, added to a 16-hour daily schedule, have left me completely exhausted. I hope the healing ministry of rest and sleep will soon prepare me for the busy months which are ahead. Meanwhile, I am using this quiet time to organize my impressions and formulate my report.

Here are some of the experiences and convictions that came to mind as I review these hurried weeks in Korea and Japan. Above all, I shall remember the magnificent fortitude of the people of Korea. There is scarcely a family there that remains intact. Loved ones have been taken away by the communists. Their cities have nearly all been destroyed, their factories bombed and their farms rendered useless for the time being. A large percent of the population are refugees, some say four million, some say ten million, and are dependent for food on friendly people abroad. Turn where you will and there you see homeless people, crying children who have been separated from their parents, weeping wives whose husbands were killed or captured, and crippled young Korean soldiers whose comrades died beside him. Yet, these are a people of an almost unconquerable hope and are still confident that their nation will survive with freedom, justice, and security. I salute them as brave people who deserve the support of free men everywhere.

The news of truce talks at Kaesong does not reach me out at sea and I am not informed as to what is happening there. These lines will appear in print many days hence and what I now say may then appear foolish or completely wrong. However, I dare to put down for the record some facts which now seemed to me incontrovertible.

For the Allied armies to have drawn a line across Korea at the 38th parallel when World War II finished looks like a tragic blunder. The separation of the industrial North from the agricultural South threw the Korean economy into disorder. There was every reason to keep Korea whole and to develop it as a unified democratic nation, but no reason except a purely military one why it should be divided into two parts. This division left Korea under a virtual sentence of death and created a festering sore which became the cause of international turmoil which eventuated in a bloody war.

The Korean people high and low and without exception so far as I know are intent on achieving four objectives:

1. To win the war;

2. National unification;

3. Adequate protection against future foreign aggression and

4. The rehabilitation of their land and people physically and spiritually.

So, they go patiently throughs of the shadow of death, grateful for the help they are receiving but convinced that it would be better to die as free men rather than to live as slaves. While on this mission I have been graciously received by Gen. Matthew H. Ridgeway and Gen. James A. Van Fleet, our supreme military leaders in Japan and Korea. One thing that has impressed me and stands out in the conversations with these distinguished soldiers, is their deep appreciation of moral and spiritual values. They do not hesitate to say that the future of the world will not be finally determined upon a battlefield but by a revival of spiritual religion. They are men of faith and genuinely devoted to those intangible but imperishable values of faith and worship. I thank God we have such men in these places of leadership.

In connection with my other duties, it has been my privilege to spend considerable time in conference with our chaplains who are with our men in the armed services. These chaplains richly deserve an increasing place in our appreciation. They risk their lives to be with our sons and fathers who fight and die to preserve freedom. In Korea, recently I spent much of one entire day with thirty-one Methodist chaplains who had been pulled back from the front lines for this conference. Already some chaplains have died alongside our men on those fiery mountainsides and others will. In hospitals with the wounded, or in training camps, they carry out a ministry of courage and consolation. They help to keep our lads clean in life, strong in the faith, and worthy of the loved ones back home. The church of the future will be stronger because of what our chaplains are now doing for our fighting men. The church of the present must see that they never lack our appreciation and full support.

While in Korea, I met and talked intimately with the leaders of government. President Rhee, who is a Methodist, gave me an hour of his valuable time. I traveled with the Prime Minister and found him a devout Catholic. Several other members of the President's Cabinet graciously entertained us. I found them all men of ability and sincerity and as I have indicated, several of the more active Christians.

We should remember that when South Korea was invaded, the new government of the Republic of Korea was just beginning to function efficiently. Under Japanese domination, Koreans were seldom permitted to hold positions of responsibility.

There was, therefore, no backlog of experienced leaders or trained administrators. However, these men whom I have referred rose to meet the challenge and when all things are considered they have succeeded remarkably. It would be unfair to judge their accomplishments by the same standards applicable to long-established and better-organized governments.

President Syngman Rhee, I regard as a strong resourceful leader. He is hated by the Communists and often accused by his supporters of being a stubborn old man, but I admire him for his lifelong devotion to the cause of Korean independence in his unyielding opposition to communism. The important thing to remember is that Korea does have a democratic government that is functioning with a minimum of inefficiency and a maximum of courage and that it steadfastly refuses to compromise with atheistic communism.

Whenever Communism invades any country, it sets out either to liquidate the church entirely or failing in that, to make it the voice and agent of its totalitarian ideology. That has certainly been true in Korea and their campaign has been one of ruthless persecution. But the church in Korea, bereft of many of its most capable leaders, with much of its physical properties reduced to ashes, and with its people in exile, carries on with surprising initiative and courage. In Pusan alone, which is a city of refugees, eleven new Methodist churches have been organized. They meet in tents, attics, or out-of-doors. Practically every Christian school in Korea has been driven from its campus, but they carry on in make-shift buildings without floors or windows, perched upon muddy hillsides. Both churches and schools refused to fold up, and as long as people who are homeless and hungry refuse to cry out or whimper but go on singing and praying compose the church, it will be deathless.

These notes which have been so personal and informal must be brought to an end. I began this journey with a prayer for God's guidance and I shall close it with a prayer of thanksgiving for what our fathers called "journeying mercies." Meanwhile, my heart is filled with gratitude for God's unfailing goodness and for a small place in the life and work of the church which follows Christ upon the broken roads to the world.

Wesleyan Christian Advocate, December 20, 1951, p. 4

The SS *President Wilson* upon which Bishop Moore sailed home from Korea.

CHAPTER ELEVEN

A Near-Death Experience In a Kansas Wheatfield

March 26, 1952

The bishop boarded a plane Thursday, March 27 at 3:20 p.m. in Colorado Springs, Colorado, where he had been presiding over a Methodist missionary meeting. It was snowing, but the sun was shining, and it was a very nice takeoff. Every seat was taken. The plane was a Braniff Airlines plane with four engines.

The fire broke out about 5:00 p.m. It was an engine on the right side of the plane, the one next to the fuselage. I was seated on the left and noticed the light, but at first, I thought the flashing was the sun playing in and out of the clouds. But some of the passengers spotted the fire, and soon we were all crowding over to the window to see. The crew turned on the automatic emergency fire extinguisher, but it did not have any effect. The flames lapped away at the wing.

It was immediately apparent that we were in great danger. We were flying at about seven thousand feet, I think, out over Kansas with no airport near us and no place to land. Time was of the essence. The pilot nose-dived that big plane and streaked for the earth like a bomber attack. Meantime, the engine had burned and had fallen off the plane. The wing had ignited, but it stayed on.

When that engine dropped out, you can imagine the horror we felt. We tried to keep everybody quiet, but, of course, there was some hysteria, though not much. I think everybody behaved very well. Two or three lost control and were quieted by others; we had to do that for the sake of the good of all. I am as susceptible to fright as anybody. I just thought it was the end. I thought that it was not a very romantic thing to do – to die out in a Kansas wheat field.

One prays more subconsciously than consciously at a time like that, I suppose. One does not have time to do much orderly thinking under such circumstances. Whatever one's impulses are – if they are those of faith and trust – those guide his reaction. I have been flying all through the world, and, except for a tornado experience on a flight in Africa, this was my only real brush with death.

While the plane was going down, some of us started opening the emergency windows – the two on the left. We could not open those on the right because of the fire and flames. Once the first fright had passed, everybody settled down into a silence you could almost hear. The pilot flashed the "Fasten Seat Belt" sign, and we were doing that when he went into the dive.

He made what I think was a pretty good landing in a Kansas wheat field. It was pretty rough, but nobody was hurt in the landing. To come down in flames like that – it is hard to describe how it is. We hit the ground and bounced – oh, very high. But the plane remained upright. We shot through two or three fences, knocked down some telephone poles, and even [crossed] a highway, but still, the plane did not turn over.

The two-emergency window exits in the door were open by the time we came to a halt, and in an incredibly short time, everybody succeeded in getting out. We had to go down a rope – slide down it because the exits were 20 to 30 feet from the ground. A good many burned their hands on the rope and some twisted their ankles, but no one was seriously hurt. I did not get any rope burns or hurt my ankle; I was all right.

Everybody was alive. We stopped once to look back at the flaming plane; the pilot motioned us to get farther away. We went a pretty good distance from it. We stood there in the wheat field – the wheat was not very high – and watched the thing burn. The gasoline tanks exploded. It was gone in ten minutes. It was a total loss.

As we stood there, we felt a deep sense of gratitude for help beyond any human source. I do not know what the beliefs of the passengers were when they boarded that plane, but there were not any atheists when we got out of that wheat field!

As soon after we landed, some cars drove up and took us into the little town of Hugoton, Kansas. It was Wednesday afternoon, and the stores were all closed. I sought out the Methodist parsonage; and when I knocked on the door, a kind lady opened it and said, "My goodness, Bishop Moore, where did you come from?" I said, "I have just fallen out of the sky, and I am scared to death. Let me in." She let me in, gave me a cup of coffee, and I got on the phone and called home. The preacher had a merchant open up his store, and I bought a new coat and a new hat. I suppose that was as close a call as I have ever had, and I have never ceased to be grateful to God for a miraculous deliverance from what seemed to be certain death.

Editor's Note: This chapter is based upon interviews Bishop Moore gave to the *Atlanta Constitution*, the *Atlanta Journal*, the *Wesleyan Christian Advocate*, and recollections in his autobiography, *Bishop to All Peoples*.

Wreckage of the Braniff Douglas DC-4 just after it crash landed on in a
Kansas Wheat field on March 26, 1952.

Bishop Moore described the decent in terms of a dive bomber making a
bombing run.

CHAPTER TWELVE
An Emergency Mission to Germany

February- March 1953

For the fifth time in recent years, Bishop Arthur J. Moore of the Methodist Church, is being sent by his church on an emergency mission to one of the disturbed areas of the world. This time he goes representing the Council of Bishops to preside over a Central Conference in Germany. At this Conference, a new bishop will be elected, and Bishop Moore will preside over the Conference and assist in the consecration of the newly elected bishop. The former German Bishop J. W. E. Sommer died last October.

Bishop Moore will depart from Atlanta on January 30, going first to Dallas, Texas, where he will deliver the Fondren Lectures at Southern Methodist University from February 2-5. From Dallas, he will fly to New York and sail on the on the RMS *Queen Mary* on February 7. He will disembark at Southampton, England, and spend two days with Methodist leaders in London. From there he will fly to Berlin, where the German Conference is scheduled to open on February 17 and adjourn on February 23. The bishop will cross the Atlantic on his return journey by air and expects to be back in Atlanta by March 1.

In 1945 immediately following the end of World War II, Bishop Moore was sent to Korea. During his four months stay, he lived with the American troops and helped reorganize the Methodist Church of Korea. In 1946 he was sent on a special mission to Malaya, Borneo, Sumatra, Japan, and Taiwan (Formosa). In 1948 he was in Germany and Norway helping to rehabilitate the church.

In 1950 he was sent again to Korea where he presided over the General Conference of his church. It was after this mission that the Republic of South Korea awarded Bishop Moore its highest civilian award. The National Medal of Honor was given to the bishop while in San Francisco last May and this metal with a strong letter of commendation from Korea's President Sigmund Rhee is proudly displayed in the Bishop's office. The Declaration refers to Bishop Moore's long ministry on behalf of Korea, especially to his interest in humanitarian relief.

In the autumn of 1952, Bishop Moore was in Austria, Belgium, Switzerland, and North Africa, and returned to America in late November. Now once more he is being sent to deal with the very critical situation in Germany. John Wesley said to the Methodists of his day, "The world is my parish." Bishop Moore demonstrates that fact in actual practice. He has flown both the Atlantic and Pacific oceans and crossed the ocean by ship nearly thirty times.

When asked to describe this present mission, Bishop Moore said, "It is not easy to picture the actual church situation in Germany to my American friends. The Methodist Church is spread all over Germany with more than half its membership in eastern Germany. One does not care to speak freely concerning church life behind the Iron Curtain. It can be stated, however, that communism has encountered what is perhaps its strongest opposition from these God-fearing Christians who lived behind the curtain in eastern Germany. The church is crowded, Sunday Schools larger than ever before, and the people showing remarkable initiative, courage, and mobility."

Where will the German Conference be held? Bishop Moore called this [primary[question. He explained that the Methodists in the Eastern Zone have applied to the authorities for permission to meet at Zwickau in Saxony which is at the center of eastern Germany. They have asked the authorities to grant me a visa to enter the Eastern Zone to preside over the conference. I have sought the advice of our Department of State and am waiting now for instructions from Washington and the developments in Germany. No one can guess whether the permit will be granted or not and even if the conference is permitted to meet. The question of an American bishop getting in for such service is yet to be decided.

"I shall not take any unnecessary risks," he added, "I will not disobey the wishes of the American authorities in Washington or Germany. I am proceeding under orders to Berlin where I shall await developments – and be ready to carry out the mission assigned to me by my church if at all possible. It would be a pale and nerveless Christianity that took no risks to keep the church alive."

Much of Bishop Moore's life has been devoted to these tense areas and he says that it is too late now for him to begin to look for a safe and easy way. The Methodists in Germany, bereft of their brave leader, urging him to come and help them and the highest authority in the Methodist Church ordered him to go. "So, in obedience to duty and in the humble reliance upon God's guiding force," says Bishop Moore, "I am going and will do what I can."

Wesleyan Christian Advocate, January 29, 1953, p. 1

February 12, 1953

Onboard the RMS *Queen Mary*, we are standing outside the harbor of Cherbourg, France, waiting for the winds to subside so that we may proceed to discharge the passengers bound for France and then proceed on our journey to Southampton, England. Standing on the deck of this magnificent ship and looking through the stormy weather at the shores of Europe has a depressing effect on at least this passenger.

This has been my twenty-fourth crossing of the Atlantic, and each visit to the shores reveals many substantial changes. Twenty years ago, I came first on a magnificent vessel known as the RMS *Berengaria*. It has long since disappeared and with it, much of what I found here on that first visit. There may remain a few misguided people living in quiet areas of the world who failed to realize that the old world is dead and that a new world order has arisen. No one can come over here and not be stabbed awake by that undeniable fact.

From February 2-5, I was in Dallas, Texas, where it was my high honor to deliver the Fondren Lectures at Southern Methodist University. There were more than a thousand Methodist preachers present for Ministers Week. It was my rare privilege to speak daily with Dr. Albert Outler, a son of Georgia who has risen to an imminent position in the theological world, and Dr. R. Y. Scott, a well-known Old Testament scholar from the faculty of McGill University in Canada.

How it happened that I was invited to appear alongside such distinguished scholars is not clear to me, and frankly, I was afraid to inquire lest it is discovered that my invitation was an accident. Anyway, while Drs. Outler and Scott gave them "strong meat," I did some "cornfield preaching" on the side, and the audience was most gracious.

A swift trip by air from Dallas to New York put me there in time to come on board the RMS *Queen Mary* early Saturday morning, February 7. This crossing has been good, especially when one remembers that this is February. The Atlantic cannot be expected to always be as docile as a collie dog. It must be allowed to roar and roll at times. I have known voyages more turbulent than this one, but there has been enough rolling pitch to keep many of the passengers in their cabins. As for me, half a dozen books have been devoured and no call to the dining room has found me without interest. Whenever possible on a trip to Europe, I try to cross the Atlantic at least one way by ship to get some undisturbed rest. The aircraft is splendid for speed but give me the good old ship for rest and reading.

When the winds have subsided, and our Cherbourg passengers disembark, we will proceed to England. My plans put me in London for two days and then on to Germany. A cablegram has reached me since leaving home announcing that the conference in Germany has been postponed for one week. This will allow me to make visits to Belgium and Switzerland where I also have some official duties. Detailed plans must wait until I reach London and have time to examine the accumulated mail which awaits me there. Already cablegrams have reached me from our chaplain station in Europe asking that I give our American troops some of my time. That I will gladly do if it can be squeezed into an already busy schedule.

Looking through the rain clouds at the coastline of France sets one thinking about the frightful storms – not of weather – but of two World Wars that have devastated Europe since 1914. Old Europe is gone. The old maps have been rolled up, and a new map is being unrolled before our eyes. When one contemplates what has been happening and what may happen tomorrow, it is a small wonder that in many sections of the earth there is a spirit of pessimism and in some places even despair. So many high hopes have been dashed to pieces, so much property destroyed, and so many thousands of brave, young men are sleeping in a soldier's grave. We who live in a quiet, prosperous America are often tempted to lose patience with Europe, but whatever our problems are, we at least are not as perplexed and baffled as those who live in Europe.

France is weak and divided and it now appears will be for many years. The Germans are rebuilding from the ashes of their bombed-out cities; but if Russia stands with hobnailed boots across the eastern half, there is not much hope for a strong united Germany. Italy will not again in our lifetime play a very decisive role in world affairs. This horrible engine of war has left destruction in its path. There is hunger, unemployment, and hopelessness in many places. The people of Europe need food not only for their bodies but their spirits as well.

The three major powers in the world today are Russia, Great Britain, and the United States of America. Great Britain with its proud history, filled with glory, honor, and prestige such as few people have known, is now poor in material substance. She has poured her treasure of men and resources into two World Wars and that has left her with insufficient material resources for the great emergency which now besets her and the rest of the world. England needs and richly deserves the patient understanding and generous support of the United States.

The two giants left in the world arena are Russia and our own country. Both have potentialities of power beyond measure. Would that Almighty God would bring us to the point of humbly seeking to know and do His will, living in helpfulness with the spirit of love and mercy in our hearts. Some will say "that will never happen to Russia," and my only answer is "it will not happen in Russia or anywhere else unless the church is strong and spiritual, and we can produce a revival of pure and undefiled religion." That is why I am over here to do my bit to keep the church of the Living God redemptively in contact with men and nations.

Wesleyan Christian Advocate, February 26, 1953, p.1

Which Way Europe?

One is forced inevitably by the frightful urgencies of the total European situation to at least attempt a realistic interpretation of the problems. Whenever a thoughtful American examines the assets and liabilities of post-war Europe, he comes at once to these two conclusions. First, there are vast and intricate problems upon whose solution the peace of the world and the happiness of mankind depend. Second, the problems are so perplexing one loses all desire to speak as a prophet.

We who live in prosperous America are always in danger of losing patience with European nations and are apt to accuse them of delaying tactics. Certainly, they do seem to lack the courage to take quick and decisive action. At least so it appears to an outsider.

What we do not always remember is that twice within the lifetime of a single generation, Europe has witnessed the devastating scourge of two total wars. Millions of men died, vast quantities of wealth were blown to bits, and entire cities and lands were ravaged. In Germany alone, there are six million more women than men because of war. We must not be surprised or disappointed that Europeans seem to lack energy and unity in cooperative efforts to prevent another war. I do not write to accuse them of their seeming tardiness, I am only suggesting that the situation in America is one thing, and in Europe is quite something else. The chief topic of conversation on both sides of the Atlantic just now is the prospect of the early ratification of the six-nation European Army Treaty.

During his recent visit to several European capitals, Mr. John Foster Dulles, our American Secretary of State sought to impress upon the leaders of these nations who are allied with us the permanent importance of their taking more decisive action if they are to continue to receive American aid. He emphasized that he would need evidence of their purpose to cooperate fully to convince America to continue its foreign aid program. He warned Europe with notable frankness that if they failed to take action, he would not be able to represent them effectively before the American Congress.

With all of that, I agree, that there is something to be said about the age-old suspicions and fears between Germany and

France, and other countries, which make quick and positive action difficult if not impossible. We have entered a long and difficult road and we must not turn back even when the pace of our partners is slower than we like. Either we stick together and thus form a coalition strong enough to deter the bold imperialism of Russia, or we fall to pieces and surrender Europe to communism by default. At least so it appears to me.

Another topic of almost endless conversation over here is the great number of German refugees who are slipping daily across the Iron Curtain from East to West Germany. The Soviets have done everything possible to stop this flow of distraught men, women, and children. As I write they continue to come. Today's paper tells of more than three thousand who at great risk of life and loss of all property, crossed the line only yesterday. The Russians have created what is known as a "Dead Zone," complete with guard towers, barbed wire, and ditches to stop the flow of refugees.

But still they come. Practically all of them cross from the Eastern Zone to Berlin for the Western or Allied Zone and are then flown out in airplanes to different places in Germany that are being occupied by America, England, and France. This great number of refugees represents all walks of life.

Let no one think that those who reach freedom do so by simply crossing the line. That would be a great injustice to the men and women who have escaped. Once having decided to leave homes, possessions, and friends in the Eastern Zone for life in an overcrowded refugee camp in the free west, they face all kinds of danger and possible death. How shall they prepare for flight, board the proper trains, or finally cross the border without arousing the suspicions of the police?

This can be done only by intelligent planning, reduction of baggage to an absolute minimum, not to mention having nerves of steel. If they are lucky enough to enter Western Germany, they face a life of poverty in a country overcrowded with refugees. How intolerable slavery must be, and how precious is the air of freedom.

We who have so much freedom in America should highly resolve that our prayers and sacrifice will always be given freely to defend and preserve the sacred principles which make for human freedom and the well-being of mankind. Long ago, William Penn, said: "Unless we are governed by God, we will be governed by tyrants." Whenever men put a superstate in the place of reference for Almighty God, their freedom is gone. Never do I come home from one of these emergency missions without an almost agonizing prayer upon my lips, "O Lord, strengthen the Christian convictions and ideals which have made my nation strong and free."

After three busy days with Methodist leaders in England, two days in Paris, and one in Brussels, where I sought to discharge official responsibilities, I reached Germany on February 19. For one entire week I have sought by whatever means possible to be of some real help to our German Methodists.

The Central Conference will begin its work tonight. We hope to elect and consecrate a bishop between now and Sunday night. Although we are now within a few hours of the opening service, we do not yet know whether any of the delegates from the Eastern Zone will be present. I simply do not know how to put down any combination of words that would describe the hopes and fears, the tears and triumphs, the assets and liabilities that would stand behind this Conference.

Wesleyan Christian Advocate, March 12, 1953

Editor's Note: The European Army Treaty would have created a European Defense Community (EDC) with a pan-European defence force. The treaty failed to obtain ratification in the French parliament, and it was never ratified by Italy, so it consequently never entered into force.

A Memorial to those killed trying to cross the Berlin Wall.

Mission Completed

This article will hardly be completed before I am back in Georgia, but today has been so unusual and important. I must begin to record something of my experiences and impressions.

Here I am in historic Frankfurt on the Main. Its history dates to the time of the Roman invasion. Last Sunday afternoon I visited a Roman fort that was created in 63 A.D. – nearly 2000 years ago. The late Kaiser Wilhelm of Germany, while still Emperor of Germany, had this fort restored. It stands today, a replica of the original fort in which the soldiers of the Roman Empire lived and from which they went forth to conquer.

Frankfurt has a population of five hundred thousand and is undoubtedly the center of the economic recovery one finds all over Western Germany. The city was heavily bombed during the last war, and practically all its historic buildings were damaged or destroyed. In downtown Frankfurt, there were thirty lovely Cathedral churches, some of them dating back to the early centuries.

Twenty-nine of the churches were completely wiped out by bombs. But with typical German industry and some financial help given by the United States, the city is being rebuilt. I went yesterday, for example, to Goethe's house which was destroyed but has now been completely restored. All the priceless belongings were fortunately stored away before the house was destroyed. Today, they are all in place and one can hardly tell a devastating war has passed by.

I took a few hours yesterday to visit the big International Fair which is being held this week. It is unlike an American fair in that there are no midways, shows, games of chance, or horse racing. This is a real demonstration of the manufacturing power of Western Germany and some of her near neighbors such as Switzerland, Belgium, France, and Austria.

One cannot help but be amazed at the quick comeback of the German industry. Here one finds machinery, automobiles, textiles, furniture, and cameras, in fact, practically all the products which made Germany a prosperous nation before Hitler came to power and brought about its downfall. The markets of the world will soon be filled with German-made goods. That is the conclusion one reaches after a visit to the Frankfurt Fair.

Frankfurt, Germany after World War II

I am supposed to be writing about the church, and the Methodist Church in particular. Like every other institution in Germany, the church faces the problems created by war and its aftermath. Here is a good place to record that all the problems of the world seem to be concentrated in a particularly acute form. This is now the battleground of powerful and conflicting ideologies. Germany had twelve years of Hitler and Nazi rule. It has now had seven years of occupation by conquering armies. Russia occupies Eastern Germany with her dogmatic reliance on the tenants of Communism. The United States, Great Britain, and France occupy Western Germany in their support to establish a democratic state. One likes to believe, as I do, that theirs is a wise, humane, and constructive endeavor.

The Methodist Church has enjoyed remarkable success in Germany. We have five Annual Conferences made up of devout, well-trained evangelistic ministers. We have more than one thousand deaconesses, every one of whom is a trained nurse and devotes her whole life to the church. We have strong, well-operated hospitals, a theological seminary, homes for the aged, etc. German Methodism for many years has had its own bishop and has been entirely self-supporting. As a result of the war, help from outside sources has been needed to rebuild bombed-out churches and restore essential institutions. It would hardly be possible to overestimate the courage, sacrifice, and hard work of the German Methodists in solving their problems. They are a proud people and do not turn easily for help from outside their own country. That makes it even more necessary that we are alert to their needs and help in every way possible. They have borrowed vast sums with which to rebuild some of their churches and hospitals. On these loans they are paying an exorbitant interest rate, but they never cry out or whimper. They are a band of brave loyal sacrificial Methodists and are living up to the best of Methodist traditions.

Bishop J. W. E. Sommer had been the gifted wartime leader of Methodism in this nation. His courage, tact, resourcefulness, and wisdom are acknowledged by all. Weary with the heavy load he carried for so many years, he passed suddenly last October to his eternal reward. It becomes necessary to hold an extraordinary session of the Central Conference to choose a new bishop. It was to preside over this Conference and to assist in the consecration of the new bishop that I was sent on this mission.

Germany, as I have said, is divided into the West and East zones with different governments. Up until now, the church has been able to escape a division such as has taken place in the nation. Our Methodist churches in the Eastern Zone have continued their work with a minimum of opposition. Large congregations have attended our services and something of a religious revival has characterized church life in that part of the country.

German Methodists desired to hold this conference inside the Eastern Zone provided permission could be secured from the authorities. We were encouraged to seek this privilege and had such encouragement from the authorities that we would be allowed to convene in Zwicken, which is in Saxony. After waiting for some time, we were requested to withdraw our application. This was done and the Conference assembled in Frankfurt, in the Western Zone.

It was a matter of genuine regret that due to lack of travel permits, none of the delegates from the Eastern Zone could be present when the conference was called to order Thursday night. It would not be wise for me to discuss in an article, such as this, the causes and conditions which lie back of this fact.

In the opening service we had a fine example of the worldwide character of Methodism. With us, were Bishop Theodore Arvidson from Sweden, Dr. Ferdinand Sigg from Switzerland, Dr. William G. Thonger from Belgium, and Rev. Ferdinand Mayr from Austria. Added to these was Pastor Martin Niemoller who fought so stubbornly against Hitlerism and is today one of the outstanding leaders of the Lutheran Church in Germany. Together we celebrated the Lord's Supper. It was my great joy also to welcome Bishop Gerald H. Kennedy of Los Angeles, who is here on a preaching mission to our American soldiers. It is on an occasion like this that the old hymn, "Blessed be the tie that binds our hearts in Christian love," takes on loving significance.

Friday morning, the conference gave itself to a prolonged session of prayer. We all felt that God must help us find the right leader for a time like this. We had the guidance of the Holy Spirit for on the first ballot cast, Dr. Frederick Wunderlich, received every vote cast, save his own. Never have I witnessed greater unity in a church conference. Dr. Wunderlich has, for several years, been the president of our theological school in

Frankfurt. He is a distinguished scholar, having studied in America, and holds a Ph.D. From Leipzig University. He is a member of one of the Annual Conferences which is now behind the Iron Curtain, but for several years his residence and work have been in Western Germany. His election was hailed with delight, not only by the Methodists but by all the Protestant leaders in Germany. I am proud to have him as one of my cherished friends. Members of the South Georgia Conference will remember his visit and message to our conference last summer in Thomasville.

Sunday, March 1, was a beautiful spring day in Frankfurt. The nearby mountains are still covered with snow, but it is a warm, sunny day. Because not one of our Methodist churches would accommodate the large congregation coming for the consecration of the new bishop, we met this afternoon in a famous Lutheran Church which bears the name "The Church of the Three Wise Men." It is the only one cathedral church left standing after the terrible bombings of World War II. Traveling from cities and towns near and far, the Methodists filled the vast sanctuary. We even had a brass band outside the church play hymns while the people assembled.

It was my privilege and pleasure to preach the sermon. The message was what God said to his people on another day when there was a grave national crisis, "Speak to the children of Israel and command them to go forward." Following the sermon, we had a most solemn and impressive Service of Consecration. I was assisted by Bishop Theodore Arvidson, Dr. William G. Thonger, Dr. Ferdinand Sigg, and a half-dozen of the leading Methodist ministers of Germany.

Thus, a high honor and an almost overwhelming responsibility were placed in the hands of a good man who values the approval of Christ above every other possession life could bestow. Let us lift this good man, his devout, and gifted wife, and four fine children, up to God as we pray from day to day.

This mission to Germany, having been accomplished, I plan to leave tomorrow morning by air for the long journey home. Thus, ends one of the memorable days of my busy life.

This article was written while I was still in Germany, but the final words must be written in Atlanta. The British European Airways plane which took me from Germany to London was forced to make its way through dense fog. The airport in London and in fact, all of England was enveloped in a typical English fog. As a result, we were delayed in London for nearly twenty-four hours. It was noon Tuesday when we were permitted to take off. Except for one fleeting glance of Northern Ireland, we flew across the Atlantic Ocean and landed at Boothbay, Labrador, without the sight of anything but clouds. The thermometer registered 11° below zero. As soon as we refueled, we were on our way to New York and arrived at midnight Tuesday. Tired in body, I slept for a few hours in a New York hotel and left early Wednesday morning on another plane that put down in Atlanta at 4:00 p.m. that afternoon.

Loved ones, green hills, a warm house, a soft bed, and a job to do makes life full of delight and challenge. I am more resolved to support every man and movement which seeks to create and develop new healing relations between the different peoples of the earth, and I shall strive to help Christ make this a safe, friendly world.

Wesleyan Christian Advocate. April 9, 1953, p. 3

Bishop Moore, Bishop Wunderlich, and Bishop Arvidson

CHAPTER THIRTEEN

On Assignment in Europe
July and August 1953

Brussels, Belgium
July 7, 1953

The nations of the Belgian Congo down in Africa have an expression to describe any great distance. It is "over the seas." I have been traveling over the seas for many years but it remains an interesting and sometimes exciting experience.

The North Georgia Annual Conference adjourned on Friday, June 26. The next day I took a train for Philadelphia to take part in the great Conference on Evangelism which had been planned to celebrate the two hundred fiftieth birthday of John Wesley. The conference had been going for two days when I arrived. Great crowds were on hand from all over America, including some certain distinguished Methodist leaders from England. Everywhere one heard enthusiastic reports of the significance and spirituality of the meeting.

It was my privilege to preach at 9:00 a.m. and 11:00 a. m. on Sunday morning in historic old St. George Church. Here was wrought out so much of the early history of American Methodism. When I reached the church, thousands were standing in the streets, hoping to find a seat. Both services witnessed the church crowded almost beyond the point of wisdom.

To sit in Bishop Asbury's chair and preach from the pulpit where this "Prophet of the Long Road" had stood so often was a moving experience. It was even more significant when I remembered that before me was seated many of the most influential leaders of present-day Methodism.

Historic St. George's United Methodist Church, Philadelphia.

The burden of my message was that we were met, not to build a monument, but to inaugurate a movement. Present-day Methodism will be only so much cumbersome machinery unless it is the instrument of God's will and the means of bringing men to experience Christ in His saving power. The afternoon service in Franklin Stadium saw 35,000 gathered despite the rain. It was all a thrilling experience.

From Philadelphia, I took a train to New York to be ready for my overseas flight which was to begin at noon on Monday. No matter how many times one is to cross the ocean, it is always something humble and sobering. This was to be my twenty-seventh crossing of the Atlantic. The Pacific has seen me as a passenger either on a ship or airplane almost as many times. Since July 1952, I have crossed the Atlantic five times, three of them by air. There is enough of the country boy left in me to make me a little afraid to start on the long flight across the Atlantic Ocean.

Accompanied by Bishop and Mrs. Glenn R. Phillips of Denver, Colorado, we left the airport in New York on a modern TWA four-engine plane. There were approximately sixty-five passengers. Four hours after leaving New York, we were on the ground at Gander, Newfoundland. There, while the plane made ready for the ocean hop, we had a cup of coffee and stretched our legs.

We took off at 7:00 p.m. for the long flight across the Atlantic Ocean. Dinner was served and it was good except for the abundance of liquors one is compelled to refuse from having his meal. It does look like these airplane companies might discover that a few of their passengers would prefer a glass of milk or orange juice instead of alcoholic drinks. By 11:00 p.m. most of the passengers had settled down for a little sleep. That I have not yet learned to do. I stayed awake and looked at a beautiful new moon that came out to guide us on our way.

At 6:00 a.m. Tuesday we sighted the Irish coast. We had turned our watches ahead five hours and that means it was only 1:00 a.m. back in Atlanta. In twelve hours, we had flown from New York to Shannon, Ireland. A steaming hot breakfast with bacon and eggs awaited us on the ground as soon as we had passed custom examinations.

We remained at Shannon for approximately two hours and at 10:00 a.m. we were in Paris, France. One hour at the airport gave us a chance to see a little of the beauty of France. Recently, I read the article in the *Saturday Evening Post* by Charles Lindbergh as he recalled his experiences on that memorable flight of his in a little one-motor plane. Certainly, in the light of his adventure, to cross the same ocean in a big four-motor plane seems to lack much adventure.

By 1:30 p.m. Tuesday we were safely on the ground in Zürich, Switzerland, and soon we were comfortably lodged in an inexpensive Christian hotel, with a meeting of the Cabinet of the Swiss Annual Conference only a few hours away.

Thursday, July 2, witnessed the opening session of the Switzerland Annual Conference. We sang the traditional opening hymn for Methodist conferences, just as we had done a few days before at the two Annual Conferences in Georgia, meeting in Albany and Atlanta. The opening verse is, "And are we yet alive and see each other's face." We have approximately a hundred pastors in Switzerland with godly and sacrificial church membership. We have two hundred twenty-nine deaconesses who devote their entire lives to the church. A network of hospitals all over Europe gives evidence of their skill and Christian devotion.

Sunday, July 5, was a high day for us. Bishop Clare Purcell of Birmingham, Alabama, who had come to join us, preached in one church, Bishop Phillips in another, while I preached in another to the Annual Conference. At the close of the services, it was my privilege to ordain four fine young ministers.

In the afternoon we enjoyed a wonderful concert by the combined choirs of several of our churches. Never have I heard better singing than in Switzerland. The closing session of the Conference began at 5:00 p.m. Again it was my joy to preach and then read the pastoral assignments for the next year.

These lines are being written in Brussels, Belgium, where tomorrow we begin the session of another Annual Conference. Not since Easter have I had a single day of rest, and when the final benediction is said here next Sunday night, I propose going to bed for about 48 hours.

So goes the travel and duties of the traveling Methodist Bishop. My friends in Georgia have insisted that I write these travel notes and have been good enough to say they read them with interest. If so, I am glad to write them. In the next article, some attempts will be made to analyze present-day conditions in Europe.

One would like to believe as I do, that a host of God's people hold them up with their prayers. For the love and prayers of dear friends, I am most grateful.

Wesleyan Christian Advocate, July 23, 1953, p. 1.

Brussels, Belgium
July 16, 1953

The Annual Conference of Belgium came to a glorious climax last Sunday afternoon in a most extraordinary celebration of the 250th anniversary of the birth of John Wesley. We gathered at Vilvoorde, which is just outside of Brussels. Here, in October 1536, William Tyndale was imprisoned, and later strangled and burned for translating the Holy Bible. His last words were a prayer that the King of England might have his eyes opened. God heard Tyndale's prayer, and one year later the King of England caused the Holy Bible to be printed in a language that the common people could read.

After the Methodist service was over last Sunday, I stood at a granite monument erected by the British Bible Society honoring the memory of this man who died so that the word of God might be made available to all. Truly, all we have and enjoy have come to us out of the slow and painful strivings of men and women who were willing to die, if need be, for the good of others.

Yesterday, I travelled across that section of Belgium and northern France where much of World War I was fought. At Ypres, Passchendaele, and other nearby territories, the British and German armies were locked for four years in one of the most terrible wars of history. Inscribed on a huge monument at Ypres are the names of 64,000 British boys who were killed nearby, but whose bodies were never recovered and had no formal burial.

In a nearby English cemetery, there are 11,876 graves, one finds the names of another 35,000 English soldiers who were buried in unknown graves. There are more than a hundred cemeteries of those who died in World War I.

It gave me a pain in my heart to think of so many gallant lads dying so early to make the world safe for democracy. Last night's sleep was far from my eyes as I thought especially of those 99,000 who sleep in unknown graves and whose names are known only to God. They were only a small part of a greater company. On one of the headstones in Tyne-Cot cemetery, I read these words: "Although wounded in the morning, he fought until the evening when he fell." Whether one fights in a war or in the ceaseless struggle to build a Christian world, there can be no finer epitaph.

We were also at Dunkirk, France, where the entire British Army, numbering 300,000, miraculously escaped from the Germans in World War II. Standing up on the beaches at Dunkirk with a powerful army pressing to enter to capture them, they beheld the multitude of boats of all sorts and sizes coming across the English Channel, a distance of approximately 75 miles, to snatch them away from their pursuers. If ever there was a miraculous deliverance, it was this escape of the British at Dunkirk. Such a day stir's one's emotions and causes one to wonder if the human race will ever learn to settle its disputes without resorting to war.

In the last article sent to the *Wesleyan Christian Advocate*, I promised to attempt an analysis of the European situation at the present moment. That was a foolish promise. First, because no one man is prepared to interpret this tangled situation, and second, because it changes from day to day. When these lines appear, the whole scene may have changed. Nevertheless, here are a few observances.

First, Moscow is having trouble. Our friends on the other side of the Iron Curtain, the oppressed peoples of those nations which have been overrun by Russia, are waging a desperate and surprisingly strong fight for freedom. Instead of keeping silent, instead of grovelling in submission, they are with their bare hands giving the Russian authorities an increasingly tough time. The fires of rebellion seem to be burning in several places.

In Russia, the power struggle has broken out in the imprisonment of Lavrentiy Beria, one of the three men to whom authority was given at the time of Stalin's death. The viciousness and bloodthirstiness that are too often characterized by Russia's treatment of other people are now showing up in their treatment of each other. In that land where evil calls itself good and where the desire to think one's thoughts is considered evil and dangerous; the power struggle is revealed in all of its naked hideousness. It is too early for us to know what Beria's arrest will mean, but unfortunately, the unbridled lust for power is endangering the future domination of this wicked thing called Communism. Let us hope so.

Second, in eastern Germany, where Russia has stood like a conquering army since the end of World War II, there have been a series of dramatic happenings. The workers, so long oppressed, have risen in protest against this tyrannical regime. Many were killed and injured in these uprisings. At the moment, the rebellion seems to have subsided, but we now know the will for freedom and the power to resist is still in the hearts of the people, and sooner or later it will express itself again.

Meanwhile, the Communist authorities, to appease these determined people, crop quotas have been lightened and the pressure on the churches has, for the moment, been relaxed a bit. It warms my heart, as an American, the see President Eisenhower standing up against the Kremlin and taking bold measures to give encouragement and practical help to those who are risking their lives to throw off the yoke of Russian domination. The Western powers must show solidarity and determination if the banner of freedom is to fly high once more all over the world.

One could write at length about recent happenings in Czechoslovakia, Romania, Egypt, and other nerve centers of this part of the world. Sometimes I feel that the average American does not realize that the struggle for the freedom of religion, of speech, of the press, of assembly, of freedom from arbitrary arrest, of freedom from the search of one's home, and freedom from the censorship of one's correspondence goes on fiercely in vast sections of the world. We cannot fashion ourselves a cozy little world and proceed to live in it by ourselves.

Fighting Communism is something far more costly than calling our fellow Americans bad names, simply because they disagree with us. It is a struggle, long and painful, to introduce all to that abundant life which Christ alone offers, and in which tyranny dies and freedom of opportunity comes, and we strive to live and grow as the children of God.

These rambling remarks may have gone too far; however, they must not close until I say that our Methodist people in Europe are worthy successors of the great Protestant leaders of other days.

If you could jhave been with me at Vilvoorde, Belgium, and heard that great congregation of Methodists singing their devotion to the Methodist way of life and faith, you would feel as I did, that "like a mighty army moves the church of God."

Wesleyan Christian Advocate, July 30, 1953, p. 4.

Editor's Notes:
1. The date of the newspaper is July 23, 1954. However, the date on Bishop Moore's letter is July 7, 1953. It seems to be an error in typesetting.
2. Beria was the longest-lived and most influential of Stalin's secret police chiefs, wielding his most substantial influence during and after World War II. After Stalin's death in March 1953, Beria became First Deputy Chairman of the Council of Ministers and head of the Ministry of Internal Affairs. In this dual capacity, he formed a troika with Georgy Malenkov and Vyacheslav Molotov that briefly led the country in Stalin's place.

A coup d'état by Nikita Khrushchev, with help from Marshal of the Soviet Union Georgy Zhukov, in June1953 removed Beria from power. After being arrested, he was tried for treason and other offenses, sentenced to death, and executed on 23 December 1953.　　(Wikipedia)

Memorial Tablet in Westminster Abbey, London.

The martyrdom of William Tyndale.

Amsterdam, Holland
August 18, 1953

This is the Sabbath day and we are in Holland. Last night it thundered, and the lightning flashed across the sky, but this morning the sun was shining and the church bells sounded across this ancient city, calling the people to worship. With all the members of our party, we attended the morning service in [De Nieuwe Kerk]. Although it is more than three hundred years old, it is still called the New Church. Here in this magnificent cathedral was held the opening service of the organizational meeting of the World Council of Churches in 1946. The service was all in the Dutch language, but despite all the barriers of language, we shared with our fellow Christians "The glory of God's presence." It was not difficult to open one's heart and soul, nourish lovely thoughts and high aspirations and resolve to make life more useful, in such a sacred spot.

The Scripture text for the sermon was I Kings 3: 12-16, "And if thou wilt walk in my ways to keep my statutes and my commandments, as thy father David did walk, then I will lengthen thy days. And Solomon awoke, and behold, it was a dream." Despite the language difficulty, it was possible to know that the earnest preacher was saying that the only safe and secure foundation upon which men or nations can build is the Word and Will of Almighty God. In a world beset by false values and ambiguous standards here was a preacher of God's Word pleading for the renewal of vital convictions about God and duty. It was a rewarding experience, as church-going always proves to be.

With a group of seventeen fellow Americans, I have traveled across France, Switzerland, Germany, Belgium, and now we are in Holland. These dear friends who compose the group are far more than tourists rushing throughout Europe.

They are team-minded, Christian men and women, alert to discover the hidden currents of life and thought which flow beneath the surface in which, after that sets in motion the forces which are made of great nations. They insist on seeing everything, and it is a pleasure to share with them the little information I possess and bring them in close contact with leaders of church and state who can supply authentic information relating to the hopes and fears of the particular nation in which they happen to be at the time.

De Nieuwe Kerk, Amsterdam

It is not easy to organize all the information one acquires, and it is most difficult to put down in written form one's impressions and convictions. Some of the volcanoes which have been erupting in Europe for many years are extinct for the moment, but from these empty craters smoke still drifts and their intermittent rumblings excite one's imagination as to what the future holds for Europe and the world.

The suspicions, conflicts, and antagonisms which turned our world into the nightmare of two world wars are still here. When one writes or speaks about Europe, he is compelled to put down both assets and liabilities and attempt to find some sort of balance.

It is not difficult to see and appreciate Western Germany, for example, the extraordinary revival of industry, factories turning out new products, and vast housing projects, either complete or under construction. Never have I seen a people so intent on rebuilding their nation as are the Germans. There are rumors here and there of a revival of aggressive nationalism and even of a return to militarism, but I do not share these fears. The people with whom I work are sick and tired of propaganda, whether it be from [the devotees of] Hitler or Stalin. They want a reunited Germany with peace, freedom, and prosperity. Before these lines appear in print, a national election will have been held and the results are not yet in sight. The present government led by Prime Minister Adenauer is friendly toward the Western powers. He is a devout Catholic and a strong and progressive leader. For good or ill, Germany is bound to be strong and united, and the whole of Europe will be in the future, as it has been in the past, greatly influenced by what happens in Germany.

France is altogether a different story. As I write, the entire nation is in the throes of a strike. Practically all transportation facilities are at a standstill, and thousands of tourists are stranded. Such a situation imposes a terrific strain upon the minds and nerves of all foreigners caught in such a situation, and I am sure the native population is equally irritated. It would be easy to blame this or that class for what is happening, but to do so would be to miss the profound significance of what has been happening in France for a long time. The blunders of the government, the distribution of wealth, the unequal burdens of taxation, and wages that have not kept pace with the rising cost of living, all are positive factors at work in this present situation, but they are not all.

For a long time, French Communists have been extremely busy and at times their activities have bordered on the revolutionary. Behind the gay boulevards of Paris and the crowded cafés, there goes on a severe struggle for dominance in the national government. Cabinet after cabinet topples and this present strike is an effort on the part of the Communists to bring about a general election with the hope that they may gain control. The challenge of Moscow hangs over France, and it requires some stern arithmetic to determine what the future hold. I do not prophesy that France will go communist, but even a casual observer can see enough dangerous signals to compel the attention of his reluctant eyes and ears. How can a strong nation be built where there is a minimum of political unity, economic strength, and religious idealism? A Europe with a sick France is not likely, and we may all pray to God to give these sorely tired

French people a new national unity and a return to spiritual values.

Speaking of religion, there is much across Europe to encourage one. I have preached on this trip in many places to vast congregations. Only this week, more than sixty thousand German Protestants are gathered in Hamburg for the German Kirchentag. From East and West Germany, these thousands have come here to plan for a national revival of the Protestant churches. When one writes of the anxieties and terrors of these disturbing times, he must also record this new search of the multitudes for God. When men recognize and serve God the refinements of civilization and the graces of Christian living grow and flourish. It is my sincere conviction that most of the people of Europe are sick and tired of war. They are wary of man-made restrictions and long for the freedom of the human spirit.

This one fact helps me to believe that before our generation passes, we may witness another revival of religion in the world. After all, the basic need of most nations is a Divine leader who can furnish authentic leadership and speak with an authoritative voice. That is exactly where Christ takes over, for in Him is no darkness at all, and when enough of us follow Him the world's darkness will turn to dawn.

Tomorrow, we cross over to England. The more I read English history, the better I know English people, and the more I look at England's beauty, the prouder I am to have come from such a noble race. Economic conditions are much better. England is slowly, but surely, recovering her place of leadership in world affairs. There may be some differences between us as to how to proceed in Korea and China, but these differing viewpoints must be resolved. The world needs concerted leadership from our two nations. My sky of hope would be greatly darkened if our two nations were ever to come to any serious parting of the ways.

August 22 will find us onboard the RMS *Mauretania* bound for New York, where we should disembark on August 28. Once onboard the ship I shall find a half dozen good books and devote myself to six days of reading and resting. Upon arrival in the United States, I go immediately to Ocean Grove, New Jersey, for my fifteenth season in that great Methodist Camp Meeting. September 7-9 finds me at Wesleyan College at our Georgia Pastors' School. Then follows a most strenuous fall and winter of hard work.

Traveling abroad has its compensations and for all of them, I am grateful. However, for me, the best part is that it gives you a chance to "come home," back to those you know and love best and the people and the work you love almost like life itself.

Wesleyan Christian Advocate, September 3, 1953, p. 12.

Editor's Note:
The German Evangelical Church Assembly or Kirchentag is an assembly of lay members of the Evangelical Church in Germany, that organizes biannual events of faith, culture, and political discussion. It sees itself as a free movement of people brought together by their Christian faith and engagement in the future of the Evangelical Church and wider society. The assembly partakes in Bible study, lectures, and discussions, and also hosts concerts. (Wikipedia)

The RMS *Mauretania* which brought Bishop Moore back to New York.

CHAPTER FOURTEEN

Duty Calls in Central Europe and North Africa

October – November 1953

Once more the path of duty takes me to far and difficult places. When these lines appear in print, I will be on my way to preside over some Annual Conferences in Europe and Africa.
When the Southeastern Jurisdiction Conference met in 1952, it placed the Atlanta Episcopal Area and the Geneva Area in Europe under the presidency of one bishop. No one seemed to realize fully all that was involved in such an assignment. Methodism in Georgia, with its two large conferences, represent a great block of American Methodism. Here are multiplied thousands of devoted Methodists, many institutions, and hundreds of churches, with devoted members and ministers. Certainly, there is enough work to keep anyone employed. But for reasons it believed to be valid, the Jurisdictional Conference added the duties of the Geneva Area to those of the Atlanta Area.

Included in the Geneva area is our Methodist work in Switzerland, Austria, Belgium, Yugoslavia, Czechoslovakia, Bulgaria, Hungary, Poland, and North Africa. In addition, there are some Methodist interests in Italy and Spain. Four of these countries, namely Czechoslovakia, Poland, Bulgaria, and Hungary, are now behind the Iron Curtain, and an American bishop cannot visit or supervise the work. The other countries, namely Switzerland, Belgium, Austria, Yugoslavia, and North Africa are accessible and Methodist work goes on with steady progress. It should be said that even in the countries behind the Iron Curtain our churches carry on.

Recently I have received pictures showing fine groups of young people being received into church membership in one of these so-called Communist countries. But notwithstanding these encouraging reports, it cannot be denied that all our churches behind the Iron Curtain struggle against overwhelming odds. The miracle is that they survive. Nothing but the help of Almighty God could sustain people under such strain.

In Switzerland, Belgium, Austria, Yugoslavia, and North Africa we face great opportunities for advancement. Our work goes on with many encouraging results. One could write at length about faithful pastors and large, efficiently operated institutions. For example, we have in Switzerland two hundred ninety full-time deaconesses operating ten wonderful hospitals. Belgium has an orphanage, a hospital, and a partnership in a theological school. Our people in Europe have been sorely tried by war and its terrible aftermath, but they have emerged from these fiery trials cleansed and strengthened. European Methodism is in every way worthy of our best traditions.

Leaving New York Monday, October 21, on the RMS *Queen Mary*, I will have five days at sea. On October 26, I will reach France, and after one day in Paris will proceed by airplane to Vienna, Austria. The Austrian Conference will be in session from October 29 through November 1.

From Austria, I will go immediately to Novi ad, where the Yugoslavian Conference will meet November 5-8. As these lines are being written, the radio and newspapers are full of comments on the possibility of trouble between Yugoslavia and Italy over Trieste.

It has not been possible for a bishop to enter Yugoslavia for several years and I certainly hope this tension at Trieste will not result in another crisis that will delay my entrance. Speaking of Yugoslavia, we have several congregations of Methodists down in ancient Macedonia; the same Macedonia mentioned in the New Testament from which a voice cried out long ago, "Come over and help us." If I get there, at least the satisfaction will be mine of being in apostolic succession, and that I am on the King's business.

From Yugoslavia, I will cross the Mediterranean to Tunis, North Africa, where I expect to arrive on November 12. In the company of some faithful missionaries, I will then visit our Methodist mission stations in North Africa. Traveling by automobile for ten days, we will visit Tunis, Constantine, Fort National, Algiers, and finally Oran.

The North Africa Conference will convene in Oran on November 19 and adjourn on November 22. It will be another thrilling experience to gather with these faithful missionaries who labor year in and year out with these Muslim people in North Africa. The work there is of great importance but difficult and slow. The faithfulness of these missionaries keeps me in perpetual gratitude for their amazing hopefulness and diligent service.

If all goes well, I will board a TWA transatlantic airplane at Algiers late in the afternoon of November 24 bound for New York. Flying over the Atlantic Ocean is no simple matter at any season, but the flight in winter leaves one praying for fair weather. My plane is due in New York on November 25. Once there, I will come straight to Atlanta and plunge once more into my "home work."

For the moment, the general life of the world, amid the many confusions of the hour, does not realize that only Christ can furnish the creative and directing energy it so sorely needs. This makes it all the more imperative that Christian people come to understand better than ever before what is the will of God for the whole world through His church. The whole inheritance of our spiritual past is a witness to our God. If we are faithful, we may see another great religious revival in our time. I hope all who love Christ will uphold me with their earnest prayers.

Wesleyan Christian Advocate, October 22, 1953, p. 7.

Editor's Note: The Free Territory of Trieste was an independent territory situated in Central Europe between northern Italy and Yugoslavia, facing the north of the Adriatic Sea, under the direct responsibility of the United Nations Security Council in the aftermath of World War II. For seven years, it acted essentially as a free city. The Free Territory was established on 10 February 1947 by a protocol of the Treaty of Peace with Italy to accommodate an ethnically and culturally mixed population in a neutral independent country. The intention was also to cool down territorial claims between Italy and Yugoslavia, due to its strategic importance for trade with Central Europe. It came into existence on 15 September 1947. Its administration was divided into two areas: one being the port city of Trieste with a narrow coastal strip to the northwest (Zone A); the other (Zone B) was formed by a small portion of the north-western part of the Istrian peninsula. The Free Territory was dissolved and given to its two neighbors (Italy and Yugoslavia) in 1954. This was formalized much later by the bilateral Treaty of Osimo of 1975, ratified in 1977 (Wikipedia).

Vienna, Austria
November 2, 1953

After the Reformation Day Service in Atlanta on Sunday afternoon October 19, I made ready to leave for the duties here in the Geneva Area. My family took me to the railroad station and once again we went through those always difficult "good-byes." It has happened to us many times as I have started to far-off places on a mission for the church. It is never easy, and to tell the whole truth, it grows harder for me every time we are called on to repeat it. An afternoon and evening in New York afforded an uninterrupted opportunity to confer with Dr. Ralph Wodge and Miss Sallie Lou McKinnon. They are the secretaries of the Board of Missions with special responsibilities for Europe and Africa.

Wednesday afternoon, October 21, found the good ship RMS *Queen Mary* slipping quietly down New York Harbor, and before dinnertime, the lights on the shore were out of sight. Once more we had committed ourselves to "the great waters."

It was possible to secure a comfortable cabin for myself and with several good books which I was eager to read, I prepared myself for five days of rest, reading, and plain lazy living. There were five dear friends from England on board who invited me to be seated at their table in the dining room but I asked to be excused. The head waiter found me a table where I had my meals in solitude.

Mr. Gandhi of India always insisted on having his day of silence and I am beginning to appreciate what he had in mind. Someone has said that "Solitude is the nursery of a full-grown soul." I only know there is too much breathless rush in my life and too little time for introspection and meditation.

The sea was kind, the books proved to be most interesting, and the voyage developed into a delightful experience. By the way, one of the books I read was about the life of Henry VIII. Some days before leaving home, my little granddaughter wanted to know how many wives Henry VIII had. My reputation with her suffered a distinct loss when I did not know. Now I am ready for her and the names of all six of those wives are being constantly rehearsed for my examination when I get home.

RMS *Queen Mary*

We disembarked at Cherbourg late Monday night, October 26. One has to be in Paris for only a short time to come under the spell of its history, its monuments, and its great traditions. Who can describe the breath-taking vistas from the bridges spanning the Seine River, the ageless beauty of Notre Dame, or the all-inspiring stained-glass windows of the Sainte Chapelle? Paris is more than a city; it is a world. It has been besieged, occupied, and liberated more than once by conquering armies but it remains changeless and yet ever new.

From Paris, I took a plane to Zürich, Switzerland, and from there on to Austria. Dr. Ferdinand Sigg, who oversees our Methodist Publishing House in Zürich, joined me and will be my traveling companion throughout this journey. It is a gracious privilege to have such a cultured Christian gentleman as a companion. He knows Europe, and his presence is an invaluable aid to me as we move from country to country.

The opening service of the Austria Conference last Thursday night was an inspiring experience. The spacious church was crowded while a choir of sweet voices led us in worship. The subject assigned to me was "The Christian Message in a Time Like This." That would have been a timely subject in America, but one has to be in Vienna to get the full meaning of the phrase "a time like this." This proud city is divided into four zones, each one occupied by a conquering army. The Russian army occupies much of the city and practically all of the surrounding country. To reach Vienna the plane on which I traveled was compelled to fly in through a specially designated corridor. Pictures of Stalin are yet hanging on certain prominent buildings and Russian soldiers walked the streets. More than once since coming I have stopped to read the notices on large billboards denouncing America. You are face to face with the real thing here. Just a few miles away in Czechoslovakia, now behind the Iron Curtain, the once flourishing Methodist Church, which I served for eight years, has been taken over by the state authorities.

Methodism in Austria is not large but is virile and evangelistic. We have some good properties, a very devout membership, and a small group of intelligent and zealous pastors. When I observed their sacrifice and devotion it shames me and makes me long to do more for my Lord.

Yesterday afternoon in the automobile of Captain Windsor of the U. S. Army drove me from Vienna to Linz where we dedicated a new church building. The captain is a devout Baptist from Decatur, Georgia. He is one army officer who brought his religion with him. He is the Superintendent of the Sunday School organized to take care of the children of Army personnel stationed in Vienna. In his school they have a hundred children enrolled and this faithful officer carries much of the load. To be a guest for dinner in their home was a never-to-be-forgotten experience.

To drive from Vienna to Linz one must travel more than a hundred miles through the Russian Zone. It is necessary to secure a special permit to make the journey. But in due time we reached the beautiful city of Linz, wherein the American Zone I found and dedicated a beautiful new Methodist Church. The story of how this congregation came into existence and how the refugee pastor and his faithful people succeeded in erecting this lovely church is as thrilling a story as I know.

Pastor Ernest Nausner I knew first in Poland where I ordained him as a Deacon in 1936. Then came the terrible war. This good man, his wife, and eight children were driven like sheep in a terrible storm. At last, he found a place of refuge in Linz, and with characteristic Methodist spirit, he started preaching. His hearers were chiefly war refugees like himself, homeless and defenseless, but with courage and faith to start life over again.

When I arrived in Linz, I found every seat in the splendid church taken. The representatives of the state and city were there along with the commanding officer of our U.S. Forces. Scores of people stood against the walls when seats were unavailable.

It is a splendid and beautiful building, built almost entirely by volunteer labor. For three summers a youth caravan, composed of consecrated Methodist young people from North Carolina, has come over and worked on this building. They were joined by groups of Austrian young people. Here is a demonstration of how young people can step across the chasm created by war and join other young people in building the church.

As I sat in the pulpit, my eyes scanned the faces of many old men and women who are refugees from Yugoslavia and other Balkan states. They were driven by the multiplied thousands from their homes by the communists and found refuge in the American Zone of Austria. Our government is housing and feeding them, but they are a sad, scattered people who have been uprooted and thrown at the mercy of the world. This beautiful chapel is their church and their spiritual anchorage. How happy and contented they appeared in their own church home.

Today, I leave Austria and push toward the South into Yugoslavia. What I will find there no one knows. The last bishop to visit our Methodists in that part of the world was Bishop Paul Garber. I think his last visit was in 1948. For more than five years those doors have been closed, but now Marshall Tito is cooperating with Western powers, and I have been able to secure an entrance visa. In another article, I hope to describe the conditions there and relate some of my experiences.

For almost a week I have lived in the presence of the Russian army. Turn where you will in Vienna and there they are. Russia is one of the occupying powers and wherever they are they occupy. Some of the leading hotels in Vienna have been taken over exclusively for their use. Enormous public buildings house their Army headquarters and their soldiers are to be seen in the streets.

Before leaving America, I secured a "gray card" which permitted me to travel through the Russian Zone from Vienna to Linz. As we started our journey on a bright Sunday morning, I was a bit nervous. It would have been much better to have been preaching somewhere in Georgia with dinner on the ground following. We drove a short distance from Vienna where we reached the American "checkpoint." The American soldiers took down our names, card number, etc., and bade us go on our way. Soon Russian soldiers could be seen mingling with the Sunday crowds. Every few miles we would pass very large military camps. Returning last night we saw several large red stars shining in the night. Even the darkness tells you of their presence. But nothing happened to mar our journey. It is only fair to say that when I was safe in the American Zone, I felt better.

There is much to gladden one's heart. The quality of sacrificial devotion these European Methodists exhibit in daily living is proof of the fact that the Grace of God is in their hearts. Vienna is trying to rebuild itself but there are innumerable scars of war still in evidence. The Austria of Maria Theresa and Franz Joseph is dead. Maybe a new Austria is being born, but if so, it is with great and agonizing struggle. The President of the nation, Theodor Körner, graciously received me last Thursday. He is a strong and kindly old man much beloved by the Austrian people.

He wished me well in my work and I certainly pray God's blessings to rest upon him and his sorely tried people.

Wesleyan Christian Advocate, November 19, 1953, p. 3.

Editor's Note: In this letter, the Bishop was longing for the preference of a "dinner on the ground." This was a common tradition in Southern churches during Bishop Moore's day. By 1953, it was not on the ground but would have been an outside "covered-dish" lunch.

Novi-Sad, Yugoslavia
November 9, 1953

My arrival in Yugoslavia was a bumpy one and my stay was a rugged but interesting experience. On Swiss Airlines, Dr. Ferdinand Sigg and I left Zürich at 10:00 a.m. on November 3, for Belgrade. Our flight took us over the beautiful Austrian Alps which were already snow-covered. When we arrived in Belgrade, the capital of Yugoslavia, such a fierce wind was whipping in from the nearby Black Sea that landing our airplane was difficult. Instead of coming down on the regular concrete runway, we came down guided by a special marker and made a safe landing on the grass. It was good to be down and interesting to be in this country which is avowedly Communist but has diplomatic and business dealings with America. One has to remain here but a short while to detect some strange contrasts.

Here is Oriental influence and Western culture, Communistic ideology, and Christian idealism, East and West living side-by-side and offering the newcomer, something unusual, different, and interesting.

Yugoslavia possesses in herself the traces of many cultures, styles, and manners of living of many different periods. The traces of these cultures and periods may be found in all parts of Yugoslavia in the form of numerous cultural and historical monuments. There are the remnants of Roman columns, Greek capitals, a palace in Venetian Gothic, or a fortress built by the Spaniards. A similar kaleidoscope is also encountered in Bosnia and Macedonia. On the former Roman ramparts rises a Turkish fortress in the vicinity that once were Byzantine basilicas or well-concealed Orthodox churches and monasteries. On the ramparts of the Belgrade Fortress at the confluence of the Sava and the Danube, one becomes aware of the blood-soaked history of the whole of Europe. Yugoslavia comprises the middle and southwestern parts of the Balkan Peninsula. It is about the size of the states of New York and Pennsylvania together, with 16 million inhabitants: Serbs, Croats, Slovenes, Macedonians, and Montenegrins.

The form of government in Yugoslavia is a Federated republic consisting of the following republics: Serbia, with its capital Belgrade (380,000 inhabitants); Croatia, whose capital is Zagreb (290,000 inhabitants); Slovenia, its capital Ljubljana (121,000 inhabitants); Bosnia and Herzegovina, whose capital is

Sarajevo (118,150 inhabitants); Macedonia, its capital Skopje 92,000 inhabitants); and Montenegro, whose capital is Titograd (13,000 inhabitants). The present social and economic organization in Yugoslavia constitutes a socialist state which is the result of the national revolution. The languages spoken by the peoples of Yugoslavia are Serbian, Croatian, Slovenian, and Macedonian.

The alphabet used by the peoples of Yugoslavia is the Cyrillic alphabet. The majority of the population read and write in both alphabets. As to their religious beliefs, the Yugoslavs are mostly of Orthodox Catholic and Muslim faith.

In the sixth century, the great South Slav migration began. Coming from the north, the Slavs settled in the Balkans. As the people took root during the next two centuries, a new civilization started and developed. Independent states sprang up from the eighth century onward, and by the thirteenth century, Slav civilization had reached a high level.

In 1389, the Turks defeated Serbia. Bosnia was taken in 1463 and Herzegovina in 1483. The Turkish invasion considerably slowed down the development of the South Slav civilization. The resistance of the Slavs continued during the five hundred years of Turkish occupation and played a part in preventing the Turks from penetrating further west. The long rule of the Ottoman Empire is evidenced by the mosques, palaces, and forts that may still be seen in certain areas of the country.

For centuries the Republic of Venice saw a foothold on the Dalmatian Coast. The Austrians and Hungarians came later and what is today's Slovenia, Bosnia, Croatia, and Vojvodina ultimately were absorbed into the Austro-Hungarian Empire. The Yugoslav nationalities retained much of their individuality and cultural identity and in many cases their civil and state administrations. The Montenegrins, high in their mountain fastness, were completely independent during this entire period.

During the Turkish occupation, a movement developed for the unity of the South Slav peoples, which grew as the centuries progressed. Typical of the many forms of the resistance was the harassing activity against the Turks in the 16th century. These patriots sniped at the occupation from the forests and hills, much as their descendants did centuries later.

The struggle for complete independence reached its climax in the last one hundred fifty years, which saw twenty-eight separate rebellions. In 1804 the Serbs carried out the first national revolution after the French Revolution of 1789. By the twentieth century, the resistance had grown so strong that it interfered with the plans of the Turks in the Balkan Wars of 1912-13 and was a factor in gaining independence from the Austro-Hungarian Empire in World War I. On December 1, 1918, an independent country was set up, called at first the Kingdom of Serbs, Croats, and Slovenians (it included Macedonia and Montenegro), and later the Kingdom of Yugoslavia.

On April 6, 1941, German troops marched into Yugoslavia. Squadrons of German planes bombed Belgrade, leaving a heavily damaged city. Estimates of the dead ranged from seventeen thousand to twenty-five thousand. On April 17, the Yugoslav government capitulated.

The country was occupied and petitioned by Germany, Italy, Hungary, and Bulgaria. Resistance continued throughout the occupation. During the occupation, Great Britain and the United States gave military assistance to the various resistance groups. In the latter part of 1944, the Partisan Army of Marshall Tito, together with elements of the Soviet army, occupied the country. On March 2, 1945, King Peter II named the new regency counsel, and Marshall Tito was chosen Prime Minister. Elections for a Constitutional Assembly were held on November 11, 1945, with the government party the victor. On November 29, 1945, the Assembly proclaimed Yugoslavia a Republic.

Yugoslavia was declared a Federated People's Republic on January 31, 1946, under a new constitution. The Constitution Assembly adopted a new basic law and named Marshall Tito to form the new government. He remains not only the leader but the idol of his people.

Methodism has been in this part of Europe for nearly three-quarters of a century. It is numerically small but is composed of serious-minded, deeply devout, and evangelistic people. It was once much stronger than at present due to the Methodists among the numerous German population which had emigrated from Germany more than a hundred years before to occupy the rich farmland in the valley of the Danube River. When Hitler came to power in Germany and began his conquest of Europe, many of these German people had visions of a Germanic Europe and many of their leaders espoused Hitler's cause. When his dreams of conquest were shattered, these German folk were left to the mercy of those who had defeated Hitler and were now in power.

One of the mass movements of distressed humanity took place as these people were driven out. They were first imprisoned, suffering unbelievable hardships. It is reported that seventy thousand died either in prison or on the march to another country. They went or were pushed across the border into Austria where, as homeless refugees, they have tried to begin life anew. These people were mainly Catholic or Lutheran but among them were practically all the Methodists who had lived in what is now the northern part of Yugoslavia. In the far south of the country is Macedonia where there exists a part of the oldest cultural history to be found in Europe.

Ancient Macedonia from which the cry, "Come over and help us," was heard has now been divided between Yugoslavia, Bulgaria, and Greece. In this old and romantic country, we have several Methodist congregations. They are a happy, carefree people and to hear their choirs singing the praise of Almighty God is a rich and rewarding experience.

In all of Yugoslavia, we have at present twenty churches with a membership of approximately three thousand members. There are seven full-time ordained pastors with numerous local preachers who help to preach the gospel. The churches are well-organized with Sunday schools, youth groups, and women's societies, all of which carry on against great odds. We also have nine Deaconesses, a finer and more dependable group I have never seen.

Our Annual Mission Conference met here in Novi-Sad from November 5-8. The preaching of the gospel and the business of the Conference was carried on in three languages – German, Serbian, and English, with a summary of the sermons given in Hungarian. We had time for much preaching, and it was my joy to speak many times. Always before and after the sermon, we would have several choir numbers. On Sunday, some of our church choirs travelled many miles to be present and on the scene for the Conference. No one seemed to be in a hurry. It is not often these Christians, now living in a "strange land," can sing the Lord's song; but when they get a chance, they certainly know how to praise the Lord with song.

At the close of World War I a noted English author produced a book under the title *Now It Can be Told.* The very title suggests there had been a lapse of time between the act and the telling of the story. It does not seem wise for me to put in this written form at the moment all my experiences or impressions. To go as the guest of the country, be received by some of its highest government officers, and then come away to write letters of criticism is hardly the courteous thing to do. Quite frankly, it would work to hurt our people who are already carrying burdens on heavy or weary shoulders.

Yugoslavia has broken her diplomatic ties with Russia and is now working with the Western Powers. She is still a Communist nation and openly declares herself to be. Her government, schools, economy, and public life were organized to serve the ideals and objectives of a Communist State. There is the claim that church and state are separate, but that hardly tells the story of outright and positive anti-Christian teaching. All of this means that to be a Christian here is a difficult and courageous business and one must pay a great price for his faith.

For a week now I have not had a bath towel or worse, any hot water in my hotel room, and that is indicative of how many of the things we Americans regard as necessities are wonderful luxuries over here.

I found the highly placed government of officers kind and considerate; for their kindness I am grateful, but that does not alter my conviction that Communism exalts the State and denies man his God-given rights. Let us hope that what Yugoslavia sees of our American Christian way of life will convince them there is "a more excellent way" than what they now practice.

The flight out of Yugoslavia on one of their airlines was without incident. The plane lacked all the conveniences one finds on an American plane. One can only hope that the motors have been looked after with more care. The Austrian Alps were glorious as we crossed over at ten thousand feet altitude. We stopped for an hour at the bombed-out airport in Munich, Germany, where I had time to reflect on what Adolf Hitler said that he could build a Germany without God. He is gone and with him his atheistic ideas.

All this gave me hope to believe that someday communism in Yugoslavia will collapse and the people will be given a chance to worship and serve God without any kind of interference from the state.

Tomorrow, by airplane, I go from Paris to North Africa where, by auto, I shall visit our churches in Tunis, Constantine, and Algiers, and hold an Annual Conference at Oran from November 19-22. But that is another story and will come later. It is a great thing to be an American with all the blessings of our Christian faith. We must all resolve to stand with sleepless vigilance against those destructive forces which are rampant in other sections of the world.

Wesleyan Christian Advocate, December 3, 1953, p. 3.

Editor's Notes:
1. The Serbian Cyrillic script was one of the two official scripts used to write Serbo-Croatian in Yugoslavia since its establishment in 1918, the other being the Latin script (latinica) (Wikipedia).
2. Yugoslavia dissolved her Federated alliances in the early 1990s. The breakup of Yugoslavia occurred as a result of a series of political upheavals and conflicts during the early 1990s. After a period of the political and economic crisis in the 1980s, constituent republics of the Socialist Federal Republic of Yugoslavia split apart, but the unresolved issues caused bitter inter-ethnic Yugoslav wars. The wars primarily affected Bosnia and Herzegovina, neighboring parts of Croatia and, some years later, Kosovo.
3. *Now It Can Be Told*, by Sir Phillip Gibbs, Harper, 1920. Sir Philip Gibbs served as one of five official British reporters during the First World War. In this book he relays the experiences of British soldiers and offers a detailed narrative of the events of World War I, while trying to draw broader conclusions about the nature of war and how it can be prevented in the future.

Dr. Ferdinand Sigg accompanied Bishop Moore on this mission to Austria, Yugoslavia, and North Africa. He was elected bishop the following year.

El-Matten, North Africa
November 15, 1953

This "travel letter" is being written from El-Matten, which in English means "Green Pastures". We are traveling in a tiny French automobile from place to place in North Africa where the Methodist Church has a church or institution. From Tunis, in the East, from where we started several days ago, to Oren in the West, where the Annual Conference will meet November 19-22, is approximately one thousand miles. At almost every turn of the road, one is faced with vivid reminders of proud civilizations which once flourished in this part of the world. How I wish my knowledge of history was a bit fresher. There once were the proud cities of the Carthaginians, Romans, Byzantines, Turks, Arabs, and now the French . One by one, these proud nations died at the heart, and the great glory ended in a dismal sight.

One day last week, I walked for hours over the vast ruins of the ancient city of Carthage. It began as a Phoenician colony around 850 BC. At one time in Carthage children were sacrificed to Moloch. There are scores of tiny granite caskets to be seen in which one finds the bones of precious children, who were once offered up in this heathenish custom.

Rome and Carthage became bitter sea rivals. Around 230 BC, Rome provoked Carthage into a Declaration of War. We recall how Cato in the Roman Senate concluded all his speeches with the announcement "Carthage must be destroyed." In 149 BC, the Romans besieged the city, fighting from house to house until out of a population near a million, only fifty thousand were alive, and these were sold into slavery. The entire city was leveled to the ground so that no stone remained standing. A century later, the Romans built another city on the old site. This new Carthage became one of the wealthiest cities of the Roman Empire. In this new Carthage, Christianity flourished. We visited the ruins of several Christian churches that in their time must have been as magnificent as the famous cathedrals to be found in Europe. Carthage was captured by the Vandals in the fifth century AD and in the seventh century was again destroyed by the Arabs.

It staggers one's imagination to conceive of the grandeur which must have been on every hand while the cities flourished. The Roman baths, which was a great social institution, something like a country club, covered an area of more than a quarter of a mile in extent. Scattered over the ground are broken pieces of marble of high quality, which must have been twenty to forty feet in height. Huge pieces of exquisite marble weighing tons upon which there are carvings of the rarest sort, are to be seen in abundance. The vast amphitheater, in which Christians were fed to the lions because they would not deny their faith, is there. The cages, in which the lions were kept in hunger, so they would spring upon their innocent victims are to be seen hewn out of the rock. I brought away with me a copper coin bearing the likeness of Julius Caesar which could have been in circulation when the Christian movement was in its very infancy. Also, I have an oil lamp made of pottery which undoubtedly belongs to biblical times. Certainly, both of these articles go back to the second or third century. Seldom have my emotions been more deeply stirred than while walking amid the ruins of these mighty civilizations which were born, flourished, played their part in the world drama, and then committed suicide.

Saturday, we visited Hippo, the city in which Augustine lived and preached. There in a modern and magnificent Roman Cathedral, they show the visitor a piece of the bone out of the good right arm of this great preacher. The relic did not particularly impress me, but to walk where a man such as Augustine had preached, speaking out against the evils of his time, did move my heart.

The relic of St. Augustine at Hippo.

The Romans must have spread their civilization all over northern Africa. Last night, a native in this remote mountain village told me the first inhabitants of this place were the Romans. I was shown a large slab flooring in the staircase hewn out of a large rock foundation as proof of the fact that a Roman civilization had once existed here where today the native Kabyle people live in squalor. And other days when there was always danger from neighboring tribes, these Kabyle people built their villages close together to be able to defend themselves. Even now they place large stones at the entrance of the village and every rider who approaches must dismount at the stones and enter the village on foot, thus preventing surprise raids.

The women all veil their faces and live in the seclusion of their homes. Marriage is always arranged by the parents and the young couple never see each other until after the wedding ceremony. The older women do leave the houses at a fixed hour to go to the wells with their water pots. The men are not allowed at the wells during the time the women are there to draw water. Entire families live together in one little house. There is some making of pottery, the gathering of wild olives, and small farming, but the people live in poverty.

Let me make it clear that I am now speaking of the Kabyle people who live up in the mountains. Down near the coast are large cities like Tunis, Algiers, Oren, and others and here one finds all the advantages of our modern civilization. Here one finds homes as comfortable as American homes. The French have built many schools and good roads, and gradually the old type of life is giving way to new ideas and better methods. The native population, made up of Arabs and Berbers, is slowly taking on some of the ways and vices of their conquerors.

Algeria is a French colony in the garden of North Africa. Morocco is on the west, Tunisia to the east, and the vast Sahara Desert to the south. The French took possession in 1830 and as I have already stated they have made valuable improvements. Vast irrigation projects are to be seen in the valleys where wheat, oranges, and other crops are growing in abundance. When one speaks of Africa, he must be careful to state what section of this vast continent he comes from. North Africa, with the Mediterranean Sea kissing it sure is a lovely country. Only when one crosses the mountains and approaches that vastness of sand called the Sahara Desert does its beauty fade. But, even the desert has a charm of its own.

Our Methodist Church has been at work in this difficult field for many years. There is no work so slow as work among Moslem people. They are loyal to their faith. At present, we are operating homes for boys in several places and likewise separate homes for girls. The French authorities will not permit churches to operate schools unless a majority of the faculty are French citizens. These boys and girls live in our Methodist homes and attend regular public schools. In several cities, we operate very successful social centers and carry-on medical missions through infirmaries staffed by capable nurses. We do have a large Christian constituency, but our people are faithful and the church is in the making. We are active in preparing and disseminating excellent Christian literature. There are approximately twenty-five American Methodist missionaries working in this field and I have not found anywhere a better prepared and more genuinely sacrificial group than we have in North Africa. As I have moved from station to station, lived in their homes, and gotten acquainted with their problems my already high estimate of missionaries has risen. They are brave pioneers ready to follow our Lord in the dangerous way of the Cross.

Let me close this message with a little touch of home. While in Tunis, I visited an English churchyard and walked from grave to grave. Here are buried Americans and English who died while living in this far-off land. Imagine my surprise to find an imposing monument marking the grave of John Howard Payne who wrote "Home Sweet Home." While serving as the American consul in Tunis, Mr. Payne died and was buried in this lovely garden far away from the home sweet home about which he sang. He died in 1852, and his body remained there until 1885 when it was removed to America. I must confess that on that particular day, I too was longing for the sight of home. The singer was right, though we wonder mid pleasures and palaces, there is one spot and one only that clings around us with multiplying association and deepening spell, and that is home. To leave home, even for a brief time on an important mission for the church, is a painful experience, and to get home after traveling in distant lands is like a mother's caress after a bad dream.

On the morning of November 24, I go on board a plane to fly from Algiers to Paris. After a brief stop-over there, I leave by Pan American Airlines for the flight across the Atlantic Ocean. Wednesday night, November 25, should find me at home in Atlanta. To get home, to be again with my family, my friends, and my work in Georgia will be an indescribable joy.

Wesleyan Christian Advocate, December 10, 1953, p. 10.

Kabyle people of Algeria

CHAPTER FIFTEEN

An Around-the-World Mission to Europe, Africa, and Asia

October-December 1956

Decatur, Georgia
September 8, 1956

September 26 will find me on board the RMS *Queen Elizabeth* sailing from New York to Europe. This will be the first step in another missionary journey that will take me around the world. From England, we will travel by air to France, Italy, Lebanon, Syria, Arab-Jordan, Pakistan, India, Thailand, Hong Kong, Japan, and possibly a brief time in Taiwan (Formosa) and Korea. The "we" in the sentence refers to the Rev. Rembert Sisson of the Druid Hills Methodist Church, Atlanta, the Rev. L. Bevel Jones, III of the Audubon Forest Methodist Church, Atlanta, and the Rev. Frank Moorhead of First Methodist Church, LaGrange, Georgia. It will be a personal joy to have these three fine younger ministers accompanying me. They will prove ideal traveling companions I am sure and as a result of what they observe and experience they will return to their churches with a deeper missionary passion in their hearts and a new note in their preaching. They will fly from New York to London.

The chief purpose of my going is to represent the Council of Bishops and the Board of Missions at the Centennial Celebration of Methodism in India. Following the celebration of one hundred years of wonderful Methodist work and witness among the millions of people in India will come the quadrennial session of the Central Conference of Southern Asia.

This Central Conference will have before it many matters of great importance. Among these will be the election and consecration of at least three bishops. Two for India and one to preside over our work in the newly created nation of Pakistan. Bishops J. Waskom Pickett and Clement D. Rockey will retire after many years of creative sacrificial service to the people of India. It will be my high honor to officially represent the Mother Church, the Council of Bishops and to assist in the consecration of the newly elected bishops. It would be difficult, if not impossible to overstate the importance of these gatherings in India at this particular time. India is to play an ever-increasing important part in world affairs and the work of Christian missions there has assumed extraordinary importance.

When our duties are finished in Lucknow, India, the seat of the conferences, we will proceed by air around the world. Our Methodist work in Hong Kong, Taiwan (Formosa), Japan, and Korea faces incomparable opportunities and some staggering responsibilities. It is my purpose to visit the missionaries and national leaders of these countries and to render whatever service I possibly can to these brave, young churches.

If our plans proceed according to schedule, and if we have journeying mercies, we hope to arrive in San Francisco around the middle of December and to be back with those we know and love best a few days before Christmas. If time permits, I will furnish the *Wesleyan Christian Advocate* with some articles dealing with conditions around the world as we find them.

This will no doubt be my final missionary journey. Since 1934 when I was appointed as Bishop in charge of all the missionary work of the Methodist Episcopal Church, South, in Asia, Europe, and Africa, I have been a missionary in heart and practice. In peace and war, I have traveled to the far and distant places of the earth on "The King's Business."

Starting on another journey, I look forward with keen delight to the fellowship that this travel will afford me to see and visit with cherished friends clear around the world. The church has given me many honors, but none greater than the privilege of having a small part in the Christian missionary enterprise. Whatever mistakes we have made despite war and the rumors of war, there are today millions of men, women, and children who are better and happier because the church is taking seriously Christ's command to preach the gospel to every creature.

The mission of Methodism has always been to help me to realize man's deep estrangement from God, which is the result of sin, and to help them to turn to Christ as the Savior of the world, and to receive Him by faith in the plenitude of His saving and enabling grace. It is the deep conviction of true Methodists that Christ died for all men and that belief leads to a concern for missions. Mr. Wesley stated the intention of Methodism in his now well-known statement, "I look upon all the world as my parish." Our missionaries and what they are doing across the earth is a logical and inevitable expression of what we believe about Christ, and His will for all men.

A great moment is impending in the life of the world. The picture seen by our natural eye looms dark and perplexing, yet there is in the hearts of those who have discovered the eternal and inexhaustible resources of faith, a deathless conviction that we may be about to witness another striking and arresting manifestation of Christ's power. Where and when it will begin no one knows, but God reserves the right to send His Spirit into the wilderness of man's earthly confusions and to give us another spiritual revival. The whole inheritance of our past is a witness to what God can do, and before this generation passes, we may see a new world take shape before our eyes. Believing this, we must follow Christ as He goes forth on this redemptive pilgrimage.

Bishop John W. Branscomb of the Jacksonville Area has kindly consented to watch over the Atlanta Area during the time I am out of the country. The District Superintendents will carry on in their usual diligent fashion and call on Bishop Branscomb only if an emergency develops that demands his presence and help.

As a growing boy down at Brookfield, I used to stand and watch the fine passenger trains go swiftly by. In my boyish manner, I wondered if ever I would ride such a fast train and have a meal in those heavenly bright dining cars. Little did I know that my duties as a Methodist preacher and bishop would put my feet on a worldwide circuit. For many busy and happy years, I have been literally "a traveling preacher." For a short time or longer season, my Episcopal responsibilities have placed me in thirty-one different nations.

Twice within the span of my ministry, the nations of the world have been plunged into war, leaving the nations, even the victorious ones, weaker than when the war began. It staggers the imagination to contemplate another war with its unspeakable horrors. The church must therefore gird itself for new crusades of love, understanding, and peace. Blindness, selfishness, and hate must give way to vision, cooperation, and respect. We dare not turn the world over to the hotheads who with their feverish, fumbling hands would start another world conflagration. The price of peace was fixed a long time ago, and the price was a Cross. We are, therefore, not at the end of Christian missions but at the beginning. The church can never stand on the sidelines and have nothing to do but get men into heaven. It must live and work for the assertion of truth, the dissipation of hate, and the conversion of men's hearts and minds. This is the idea and purpose which has called hundreds of our sons and daughters into missionary service. By their witness and work, they are doing more than we recognize in building a safe world, and to make secure and strong the church of tomorrow. To go and stand at their side for even a little while is a high honor.

In route to India, we will spend a few days in London, Paris, and Rome. If the Suez Canal problem does not worsen, we will devote a few days to Palestine and stand in reverence at so many places intimately associated with the earthly life of our blessed Lord. Our main business will be in Lucknow, India, where from October 25 to November 12 we will be with the Methodists of India as they assemble into magnificent historic gatherings. From there as indicated, we will return home through Hong Kong, Taiwan (Formosa), Japan and Hawaii, and maybe Korea. At sea and in the air, we will require God's watchful care. I sincerely hope our friends will lift us daily in arms of love and faith for God's unceasing protection.

Wesleyan Christian Advocate, September 6, 1956, p. 11.

At Sea aboard the RMS *Queen Elizabeth*
September 30, 1956

Last Sunday, I was in Atlanta preaching for my dear friend, Dr. Louie D. Newton, in the great Druid Hills Baptist Church. Today I am at sea approaching the coast of England, on board the largest and potentially the fastest ship that was ever launched, the RMS *Queen Elizabeth*. In another hour I shall go to church and listen to the Commander read the always moving and stately worship service of the Church of England.

Although, I have known for some time that this long and strenuous journey was ahead of me, the time to say goodbye took me by surprise. Never have I known a year when there were so many Methodist conferences. Since last May we have had the General Conference at Minneapolis; the two Georgia Annual Conferences, one in Waycross, the other in Athens; and the Southeastern Jurisdictional Conference at Lake Junaluska, which met in July. September witnessed the World Methodist Conference and the organizational meeting of the Board of Missions, both held at Junaluska, and these were followed by the Atlanta Area Planning Conference held at Epworth-by-the-Sea. When the last of these conferences was over, there were only four days left for last-minute preparations and final goodbye.

Since 1934, the church has been sending me on these missionary journeys. I have always gone promptly and gladly. Frankness compels me to say that travel and long absences from my family are more difficult for me than ever before. I am not a young man any longer, and the journey which I have only just begun is more suited to a young man than one of my age.

However, I am grateful for good health and the further fact that the passing of the years has not taken from me that exultation of spirit that always comes from participation in the missionary enterprise. So here I am on my sixty-eighth crossing of an ocean. My strength comes from the knowledge that many are praying for me and also, that I am on "The King's Business."

Perhaps a word should be written concerning this wonderful ship. It has been called "human audacity in steel." Certainly, it is the symbol of the strength of purpose and the daring vision of a nation whose courage in war determines the future of the world. The RMS *Queen Elizabeth* is one thousand thirty-one feet long which one can easily see is one-fifth of a mile in length. It has fourteen decks and can carry thirty-five hundred passengers and a crew of twelve hundred. It is in reality a floating city with shops, playgrounds, banks, and all that would be needed by a city of several thousand. For six years during World War II, this proud vessel carried hundreds of thousands of fighting men to the war fronts. Despite all its elegance, one can still find here and there the initials of soldiers carved into the guardrails. Because this is the off-season, I have been given a cabin to myself and I am enjoying the long hours of uninterrupted reading.

Tomorrow, Rembert Sisson, Bevel Jones, and Frank Moorhead will leave Atlanta by air for New York. They will fly the Atlantic Monday night and reach our hotel in London at approximately the same time I will arrive. This is a good illustration of how travel has been speeded up by air. I have done and will do my share of travel by air, but I confess the quietness and comfort of a good boat still appeals to me.

The first land we will sight tomorrow morning will be the islands of Jersey and Guernsey. Alfred Tennyson lived on Jersey in his later years. The average American will recognize the names of these islands because some of our finest cattle bear these names. Soon after breakfast, we will drop anchor in the beautiful harbor of Cherbourg, France. One never approaches the French coasts without being reminded of the great history wrought out by these people. Unfortunately, too much of it has been the kind of history made by war, and today France is weak and divided. The beauty of the countryside is still here, but no nation can sacrifice practically a whole generation of its manpower and not stagger for a long time.

Our stay in Cherbourg will be for only a couple of hours to allow many of our fellow passengers to disembark. Then we will move slowly across the English Channel and reach Southampton early in the evening.

My blood always runs a little faster, and I stand tall when travel brings me once more to England. I have seen these people in war and in peace, in success and in great financial depression, but always they have been a gallant, brave people. Never have jokes which make fun of the English seemed funny to me. They shouldered a staggering part of two World Wars that were fought to preserve our Christian civilization and carried them a long time before we finally came to their side.

In a few hours, I will be near the port from which those God-fearing and liberty-loving men and women, who landed at Plymouth Rock, sailed. They brought with them in the *Mayflower* the ideals from which sprang our democratic institutions and Christian convictions. They perceived the vital connection there is and must be between the strength of religion and the welfare of the nation. They believed that faith in God is the indispensable support of national stability. So many modern Americans do not seem to realize that these imperishable ideals will be of little worth to our present-day America unless we who are now alive meet the organized enemies of religion with equal faith and fortitude.

Tomorrow will be our first day in London, and it is easy to see that it will be busy. Dr. Edward McLellan, who has visited us so often in Georgia, will be our guide. He is eighty-four years of age, but it will not be two days before some American preachers will be begging the doctor not to walk so far or so fast. Tuesday afternoon Dr. and Mrs. Ronald V. Spivey will entertain us at an afternoon tea in the parsonage at Wesley's Chapel. What a privilege it will be for all of us to visit this "Westminster Abbey" of Methodism and see it all through the eyes of Dr. Spivey, who is the pastor, and loves it so dearly.

In the evening we go to a dinner party given for us by Dr. Benson Perkins in the National Club. But I must not anticipate but wait until the events have occurred and then give a report. That I promise to do. I shall be glad to visit the many wonderful historic sites in London, but I shall have an even greater joy to see and share all these wonderful places and experiences with my three traveling companions who are here for the first time.

Wesleyan Christian Advocate, October 11, 1956, p. 12

Paris, France
October 8, 1956

One would judge from reading the newspapers, which are available over here, that all America is talking about and thinking about these days is baseball and politics. It is interesting to observe what commands the attention of the British and the French.

In England the main subjects of discussion were the poor weather which has characterized the entire summer; Prince Margaret's royal visit to Zanzibar and Tanganyika and other places to build up goodwill for the Empire; and of course, the repeated assassination of British soldiers who are trying to put down the rebellion in Cyprus. In France, the subjects of the day have been the Suez development in the continuing crisis in Algiers. But life goes on as it does elsewhere, and the people trust that solutions for all these problems will be found somehow and somewhere.

From Southampton, where the RMS *Queen Elizabeth* docked, to London is only two hours by train. I was hardly in our London hotel before my three traveling companions, Sisson, Jones, and Moorhead arrived. They had left Atlanta a week later than I had, but by crossing the Atlantic Ocean by air they arrived in London as soon as I did. We were quartered in a new London hotel called The Westbury. It is operated by American management and while one is staying there it is difficult to realize he is in a foreign land. We were all quite comfortable there.

Dr. Edward McLellan, who has been our guest in America several times, was waiting for us, and immediately we plunged into a round of sightseeing. Westminster Abbey, the Tower of London, St. Paul's Cathedral, Wesley's Chapel, in fact nearly all the places of historic interest found us as visitors there. We were especially fortunate to have the honor of tea with the Rev. and Mrs. Ronald Spivey, the minister at Wesley Chapel, who gave us a personally conducted tour through this "Holy of Holies," of World Methodism. To bow in the room where John Wesley prayed for an hour each day and the very room from which he went to be with God stirs one's emotions and causes him to resolve to be a better man. My traveling companions were seeing these places for the first time, and I rejoiced to see their deep interest and response.

On my first night in London, I was entertained at dinner in the famous Liberal Club which was founded by the great prime minister, William Gladstone. My host was Methodist leaders from both England and Australia. This Methodist fellowship not only reaches around the world but is genuinely rich and rewarding.

After four days in London, we crossed the English Channel in a modern airplane, and in one hour and a half, we were aB another culture. I have been coming to Paris for twenty years and have seen it in hard times and better times. The economy seems more stable this year despite their worries over a war in Algeria and the possibility of another over the Suez Canal Crisis. Prices have sky-rocketed, and one pays dearly for everything he purchases. But France still has its appeal and for three days we have gone, without much stopping, to the places which show interest for all lovers of history. While I write these lines, my companions are on a half-day trip to the famous palace at Versailles. Yesterday we visited the Louvre, and Notre Dame Cathedral and also attended church in the morning at what is known as the American Church.

The lovely sanctuary was crowded, and we heard a good sermon. I suppose the many Americans present were drawn largely from the families of American military men who were stationed in and around Paris.

One never grows weary of the inspiring spaces of Notre Dame. Here much history has been enacted. The cathedral was built by Maurice de Sully, Bishop of Paris, in the twelfth century to take the place of two churches that stood on the same site, Notre Dame and St. Stephens. Pope Alexander III laid the foundation stone in the reign of Louis VII in 1163; the high altar was consecrated in 1182; the choir was finished in 1177, the nave in 1208, the West front and towers in 1240; the chapels were added between 1240 and 1325; the South Door dates from 1245 and the North from 1250. The church underwent a thorough restoration during the nineteenth century at the hands of the architects Lassus and Viollet-le-Duc, being reconsecrated in 1864 by the Archbishop of Paris. It was honored with the title of "Basilica" in 1805.

Dr. William G. Thonger, the superintendent of our Methodist Church in Belgium, has come down from Brussels to Paris to act as our guide. He was born in Paris and therefore knows it well. Many of our churches in Georgia give missionary gifts to sustain our work in Belgium. Frank Moorhead took an extra day to visit a church in Belgium where the pastor is the special missionary of First Church, LaGrange. I was sure both Druid Hills Church and Audubon Forest carry special advance gifts for Belgium. To have Dr. Thonger, with his love of history and his intimate knowledge of Paris, show us around the city has been an unusual privilege for us.

Early tomorrow morning we go on board a Pan- American airplane and begin our journey to Rome. We will fly over the Alp and should be in Rome by the middle of tomorrow afternoon. There the Rev. Mr. Kissac, will take us in tow. He is an English Methodist minister and lives in Rome where he serves as the superintendent of the English Methodist Church.

My stay in Rome will be brief as I must leave there on October 11 for a long air journey to South Africa. My flight will take me to Athens, Greece, Cairo, Egypt, and then southward along the Nile River. Then to the Belgian Congo, coming at last to Elizabethville, where I will officially represent the American Methodist Church at a Central Conference. The conference will be in session for ten days, and I am to preach each day. When my duties in the Congo are over, I will fly back to Egypt, out across the Middle East, and on to Pakistan and India.

My traveling companions will be on their own in Beirut, Damascus, and Jerusalem, and I shall rejoin them in Delhi, India, on October 25. We will then proceed together to Lucknow, India, where October 31 to November 11, we will attend the Centennial Celebration of Methodism in India. I hope to write about all this at a later time.

Two weeks have passed since I left home, yet the time seems much longer. Day by day the work of all our churches in Georgia is upon my heart. These fine autumn months allow us to make large plans and set before our eyes goals that will summon us to a high and holy endeavor. Our blessing should move us to genuine Thanksgiving and the only way to show our thankfulness is to love and faithfully serve the gracious Heavenly Father, who has so abundantly blessed us.

Wesleyan Christian Advocate, October 25, 1956, p. 4.

Elizabethville, Belgian Congo
October 16, 1956

To visit and study in London, Paris, and Rome in a few days is to suffer from historical indigestion. In previous articles, I have written about London and Paris. Although these lines are being written from Africa, something of our experiences in Rome must be said.

Rome is the Eternal City, the place of the Caesars, the Forum, the Coliseum, and the Catacombs, to mention only a few of the attractions for which this city is so well renowned. It is the capital of the Roman Catholic religion and the mecca to which believers of that faith come from all over the world.

We were met at the beautiful International Airport by the Rev. Reginald Kissac, pastor of an English Methodist Church in Rome. He is a great scholar, and fully at home with all the history that tumbles over itself in this ancient city. He gave us practically all of his valuable time for three days and was a most gracious host. As we drove down from the airport into the city, he reminded us that we were traveling over the Appian Way and that the very stones in the highway had no doubt, felt the pressure of the feet of Paul and Peter. It was a stirring experience to travel along this path of history and to approach the city with so much history, both profane and sacred that had been wrought out. Once one is in Rome he feels that he is at the very source of our Christian civilization.

Since the history of Rome is not only the history of the city itself but that of all the Mediterranean world during one of the most important periods of human development. If one has any imagination whatsoever, he can stand amid all these historic places and imagine the successive evolutions of history.

In Rome, one also has some understanding and appreciation of a people who at the price of heavy sacrifice conquered an Empire and in so doing opened up ways for the Christian conquest of the world. Here are to be found buildings that were erected before Christ was born, some of which are dated from the sixth century BC. Rome is more than the place where the Pope lives, it is the city where events transpired that profoundly altered the whole course of human evolution. One who visits Rome should be prepared to read history again and appreciate how the city grew from modest beginnings to a place where kings, emperors, and popes live and have lived in unbelievable splendor.

Before we registered at our hotel, which proved to be an excellent one located just across the street from the American Embassy, we went for a visit to the Catacombs. My first discovery there was the fact that there was not one, but several of these underground burial places. The one through which we were shown covers eleven acres underground and in this space are buried ninety-three thousand bodies. The earth is of soft rock and these graves or niches were cut into the side of the wall, the body was placed inside, and the niche was sealed up. When wicked rulers' intent on the destruction of a new religion called Christianity came to power, the early Christians were driven into these catacombs and there they lived, worshiped, and kept alive the flame of their faith. Seldom have my emotions been more deeply stirred than while standing in this underground chamber where so many men and women lived who loved our Savior enough to die for Him.

On the second day, we went to the Forum and the Coliseum. Tradition attributes to the first years of the fifth century BC, the erection of two temples: that of Saturn in 497 BC, and that of Castor and Pollux in 484 BC. Originally the Forum was the political and religious center of the city and in the later years the body of Caesar was burned inside its walls. Nearby was the prison in which St. Paul languished and went forth to die. Finally, with the passing of the years, Christianity began to grow and flourish and gradually many of these ancient Imperial buildings were transformed into places of Christian worship. I can assure you that a visit to the Catacombs, to stand in the Coliseum where Christians were burned at the stake and fed to the lions, and to stand and gaze upon all these ruins of antiquity is such a moving experience than an attempt to describe what one saw would bankrupt the English language.

In the late afternoon of October 11, I said goodbye to my traveling companions and went on board a plane that carried me from Europe to the Belgian Congo far in the South of Africa. In route, a short time was spent in Athens, Greece, and then we plunged into the land of the Pharaohs. At midnight we were flying over brilliantly lit Cairo and nearby were the solid masses known as the Pyramids. As I flew over the city and thought of the present world tension caused by Mr. Nasser of Egypt over the Suez Canal, I breathed a prayer for the peace of the world. I am to have a little additional time in Egypt as I go from Africa to India. They say there is tension there but there is no danger to a foreigner provided he stays in the center of the city. That I propose to do.

We left Cairo in beautiful moonlight and soon we were flying over the Nile River, lined with temples and tombs. Then came the heat of the desert as we plunged southward into the heart of Africa with all of its wild and awe-inspiring sights. In Africa, nature is so vast that whether in the desert or the jungle you were either inspired or depressed by it. In Africa, also was found all the animals one can imagine; those that fight and devour, whistle, sing, crawl, or leap. Stretching across the middle of this vast continent is the Congo River, a mighty waterway upon whose banks great cities such as Leopoldville have been built.

While we were flying over Sudan, the next country south of Egypt, one of the motors of our magnificent airplane began to "act up" and we were forced to land at Khartoum. It grieved me to hear the announcement that twenty-four hours would be required to repair our engine and that we would remain in Khartoum for a day and a night. Hotel accommodations for nearly sixty passengers could not be found, and we were put up for the night in some soldiers' barracks. Not soon will I forget the hard cot on which I tried to sleep, or the excessive heat. If I should attempt to tell my readers actually how high the temperature registered during the day, they would accuse me of exaggeration. Finally, the night passed, and we were again on our way. Noon found us at Stanleyville at the headwaters of the Congo River. While waiting for our plane to leave for Elizabethville, my final destination, I noticed that cold Coca-Cola was on sale and I felt the blessings of prosperous America were coming in sight.

In the afternoon we were on the ground at Elizabethville with Bishop Booth and several missionary friends waving a hearty welcome. The Central Conference is now in session. I am living in a school building with the missionaries, preaching twice each day to the Conference and enjoying the fellowship of these Christian people. In my next letter, I shall attempt to describe the work of Methodism in this no longer "Dark Africa" but "Awakening Africa." Meanwhile, I send my affectionate greetings to all my friends back home.

Wesleyan Christian Advocate, November 1, 1956, p. 1.

Elizabethville. Belgian Congo
October 21, 1956

Early tomorrow morning I begin the long journey from Southern Africa to India. This trip will require practically all four days traveling by air. My route takes me back to North Africa where I will have a brief stop in Cairo, on across Arabia, over the Holy Land, which I wanted so much to see, then into Pakistan; and if all goes well, I will be in Delhi, the capital of India by Thursday night.

This is my fifth trip to Africa. The first was in 1936 when it required six days by air on a slow plane. The second was in 1939, and while I was here World War II began and I had to go home by way of South America. In 1952 and 1953, I served as the bishop in charge of our work in North Africa and traveled widely in Tunisia and Algiers. Today, a civil war is raging throughout these countries and France is in difficulty. When I leave Cairo Wednesday morning, I will have spent two weeks on this visit. Flying down from Cairo, Egypt, to the border of Rhodesia and then back to Egypt has given me a splendid opportunity to see the people and to observe the tremendous changes which are taking place before one's eyes. The difference in the Congo since I was here seventeen years ago is simply indescribable. Often have I said that if one wants to see the world's biggest show during the next fifty years, he should get a seat close enough to observe the changing scene in Africa.

No one can put together any combination of words that will adequately describe or interpret Africa. It covers nearly twelve million square miles and includes one-fifth of the land surface of the globe. Here lives two hundred million people. There are sixty million people who are Moslem in their religious faith, twenty million who profess the Christian faith, leaving one hundred twenty million who have no vital religious faith whatsoever. There are more than seven hundred different dialects spoken throughout the whole continent.

To state these facts in another way, Africa is four times larger than the United States of America. Here is to be found ninety-eight percent of the world's diamonds, fifty-five percent of its gold, thirty-two percent of its copper, and no one yet knows how vast are its stores of uranium. Also, there are vast quantities of cotton, rubber, and coffee grown here. It is no wonder to me that many nations have cast covetous eyes on this rich and expanding continent.

There are many Africas but they fall easily into two main divisions. Northern Africa is more highly developed and is very much like Europe. Then comes the Sahara Desert which is a wilderness of sand separating North Africa from the rest of the continent. The desert is both a bridge and a barrier. The civilization of North Africa is very old, whereas Africa below the Sahara and the equator did not begin to open up and develop until the 19th century. Today the whole continent is in a state of ferment and with exaggerated speed is rushing into all the gains and losses of our modern times. It was Jan Smutz, that great African statesman who lived and died here, who once declared "for better or worse, the old Africa is gone, and the white races must face the new situation which they created." There is more racial tension down at the tip of the continent than anywhere else in Africa, but everywhere these millions of black people are awakening and demanding more and more of a share in the total life of their country.

No longer can one think of Africa as composed of pagan people pursuing their primitive tribal ways. There are remote sections where life is still primitive and backward, but as I sat waiting for my plane the other day at Stanleyville, I observed the people were well-dressed, big American tractors were moving earth nearby and so many automobiles were in sight, one had to watch when crossing the highway. All of this alongside a modern airport in which planes from all over the world landed and took off. Perhaps the darkest thing about modern Africa is the ignorance of most of us about it.

As one moves about and observes, certain questions keep coming up again and again. Questions such as these: What chance does Communism have here? Is the white man to have any place in the Africa of tomorrow? Are the Africans ready to assume leadership of their expanding political and economic life? These and a hundred other questions plague one's mind if he comes here to be anything but a tourist. The answers to all these questions are hard to find.

The total picture is perhaps brighter in the Belgian Congo than in any part of Africa. The Belgian government in Brussels seems to be pursuing a policy of partnership rather than one of exploitation. To be sure vast wealth is being accumulated by big Belgian business concerns, but the national policy is humane and progressive. Natural resources have been and are being developed; scientific agricultural methods are being introduced; communications have been expanded and speeded up, and with the help of Christian churches a most extraordinary job is being done in the field of education. So runs the story but the half cannot be told. Keep your eyes on Africa.

This is one of the largest and most rewarding fields for Christian missionary endeavor. Methodism has taken root in African soil and is already a flowering tree. Everywhere one finds evidence of the growing maturity of the church. From the report rendered by Bishop Newell Booth to the Central Conference and from other sources I have garnered the following pertinent facts: Of the total missionary staff of three hundred sixteen in the Elizabethville area, two hundred sixty-six come from America. There are also fifty from other countries. These missionaries joined with about four thousand full-time African workers from nearly fifty different tribes working in fifty languages in carrying on the Christian program in three thousand four hundred seventy-three congregations, five hundred sixty-nine schools, forty-nine medical units, seven colonies for leprosy patients, fourteen farms, four presses, and ten urban centers.

The need for missionaries is still urgent and at least twenty additional missionaries are needed if we are to meet the strategy of the "Lands of Decision" program and strengthen our ministerial training. We have had an increase of two hundred eighty-eight teachers and thirty-five ministers and other church workers and fifty medical staff members in the last four years.

In Africa, we face tremendous problems; a people less than ten percent literate, amid revolutionary changes in the economy, industrialization, the breakdown of the family, and other restraints because of the movements of populations. During the quadrennium, the total membership of the church has increased twenty-two percent, from one hundred seventeen thousand six hundred fifty-three to one hundred forty-three thousand one hundred thirty-nine. The joy of a keen growing edge and the tragedy of inadequately trained pastoral workers are both revealed in the fact that although more than forty thousand new believers have been enrolled during the quadrennium an increase of only twenty-six thousand has been registered. There just are not enough workers with the training essential for the shepherding and the integration of the new converts into the life of the church. Another evidence of the outreaching growing edge is the record of the opening up of six hundred eighty-three new congregations, more than three a week throughout the four years.

There is an average of more than a dozen preaching places for each ministerial member of the Conference. This points up both the extent of the lay ministry which maintains regular services and the massive task of training those lay workers in service and providing training for ordained ministers. As it is, the trained ministry is involved in the administration of large circuits, and the pastoral work and preaching are mainly done by those with little training for it. At present, there are seven schools on three different levels for the training of pastoral workers. The Board of Missions in America has agreed to try to provide an additional couple for each of the five conferences to strengthen this work of ministerial training.

Real advances have been made in the medical work in all the Conferences. New people have been trained, more buildings provided, and better equipment purchased. We have brought health services to more people than ever before . New drugs for the treatment of leprosy patients have made it possible not only "to make them clean" but to be able to send hundreds back to their villages able to take up normal life again.

In twenty-one of the thirty-three districts, African ministers have been appointed as heads of the districts. In addition to the twenty-one, there are assistant district superintendents in six other districts who are carrying a great share of the load of administration even though for special reasons it is not yet been deemed wise to appoint them as superintendents. Even though there is not even one who has had college or university training and although you could count on the fingers of one hand those who have had high school studies, the African ministers have demonstrated again the ability of the Master to call followers and turn them into effective apostles.

The ministerial membership of the Conferences has increased forty-three percent since 1948 reaching a total now of two hundred sixty-six with fifty-four more as ministers on trial, making a total of three hundred twenty. Seventy-six of those are missionaries. In the Belgian Congo, in only a little more than forty years, two Annual Conferences have been formed with one hundred twenty-eight Conference members supervising the work of more than seventeen hundred congregations. The reasons that these facts are outlined in some detail are (1) to show the success of our church in this land, and (2) to reveal to many churches in the two Georgia conferences what a large share they have had, by their Advanced Special gifts, in this growing church. Everywhere I have received thanks for what our churches in Georgia are doing to promote this part of our Lord's vineyard.

During the ten days of the Central Conference, I have preached twice almost every day and it has been a happy ministry for me. It has been my privilege to live with the missionaries in one of our modern school buildings and they have extended me every courtesy. Several of these missionaries are from Georgia. Due to the growth of the church in these parts, the last General Conference authorized the election of an additional bishop for Africa. Dr. Ralph E. Dodge, who once served as a missionary in Angola, but who for the last few years has been one of the secretaries of the Board of Missions in New York was elected on the first ballot. He was advised of his election by cable and came immediately by air for his consecration. At the 11:00 a.m. service, in the presence of an overflowing congregation, Bishop Booth and I assisted by certain pastors, solemnly consecrated Bishop Dodge. It was a moving ceremony and made one happy to be part of a great church that carries the whole world in its concerns. This marks the consecration of the first Methodist Bishop ever to be elected and consecrated in Africa. Thus, we made history.

Wesleyan Christian Advocate, November 8, 1956, p. 4.

New Delhi, India
October 30, 1956

If my memory serves me right my last letter to the *Wesleyan Christian Advocate* was written somewhere in Africa as I was about to begin the long journey from the Belgian Congo to India. Although I am now in the capital city of India, it seems well to write one article describing some of my travel experiences. In a subsequent article, I will attempt some description of this vast country in the work of Methodism during the last 100 years.

The Central Conference in Africa closed Sunday, October 21. I left at 6:00 a.m. on Monday to get up to Stanleyville where the larger international planes take off for various corners of the earth. I was compelled to ride in a small two-motor plane for nearly two thousand miles. This lap of the journey required a whole day because the plane was a local one and we stopped for twenty minutes at several villages. The natives came at every stop by the hundreds to see the plane and stood with their native goods about them hoping for a sale.

I was glad to ride this slow plane because it stopped at Kindue, a growing African town, where Henry Wheeler and his lovely wife live and labor. They have been my dear friends for many years. If ever missionaries deserve the term "pioneer missionaries," they do. Wheeler was the first African missionary to introduce the natives to the idea of building roads in the Congo. In Kindue, where they now live, there is a fine brick church building, a testimony to their fine sacrificial administration. They met me at the airport and for a brief twenty minutes, we crowded in the memories of twenty years of Christian fellowship. What a privilege it was.

Stanleyville, where I spent Monday night, is a growing "cross-road" in the Congo. The Belgian Air Lines have built a comfortable rest house there in which I spent twenty-four comfortable hours. At 3:00 p.m. on Tuesday, I boarded a large four-motor plane for Cairo, Egypt, there to make connections between Pakistan and India. After a few hours of sunlight, night overtook us and soon we were flying over the vast stretches of Sudan. About 8:00 p.m. we flew over Khartoum, where we had been forced down two weeks before. Looking down into the desert, one could occasionally see lonely campfires which we were told the natives build at night as protection from wild animals. Midnight found us approaching Cairo, a city toward which the attention of the entire world is turning these days and where all the combustible materials are ready to set the whole world on fire.

Little did I expect to find and feel any of the tensions when I disembarked to spend the night in that nerve center, but I was soon to discover the contrary. Upon entering the large International Airport building, I went through the usual passport examination which is found everywhere in this part of the world. After I submitted my passport and went on to the customs office to claim my baggage my real examination began. I was recalled to the passenger office and there for more than an hour was held up. It was evident that for some reason unknown to me I was a "suspect." The authorities asked a few questions of me and seemed intent on finding my name in their records. I sat silently while they searched to see if I was not a dangerous person. After a long wait, the reason for my detention was revealed. It seems there was a newspaper editor in India whose name was identical to mine, and he had been very critical of Egyptian politics. At long last, my vaccination certificate seemed to convince them that I was a harmless preacher and not a politician, and they allowed me to go. It was then 1:00 a.m. and a good ten miles to my hotel down in the city of Cairo, and I was to be back at the airport in time to catch an 8:00 a.m. plane for Pakistan. I was not in the best of humor but had sense enough to keep my mouth shut. After a few hours in a magnificent Cairo hotel, I was up at 6:00 a.m. and on my way back to the airport, ready for nearly three thousand miles over historic ground.

The big and comfortable Australian plane bound for Sydney took off at 8:00 a.m. It was a beautiful sunny morning, and all of ancient Egypt stretched out below us. In a few minutes, the now contested Suez Canal stretched beneath us like a ribbon.

One could easily see ships passing through while others were anchored waiting, I suppose, for pilots.

Then we flew on across Arabia where so much history, vitally related to our Christian religion, was enacted. In a few hours, we were far out over the Persian Gulf, a part of the world where again history reaches almost staggering proportions. It all sets one to thinking about those nations which were born, lived, and flourished, played their part in the world drama, and then, began to decline, with their bright morning turning to night. Gigantic forces are glaring at each other in that part of the world, and I would not be surprised to see war break out at any time. One could write at length about this vast Arab world, stirring such a deep sense of oppression. Everyone will do well to keep an eye on Egypt, Israel, Syria, Jordan, and, in fact, this whole part of the world. At this moment it is a vast tinderbox, and a single incident can set it ablaze and the whole world would be in danger.

Late Tuesday night we landed in Karachi, an important city in the nation of Pakistan. Here one finds a few American manufactured goods in the shops, and the atmosphere is much more cordial because America is giving economic aid to Pakistan. This fact pleases them very much but leaves India unhappy. But more of that later.

After a little rest in Karachi, a small plane brought me to New Delhi, the proud and magnificent capital of India. It is from the Claridge Hotel in that city I write. Already I have been received by some high government officials and preached to good-sized congregations of Americans.

For more than a month, I have been under the pressure of many duties. Before moving on to Lucknow where I shall be in attendance upon the Centennial Celebration of Indian Methodism and a Central Conference, I am trying to rest a bit from my African duties and to prepare mentally and physically for some more strenuous days in India.

Mail is slow out here, and I am in the dark as to how the presidential campaign and other matters back home are moving. On the other hand, I am where it is easy to see the growing edge of the Christian church, and that after all, is my main business in life. My three traveling companions have now re-joined me after some exciting experiences in Jerusalem, Baghdad, and other places. They are working seriously at the job of studying men and movements, and I predict this will make each and all of them more world citizens than they ever could have been without these experiences. We are all keeping well, and all have a touch of homesickness now and then, but that will only increase the joy of getting home one of these days.

Wesleyan Christian Advocate, November 22, 1956, p. 12.

Lucknow, India
November 11, 1956

India has a population of three hundred seventy million souls. These lines are being written in Lucknow, which has a population of six hundred thousand and is the ninth most populated city in the nation. The ancient name for India was Hindustan which meant "The Land Beyond the Indus River." It was the lure of India's wealth that led Columbus to discover the New World.

India is a land of striking contrasts. From the snow-clad Himalayas dominated by Mount Everest, which rises 29,141 feet, to the plains of the South. Before the Egyptians had built the pyramids, great discoveries in art, literature, and science have been made by the people of India. This is a land where ancient religions, many cultures, and twentieth-century progress can be found side by side.

There are striking contrasts in climate, population, and natural resources. Some of the people live in modern splendor while millions are not far from starvation. New Delhi is the proud capital with imposing buildings, but not far away thousands try to exist in frail tents or crude shacks. This is the land of the indescribable Taj Mahal before which I stood in amazement last week, but it is also the land in which multitudes go hungry. On every hand, one looks upon the lean faces of hungry little children and decrepit old men and women. To describe the total scene would go far beyond all the adjectives that are in my vocabulary.

India, by the consent of Great Britain, achieved its national independence in 1947, and the English who had been here in power for nearly two centuries turned the control over to the

Indians. The late Mr. Gandhi whose tomb I saw here recently, had done much to create the demand for independence, and leaders like Mr. Nehru, the present Prime Minister, have skillfully guided the young nation through all the pitfalls of national immaturity.

To look, as some American tourists are inclined to do, at the mosques, tombs, stately old forts, or even at the apparent poverty of so many is to fail to see how very far these people have come. A significant social and economic revolution is taking place here without influences that are bound to affect the rest of the world.

Everywhere one discovers evidence of the long stay of the British. It is quite the popular thing these days to decry colonialism and I certainly make no plea for its return. We all realize that a larger and better day is dawning in the field of human freedom.

But no one can fail to see that England left much of permanent value in India. The simple fact that the English language was almost universally used, gave the people a sense of unity and a voice for their aspirations. I have heard more than one thoughtful Indian say that England helped to prepare India for self-government. India is today a member of the British Commonwealth and trade between the two countries reaches a very high level.

My missionary service placed me in China long enough to know a little about those ancient and inscrutable people. There are nearly 500 million of them now undergoing all the turbulence of a revolution. Within the month I have traveled widely in once dark, but now awakening Africa. There another two hundred million aspiring people are awake with new ambitions. Add to those facts the tremendous and significant changes taking place among the nearly four hundred million Indians and you can easily see possibilities both for good and evil are wrapped up in these countries and continent. What they ultimately decide will influence the shape of things to come. They do not seem to trust the Western powers very much. The idea of India, as its leaders assert, is to remain neutral and thus prevent the collision of Communism and Capitalism. One cannot help but appreciate their deep desire to avoid involvement in another global war. It is not easy for me to write even these elementary facts and conclusions because to see India and look upon her strength and weakness is to lose all desire to speak as a prophet.

Throughout the last week, the Americans who are here have hovered over the few available radios to hear developments in the Suez Canal Crisis. We do not get a very full picture of what is happening or why England and France felt compelled to initiate war measures. It is quite evident that all the Indian leaders expected America to play a decisive role in preventing another global conflict. Today the tension seems a bit less and we devoutly pray that another crisis has been averted. The uprisings in Poland, Hungary, North Africa, and now in Egypt and Israel are but eruptions that indicate the smoldering fires of unrest. One does not feel happy to be so far from home when the world is thinking of going to war.

The days we spent in New Delhi were crowded with inspection visits to our churches, schools, and medical clinics. I was most favorably impressed with the medical unit in a village some miles out from New Delhi. There, a doctor, a nurse, and several pastors ministered physically and spiritually to a large crowd of sick and needy, some of whom had walked many long miles. Methodism's strength and growth in India are the results of its steady devotion to the needs of the people. Our schools are among the very best and in a thousand ways, we serve the people where they are.

Sunday morning, October 28, found me preaching to a congregation of more than one hundred fifty Americans. The service was held in the private home of a high official of our American Embassy. This congregation does not have a regular minister but meets every Sunday with a visiting preacher and, if none is available, one of the laymen takes the service. The average American living abroad is not famous for his church attendance and to find this large group of Americans giving attention to their spiritual needs was a most encouraging experience. I enjoy preaching to them.

We have now been in Lucknow for twelve days. Sisson, Jones, and Moorhead are quartered at the local hotel while I have divided time between "Government House" and a dormitory at Isabella Thoburn College. For four days all the bishops were royally entertained by the governor of the state or province in which we are meeting. We found in the most luxurious quarters of what is known as "Government House" most cordial hospitality.

Everything was according to protocol. Even our seating arrangements at the dining table were printed in advance of each meal. The Governor and his gracious wife are devout Hindus but they extended us every courtesy and I enjoyed our stay with them. Later I moved to a simple room at the college where my roommates were Bishop Ivan Lee Holt and Bishop Raymond Archer of Singapore. We have enjoyed the finest fellowship and had time to discuss many matters of common interest.

The first great gathering of Methodists of which we were a part was a Centennial Celebration and Exhibition which was held October 31-November 4. A very large and many-colored tent which is called a "pandal" had been erected as an auditorium for the large crowds. It would seat ten thousand and at times was filled. At one service of Holy Communion, more than four thousand took the symbols of our Lord's death from the hands of more than fifty pastors. Several of the best choirs from our churches scattered over a wide territory gave us excellent music. The people assembled from all over this vast nation in reverent praise and worship as the Methodist Church in India stands at the end of one century and upon the threshold of another. It was a notable celebration and the inauguration of the new program of service. For three years plans for the Centennial Celebration and marvellous exhibit have been underway and the people responded loyally and joyfully. I count myself fortunate to have been the official representative of the Mother Church in America.

The Centennial Celebration closed at noon on Saturday, November 3, and the Central Conference opened in the afternoon of the same day. A Central Conference overseas is the equivalent of a Jurisdictional Conference in America. We have now worked morning, noon, and night for more than a week on the organizational problems of Indian Methodism. Those who are delegates are men and women of good training and unquestioned devotion.

This conference is composed of one-half ministers and one-half laymen. Of the total number, there are approximately twenty women and about the same number of missionaries. The church in India is no longer a foreign importation.

The one event toward which everyone looked with great interest was the election of two bishops. Bishop J. Waskom Pickett and Bishop Clement D. Rockey have served the church long and well. Bishop Rockey was born here to missionary parents and Bishop Pickett has been here forty-seven years as a missionary and as bishop. The full story of their devoted and effective leadership can never be told, but the time of retirement had come and their successors were to be chosen.

On the fourth ballot, Dr. James Matthews, Secretary for India in the Board of Missions was elected, but after a night of reflection, announced that he thought he could serve best as a Missionary Secretary. It then became evident that the conference would elect only Indians as their bishops. It required twenty-two ballots for them to make a choice.

On Thursday, November 6, on the 22nd ballot, the conference elected Dr. Mangal Singh and Dr. Gabriel Sundaram Bishops of the Methodist Church in Southern Asia. The announcement of the results of the ballot was greeted with enthusiastic applause, and the new bishops were escorted to the platform. A recess was called, and the conference delegates and assembled visitors gathered around to congratulate the newly chosen leaders of the church and to express satisfaction regarding the result of the election.

The Rev. Dr. Mangel Singh enters the episcopacy after a long period of devoted service as a teacher, headmaster, minister, and administrative leader. He was born in Pauri-Garhwal on December 31, 1901. His oldest son is now studying at Asbury College in Wilmore, Kentucky, and the second is studying at the Leonard Theological College. The two daughters are both students at the Lal Gagh here in Lucknow.

Dr. Singh has been for some years the popular pastor of Christ Church in Delhi. He has served as Secretary for the Advance for Christ and as District Superintendent. He is a member of the Executive Board and Interim Committee and the chairman of the India Economic Development Committee. He was a delegate to the Central Conference in 1938 and the General Conference in 1948 and 1956. He thus comes to the episcopacy with considerable experience in both the ministerial and educational work of our church.

Dr. Gabriel Sundaram comes from the south, having been born in Hyderabad State in 1901. He received his BA Degree from Madras University and was awarded the Doctor of Divinity degree from Baldwin Wallace College in Berea, Ohio, this year while in the USA attending the General Conference. Dr. Sundaram, began his service in the ministry, having been ordained a deacon in 1922, and an elder in 1924. His greatest contributions have, however, been in the field of education. As headmaster and then as principal of the Methodist Boys' School in Hyderabad he made that institution one of our outstanding secondary schools. He has given outstanding leadership, especially in the field of organizing and conducting profitable institutes on various aspects of the educational task.

These are an ancient people, but as a nation they are now, enjoying all the privileges and making many of the mistakes of national immaturity.

The rising tide of nationalism and a revival of their ancient religions could become a force standing squarely in the path of the Christian church in India. Only time will reveal what happens and which road India will travel. Their leaders both in government and the church are strong men and I feel confident India will remain a democratic nation and a rich field for Christian growth.

The consecration of the two newly elected bishops brought to a close the session of the Central Conference. The large and beautiful sanctuary of our Central Church was crowded, the music inspiring and the ritual most impressive. It was my privilege as the representative of the Council of Bishops to participate in the Service of Consecration. I have now helped to consecrate our overseas bishops in the following countries: Germany, Switzerland, Malaya, Korea, Africa, and India. Here is another proof that Methodism is truly a world church.

Tomorrow morning, we take a plane for Benares where we shall see the thousands bathing in the Ganges River in an attempt to wash their sins away. From there we go to Calcutta which I am told is the most overcrowded city in the world. Then on to Bangkok in Thailand, Hong Kong in China, and from there to Japan. We are now eleven hours ahead of Georgia in time and when we turn our faces homeward from Japan, we will cross the International Date Line and observe the same day twice to adjust our calendars.

As one leaves this unpredictable land called India, he can but hope that the early visit of India's prime minister, Mr. Nehru, to Washington will bring our two nations into a better understanding and closer cooperation. Both countries are democratic, and both believe in the dignity and rights of mankind. Together, we can do much for the peace of the world and the building of a better society. I pray that it may be so.

Wesleyan Christian Advocate , November 29, 1956, p. 9

Tokyo, Japan
November 26, 1956

On a luxurious Pan-American Clipper, we were flying toward Tokyo. It had been a smooth flight from Hong Kong, China, two thousand miles away. From our lofty position we had looked down on Formosa where Chiang Kai-shek stands ready to occupy the mainland of China when it seems feasible; the island of Okinawa, where so much of our air power is concentrated; and the wide seas in which our American Seventh Fleet keeps watch over this part of the world where another world war might break out.

As I look down on the lights of Tokyo, the third-largest city in the world, my thoughts go back nearly twenty-five years. It was in 1935 that I first saw this once "hermit" nation. In 1854, Commodore Perry had pushed open its unwilling doors and opened it to foreign trade and influence. In less than a century, Japan accepted the ways of the Western nations and took its place as one of the great nations of the world. In 1894, its armies had conquered ancient China and in 1904 its powerful navy had brought Russia to its knees in surrender. It is small wonder that by 1937 it had grown so strong and conceited it imagined itself ready for new conquests.

The result was the invasion of North China in that year and a war followed with the armies of Chiang Kai-shek. Even before that had been finished Japanese warplanes were dropping death on our ships at Pearl Harbor and Japan and the United States were locked in one of the fiercest wars of history. As a result, Japan's fleet was sunk in the South Seas, her once proud armies crushed, her cities were in rubble and ashes, and conquering armies stood astride her once proud nation.

This is not the place to describe the magnificent work done by our American forces under the superb leadership of General Douglas MacArthur. Suffice it to say, but for his knowledge of Japanese history and his unparalleled statesmanship, history might have taken a different course and left us in a far more difficult position. Much of this history and a great deal more went through my mind as I looked down on the lights of Tokyo. While I have sometimes been called Japan's critic, I have always known there were two Japans. One, that mad military Japan which ran amok, and the other industrious, polite, peace-loving Japan which I appreciate so much.

As soon as our plane came to a halt, we were once more in the hands of gracious missionary friends and soon on our way to the well-known Imperial Hotel in Tokyo. The next morning at an early hour we went on a tour of Methodist institutions in and about Tokyo, all of which are now a part of the United Church of Japan. While not all the denominations have come into the United Church, many of them have, and church union in this land where Christianity is numerically small is proving a great success.

Before the day was finished, we visited the International Christian University, Aoyama University, Union Theological Seminary, and the Language School, where all our missionaries go to familiarize themselves with the Japanese language. We had lunch with a group of students, a delightful experience. All our institutions are flourishing. Aoyama University built and staffed by Methodists has a student body of ten thousand. Japanese youth demand education and it is well we train as many of them as possible.

The International Christian University was born at the close of World War II. Perhaps Dr. Ralph Diffendorfer of our Methodist Board of Missions was the first one to conceive of such a university. It is housed chiefly in a building something like the Pentagon in Washington, D. C. The building was originally constructed to design and build airplanes. Today it houses one of the most unique Christian institutions to be found anywhere. Nearly fifty years of contemplation, prayer, and effort of Christian leaders in Japan and America preceded the establishment of the ICU. They were united in hope for the Christianization of Japan by a common understanding of and critical reflection on human history. Prompted by the history-making changes confronting Japan as well as the world, ICU became a reality at long last through international cooperation. Chronologically stated, the Japan International Christian University Foundation was organized in the United States in November 1948. On June 13, 1949, the ICU Board of Trustees was organized and on June 15 these bodies adopted a new constitution and elected the first officers. The ICU campus was dedicated on April 29, 1952, and the charter for its College of Liberal Arts was granted on March 23, 1953. The opening ceremony of ICU College of Liberal Arts took place on April 29, 1953.

The ICU lands comprise some three hundred sixty-eight acres divided into academic campus, residential area, cultivated farm area, forests, and gardens. There are two land levels, with rice fields and an adjacent small stream between. The higher level, where most of the buildings are located, provides for the academic and residential sections with some wooded areas. The lower level contains the farm area, forests, and gardens.

There are now more than fifty buildings on the ICU property. The ICU church building, University Hall, and the hanger, soon to be rehabilitated as gymnasium and assembly hall, comprise the principal academic group. Two dormitories accommodating seventy men and fifty women have been in use since January 1955. The first section of the central dining hall has been in use from the same time, along with a central heating plant for the dormitory areas.

Additionally, two dormitories, one for seventy-two men and one for seventy-two women were opened on November 1, 1956. There are twenty-seven independent residences occupied by the faculty and staff and two apartment buildings, one accommodating six units, and one with ten furnished apartments for single faculty women. The independent houses are divided between twelve Japanese-style and sixteen Western or semi-Western-style residences. In the farm area, there are eleven different buildings for the various farm enterprises.

Plans are now actively under consideration for the building of the Diffendorfer Memorial. It will serve for student activities, auxiliary to the church needs, a small assembly hall, and a residence for graduate students. Faculty members are sought not only in Japan but widely in the world among Christian scholars and educators of superior academic and personal qualifications. Students are carefully selected from qualified applicants based on character, life purpose, health, academic ability, and leadership potentiality regardless of race, nationality, sex, or religion.

It is to these Christian colleges and churches we must look for a foundation upon which world peace is to be based. Japan is now negotiating a trade policy with Russia and that makes it necessary that all the ties which bind Japan and America together be maintained and made more secure.

The basic policy of Japan continues to be friends with the nations of the free world and concurrence with the principles laid down in the charter of the United Nations. The agreement with Soviet Russia, when it is ratified, will not mean that Japan is going to become part of the Red Bloc or in any way subservient to the ambitions of Moscow.

It must be recognized that the Russians will take advantage of every opportunity to strengthen their ties with Japan. It must be expected that numerous "exchanges" especially in the cultural field, will take place. This may place a severe test upon Japanese American relations, and this will be particularly true if the United States should read too much into Japan's new relationship with Russia. It is also probable, on the other hand, that the mere fact of an agreement coming into force will have the effect of making many Japanese cautious about any advances Moscow may attempt to make. Moreover, it will be realized afresh that treaties that will bind Japan and the United States together are remarkably strong ones although at times their nature and strength are apt to be somewhat obscured under the strain of passing events in which they may not always see eye to eye.

There are differences, of course, between the United States and Japan. That is only natural. The two countries have different national and regional interests. They differ in background. But these differences do not detract from the fact that the two countries are agreed with the other Western Powers that democracy must be kept alive, that international communism must be stopped, and that the free world should provide the stabilizing influence in Asia and the rest of the world. These, after all, are the important things.

Americans must accept the fact that a nation can have a separate and independent policy from that of Washington and still be very much the friend of the United States. The Japanese must learn to act as if having an independent policy is the most natural thing in the world.

Let us recognize the hard fact that the United States does exercise a strong measure of influence over Japan. After all, all are the outstanding champions of the free world against the incursions of the Communists.

Let it also be emphasized that acceptance of this influence is voluntary and is of the nation's own free will, without compulsion or coercion. This is very different from the case of Hungary, if the Japanese need this as a reminder to bolster their pride. The important thing is that both of us act like friends and equals – decide what we think without shouting, without rancor, without self-abasement, emphasizing our common purpose and common goal, not our points of difference, and always with the thought in mind that friendship with all nations is our aim.

For many years Dr. Zensuke Hinohara was the president of our Methodist Girls' School in Hiroshima which was tragically destroyed by the atomic bomb. He has been my close friend through all these years. This young doctor came to Atlanta a few years ago for post-graduate study at Emory University Hospital. While there he was often a guest in our home. When he heard of our return to Japan, he wrote asking that we have a typical Japanese dinner in his home at noon on Japanese Thanksgiving Day which is one day earlier than ours. Sisson, Jones, and Moorhead were included in this invitation, and they will testify that with this fine Christian doctor and his family, we participated in one of the most enjoyable Thanksgiving Dinners

261

we have ever known. The evening of the same day found us in the company of twenty American missionaries enjoying a typical Thanksgiving Dinner. Not soon will we forget this day made so bright for us, even though we were so far from our firesides.

At a late hour that night, we took a train for Kyoto and Kobe. We were met in Kyoto by Rev. John B. Cobb and Rev. P. Lee Palmore and spent much of the day in this ancient capital of the Japanese Empire. From there we proceeded to Kobe, where seventy years ago Dr. J. W. Lambuth established the work of the Methodist Episcopal Church, South. Yesterday it was my privilege to preach in our Central Church in Kobe which stands on one of the principal streets and to join in the afternoon with many Japanese and missionary friends in the anniversary celebration of Palmore Institute where thousands of Japanese businessmen have been trained. It was in and about Kobe that my duties took me for several years and it pained me to say goodbye to so many dear friends after being with them for only two days.

Last night in an upper berth on a Japanese train, which is an experience, we returned to Tokyo. In a few hours, I will go to Yokohama to board the SS *President Cleveland* for an ocean voyage which will give me some rest after a long and strenuous journey that has carried us literally around the world. My traveling companions – and they have been delightful ones – will leave tonight by air to be in their pulpits Sunday, December 1. My ship will bring me to San Francisco on December 8 and from there I hasten to Pasadena, California, for the regular meeting of the Council of Bishops. In one concluding article, to be written while at sea, I hope to jot down a few of the unforgettable experiences of this long and rewarding journey. I hope to be in Atlanta on December 18.

Wesleyan Christian Advocate, December 20, 1956, p. 6.

Editor's Notes:

1. The Suez Canal Crisis and the Sinai War, was an invasion of Egypt in late 1956 by Israel, followed by the United Kingdom and France. The aims were to regain control of the Suez Canal for the Western powers and to remove Egyptian President Gamal Abdel Nasser, who had just nationalized the foreign-owned Suez Canal Company, which administered the canal. Before the Egyptian forces were defeated, they had blocked the canal to all shipping by sinking forty ships in the canal. It later became clear that Israel, France, and Britain had conspired to plan out the invasion. The three allies had attained a number of their military objectives, but the canal was useless. As a result of the conflict, the United Nations created the UNEF Peacekeepers to police the Egyptian–Israeli border, British prime minister Anthony Eden resigned, Canadian external affairs minister Lester Pearson won the Nobel Peace Prize, and the USSR may have been emboldened to invade Hungary.

2. Lubumbashi formerly known as Élisabethville is the third- largest city located in the country's southeasternmost part, along with Zambia.

3. Bishop Moore was referring to the presidential race between incumbent President Dwight D. Eisenhower and Democratic challenger Adlai Stevenson II. President Eisenhower won with 457 electoral votes to Stevenson's 73.

4. Although James Matthews declined his episcopal election in 1956, he was again elected in 1960 and accepted the assignment. He served in multiple areas. He was the son-in-law of Dr. E. Stanley Jones, evangelist and missionary to India. Bishop Matthews died on September 8, 2010. He was one of the longest-serving bishops of the church.

The SS *President Cleveland*

Hong Kong
November 20, 1956

When one has been traveling for some time in the far distant places of the earth he is greatly comforted when at last he turns his face homeward, even though the distance yet to be traversed is considerable. We are still nearly ten thousand miles from Georgia, but we have passed the halfway mark in our journey around the world, and every mile from here on will bring us nearer to our beloved ones. Already I have covered twenty-two thousand miles on this journey. More than nine thousand of those were inside Africa. When one starts at Cairo in North Africa and travels to South Africa, then traces the steps whatever the method of travel, he has covered a considerable distance.

We left Bangkok in Thailand last Saturday morning and before nightfall, we had greeted dear friends in Hong Kong and were comfortably housed in a modern hotel. I do not want to intimate that our entertainment elsewhere has not been cordial, but frankness compels me to say that beds in India are not made of feathers such as my grandmother used or of foam rubber as the modern advertisements offer. They are by design very hard, and I suppose are appropriate for that climate. The first thing I look for in our hotel upon arrival in Hong Kong was a bathtub with plenty of hot water. If ever a monument is proposed to be erected to the man who first invented the bathtub, I shall make a liberal donation. The beds here have been soft with springs, and I had to get accustomed again to sleeping in such comfort.

Hong Kong is one of the most fabulous cities in the world. It is very much like San Francisco and that it has been built upon the mountains which come down to the sea. To stand on either side of the harbor and look across at the brilliantly lighted houses climbing up these mountainsides is a thing of indescribable beauty.

Among all the cities in the world, Hong Kong stands high in my book for its location, beauty, and trade. Communist China's border is only twenty miles away from our hotel. Yesterday, we drove out and stood near the line. Only a short distance away stood the observation towers from which the Red Army looked ever toward this proud city which undoubtedly they would like to possess. Let me say a little more about Hong Kong itself. It is a British Crown Colony. It was a barren rock one hundred fifteen years ago when it was ceded by China to Great Britain. It commands a strategic position astride the principal sea and air routes of the far east and throughout its history, it has played a most significant part in commerce between the East and the West, and in bringing the East and the West together.

Originally, Hong Kong – in Chinese meant "fragrant harbor." It was the name of the island on which the city of Victoria stands. But today, the name Hong Kong includes the whole British colony – subsequently, China ceded the Kowloon Peninsula and Stonecutters Island, and the ninety-nine-year lease of New Territories which extends to the Chinese frontier and embraces several smaller islands. Kowloon which in Chinese means "nine dragons" refers to the mainland part of the colony.

The official guidebooks give the area of the entire colony as 391 square miles. It is larger; for during the one hundred fifteen years of its history, the colonies' land area has been enlarged by several major reclamation projects the latest of which is now going on between the Royal Naval dockyard in the Hong Kong terminus of the cross-harbor Star Ferry service.

Hong Kong is just within the tropics. The climate is sub-tropical, governed to a great extent by the monsoons. The great majority of the estimated two million, five hundred thousand population are Chinese. There are about fourteen thousand Europeans and Americans permanently residing in the colony. This figure includes some nine thousand five hundred British subjects from the United Kingdom and Commonwealth countries, but not including service personnel and their families.

The population has increased by at least two million since mainland China fell into the hands of the present Communist government. There is hardly a Chinese now living here who has not passed through some great upheaval that affected almost every phase of his life.

Many rich Chinese came here in the first days of the Communist rule while it was yet possible to get out of the mainland of China. They brought with them some of their wealth and they have re-established themselves in comfortable homes. However, this group composes only a fraction of the refugee population of Hong Kong. Those who came after China was under Communist domination left everything behind and came here to start life anew in a place where there was at least an air of freedom for them to breathe.

Since coming here on this trip, I have talked intimately with some new arrivals. Last night at dinner I sat next to a lovely, well-educated, young Chinese woman who within the last two months rejoined her husband after a separation of eight years. Her story goes beyond the Old Testament story of Ruth and her selfless devotion. Not soon will I forget the light in the eyes of two dear little girls, who within the month, with the help of friends were able to escape and join their parents from whom they had been separated for six years. Practically every refugee in Hong Kong carries in his heart a heavy load of pain and loneliness. They are besieged by fierce perplexities. The familiar landmarks have been removed, old security snatched away from them, and the occupations and way of life they have heretofore known have been banished and likely will never be restored.

Despite all I have described, these people carry on with tenacious courage. I have not heard a single one cry out or complain. Last Sunday morning, I preached at one of our Methodist churches. It is known as "The Church in the Garage." Some unused garages have been converted into places of beauty. If the building itself is lacking in beauty (and it is not, for I was amazed at its transformation), the people when assembled for worship made it beautiful.

Some two hundred fifty worshipers were seated when the choir stood to sing "The Morning Light Is Breaking." The music was superb and I have seldom preached to a more responsive audience. In that company were many old friends of mine whom I had known in Shanghai when I was the bishop of our church in China. What a reunion we had after the benediction.

The brilliant young pastor, the Rev. Timothy Wang is a sample of young, free, Christian China. Educated in the United States, he might have remained out of this zone of conflict, but he returned to suffer with his people and to minister to them in Christ's name. It gave me great joy to say to the fine choir of this church that I knew where $2000 could be had with which they are to purchase a Hammond Organ.

If people can sing the Lord's song under such difficult circumstances, they are entitled to have an organ. I do not want to leave the impression that this was my gift. It so happens that a Christian woman who loved China many years ago left a considerable sum of money, the interest of which was to go to China. As one of the three trustees of this fund, I was able to assure the congregation that $2000 would be made available.

One of the rare privileges associated with these days in Hong Kong has been the opportunity for fellowship with some of the great missionaries of our church. They are Bishop and Mrs. Ralph Ward, the Rev. and Mrs. Sydney Anderson, and the Rev. and Mrs. Carlisle Phillips. There are also two fine lady missionaries, Miss Nagler and Miss Smith representing the Women's Division of Christian Service.

Carlisle Phillips and his lovely wife and three children, a baby only two weeks old, are from the North Georgia Conference. Druid Hills Methodist Church in Atlanta may well be proud that they raised and gave to the church two missionaries of such statute and devotion. Rembert Sisson preached for the Chinese congregation last Sunday morning where Brother Phillips is the regular missionary. I heard fine reports concerning the service and the sermon.

Sid and Olive Anderson have been dear friends for almost a lifetime. They have been in China for nearly forty years and if ever there were two wiser, more consecrated, and effective missionaries I have not met them. Mrs. Moore and I lived with them in Shanghai and our debt to them are beyond computation. I was with them throughout those hectic years when the Japanese army was all over China. You who read this can easily imagine how we have snatched every opportunity to talk about those good, exciting days back in Shanghai before China fell into the ruthless hands of atheistic communism.

Bishop and Mrs. Ralph Ward are for me an illustration of Christ's compassion. They went to China many years ago and both of them served with distinction. Bishop Ward was elected as one of our bishops in China and remained there until he was imprisoned by the Japanese army. He spent three years in a horrible prison for no reason in the world except that he was a courageous Methodist leader. Since his release from prison, he has been the bishop in charge of all Methodist work both in Taiwan (Formosa) and Hong Kong.

He reached the age of retirement at the last General Conference and might have easily said "I've done my share," instead he responded to the request of the Council of Bishops to continue for another four years in this strategic post. No one knows the great need for leadership, both in government and the church like Ralph Ward. He seems to be an indispensable man for service in one of the nerve centers of our Methodist Missions. Mrs. Ward is a gracious lady and devoted as the Bishop to the task committed to them.

Bishop Moore and Bishop Ralph Ward

There was no work in either Taiwan or Hong Kong under the auspices of American Methodism before China was taken over by the Communists. Thousands of our finest Methodist leaders are now living there. Generalissimo Chiang Kai-shek is the beloved leader of the Chinese nation driven from the mainland to Taiwan (Formosa). There are some nine million inhabitants in Taiwan. Naturally, everyone longs for the day when the present regime in China will collapse and the Chiangs can reestablish the capital in Nanking. While I would like to see that happen, there is little evidence that such a desired result is near at hand.

Meanwhile, we have an obligation to those thousands of loyal Methodists who fled to Taiwan to escape the Communists. We have established churches in the main centers and have two missionary couples at work in those centers. Our next great project is to reestablish Soochow University which was the pride and joy of our Southern Methodist Church. The school is already in operation with hundreds of students meeting in inadequate and cramped quarters. The Southeastern Jurisdiction has pledged itself to raise at least $50,000 with which to construct the first building of the reborn Soochow University.

I had hoped to complete and mail this letter in Hong Kong, but there was so much to do in the last hours that I failed to finish it. As a result, these last paragraphs are being written while we fly at an altitude of seventeen thousand feet, between Hong Kong and Tokyo, Japan. During the last two hours, I looked down upon both Taiwan and Okinawa. Somewhere beneath me, the United States Seventh Fleet is on patrol, making sure that Taiwan is not captured by the Communists who threatened to do so. There are thousands of Americans living in Okinawa and I salute them for their heroic service. It should be said, however, that if our government thinks these places valuable enough to defend, the Christian church should think them equally important and see to it that the gospel of Christ is also offered.

We are due to arrive in Tokyo at six o'clock this evening and once again I will be on familiar ground and among dear friends. But the story of what we do during the next few days must be told in a subsequent letter. On Monday, November 28, Brothers Sisson, Jones and Moorhead will bid me goodbye and continue the journey homeward by air. They plan to preach in our churches on Sunday, December 2. They have been ideal travelling companions. This for them has been far more than a "trip abroad." They have been keen minded students bent upon learning more about the world in which we live and especially what part the Christian church must play in making this a safe, friendly world such as Christ would have it to be. They have cheered me on my way and always been diligent in carrying more than their share of the responsibilities. My week with them will always be for me a happy memory.

The Council of Bishops meeting which I must attend convenes in Pasadena, California, December 10, and because I long for some great days at sea, I go on board the SS *President Cleveland* the same day as my companions leave. After twelve days, upon what I sincerely hope will be a kind sea, I hope to reach San Francisco on December 8. Meanwhile my greetings go to all the friends there in Georgia.

Wesleyan Christian Advocate, January 3, 1957, p. 4

At Sea

December 7, 1956

Tomorrow morning, we are due to sail beneath the Golden Gate Bridge at San Francisco and by noon, we should have our feet on the soil of our own beloved country. After three months of travel – a journey which has taken us entirely around the world – to "come home" will be a thrilling experience. Years ago, Doctor Henry Van Dyke wrote a stirring poem in which he spoke feelingly of a country where "the air is full of sun-light and the flag is full of stars."

On this particular mission for the church, I have traveled approximately thirty-five thousand miles by ship, air, and train. We have been in Europe, Africa, and Asia, and while such an experience gives one a more international outlook, for me at least it also increases my love and appreciation of my own country. It will be good to get home.

From time to time I have "jotted down" some of my experiences and impressions. These travel letters have not sought to be well-rounded, documentary statements concerning the countries visited or conditions there. They have been written while flying over mountains, crossing seas, or in my hotel room late at night after a hard day's work. They have been chatty and I hope informative – the kind of letters one would fling back to his immediate family, while far away. Already many expressions of appreciation have come from readers of the *Wesleyan Christian Advocate* and for them I am grateful.

In this concluding letter, I shall try to describe a few of the places, people, and events that have left an indelible impression on my thoughts and life. Traveling to distant places is somewhat like going into an art gallery to gaze at some of the great paintings to be found there. It takes time to fully appreciate the tone, color, meaning, and message of the paintings. When one moves from country to country, he has to be on guard against hasty and immature conclusions. Once I heard a man lecture on Rome – The Eternal City – and during his lecture, he disclosed that he had spent only a portion of one day there. The longer one stays the more he knows about the hopes and fears, problems and possibilities of the people, and the less inclined he is to speak as a prophet. Our times are so incoherent and chaotic that understanding its problems and clarity of statement about its needs require years of study.

The physical scars of two world wars are disappearing. What has been done in western Germany, England, and Japan, and rebuilding the war-destroyed properties is simply incredible. It is a striking tribute to the indomitable courage of the human race. It will, of course, take much longer to do away with the hurt that war always brings to the inner life of the people. Whole sections of the earth have fallen in the hands of plunderers. The nations of the earth have been divided into opposing camps. Vast quantities of wealth which might have been used to give health and education to the needy of the world have been blown to bits. For millions of people, the ways, habits, and occupations they have heretofore known have been banished and may never return. No comfortable American dare ignore all these harsh facts nor all these harsh facts and proceed to fashion for himself a cheap Pollyanna notion that refuses to recognize anything that does not fit into his cozy, little world. While we are thankful for the physical restoration and material improvement in so many places, we must not fail to comprehend the tremendous impact spiritually and socially of what is happening all over the world.

In the opening paragraph of this article, I promised to put on paper some of my unforgettable impressions, but so far this sounds like a sermon. That is not what I started to do. Let me then get on with the main idea. Here follows a few of those experiences which will be forever stored in my memory. Some of them bless and some burn.

I am thankful for the quietness and healing effect of a sea voyage; there is too little time in my life for meditation, self-examination, and reading. The voyage from New York to Southampton in September on the RMS *Queen Elizabeth* in these twelve days crossing the Pacific on the SS *President Cleveland* has given me a chance to "take stock," to rest my body, and what is even more important to feed my mind by reading.

I am thankful for the friendliness and assistance rendered by dear friends in almost every place to which we have gone; Dr. McClellan in London and Dr. Thonger in Brussels, Dr. Kissac in Rome, Glenn Bruner in Tokyo, John Cobb and Lee Palmore in Kobe, Homer Morgan in Calcutta, and Marvin Harper in

Lucknow. These are only a few of the great company that gave me so freely of their time and strength so that we might see clearly and understand better. I shall always be grateful for the friends God is given me around the world.

I am thankful for those whose names I have called who are missionaries. I must once more record my deep and genuine appreciation of all our missionaries. Honestly, I believe that the most notable and unselfish outpouring of life in the service of others to be found anywhere in the world is exhibited in the daily living and ministry of these missionaries. Through them, uncounted numbers find Christ and enter upon a more abundant life. There is an enormous contribution to the church and the world that cannot be overestimated. In every place, I have found them consecrated and gallant. For all their ministries to this "traveling Bishop," I am deeply grateful.

I am thankful for the masses of people in every place – toiling and hopeful of the future – I will not soon forget this. In India especially, I was impressed by life in the villages. Everywhere one goes – if he walks, he must be careful to avoid brushing against the mud-splattered hides of innumerable cows that wander lazily wherever the family seems to take them. These cows go quietly on their endless way, paying little or no attention to the small boy who tries so hard to keep the herd together. On the same roads, one sees ancient bullock carts with their wheels shrieking at every turn in protest of the dry state of the axle which has not been greased in many years. India with its scientists and snake charmers, its strength and its weakness; yea, all the contrasts linger long in my memory.

I am thankful for the natural wonder of the desert in Africa. It always makes me bow down in awe. It is a wilderness of sand, overheated and wind-swept. To look upon it even from an airplane gives one a feeling of insignificance. The jungles and the mountains inspire and uplift me, the desert almost frightens me with its immensity.

I am thankful for the history of the cities to which I have gone. I think Rome impresses me most. So much of the history of our Christian faith was made there. The catacombs and the Coliseum, where so many died for our Lord put iron in my blood encouraging my heart. Never shall I read Paul's magnificent statement "I am ready to preach the gospel to you that be in Rome," without a fresh understanding of the creative and redemptive power of our glorious gospel.

My early morning visit to the Ganges River at Benares, India, is not easy to put into words. It was perplexing to see thousands going up and down this river and to watch them exercising their faith, attempting to wash away their sins in its dirty water. To look upon the numerous funeral pyres where families stand by to watch the cremation of their loved ones – brought an unutterable longing that they might know the redeeming love and measureless mercy of Him who is the Savior of the world.

I am thankful for the days in Hong Kong, off the mainland of China, where I met again old and cherished friends, every one of them refugees struggling to make a new start after having been driven from their homes by atheistic communism. It gave me a deeper insight into the menace of evil things and a hopeful insight when visiting a church service held in a garage. I heard lovely music and preached to one of the bravest congregations I ever saw.

My visit to Kobe, Japan, took me once more to the scene of some of my happiest labors. They were celebrating the seventieth anniversary of the coming of Dr. J. W. Lambuth, one of the greatest missionaries the Methodist Episcopal Church, South ever set forth. This grand old man died after establishing the church in Japan with the words upon his lips, "I die at my post." His grave is nearby and is carefully attended by Japanese Methodists. Mrs. Lambuth sleeps in a little graveyard in Shanghai, China. When her famous son, Bishop Walter Lambuth, after planting missions all over the world, died in Yokohama, Japan, his ashes were taken to Shanghai and placed in the same grave with his sainted mother. All this is, for me, sacred history and my visit to Kobe warmed my heart.

Tomorrow, after all these wanderings, I come to my land, grateful to God and my church that it has counted me worthy to have a part in the Christian Missionary Movement. Almost immediately I will be with the Council of Bishops in their meeting at Pasadena. Then, I shall hurry on to San Antonio, Texas, to visit our daughter and preach at Travis Park Church.

It was there I spent some of the happiest and most creative years of my life.

On Tuesday morning, December 18, I hope to be in Atlanta and again with those who know me best – my own dear family, for their brave and uncomplaining willingness to carry on while I go to far and distant places on the King's business. I shall ever be genuinely grateful. Never was I happier than in the service of the dear people of Georgia than now. If I can rightly interpret my heart, I long above all things to be a good and faithful servant of my Lord doing willingly every task committed to my hands.

In conclusion, let me say once again. The gospel is not for an age, but all ages. It is within the framework of current hopes and fears that we are to preach the gospel to the whole creation. If we look at the angry inferno of the world's life, we must also behold the golden spires of the City of God, coming down out of heaven to be built on the earth. We must not brood over the problems which are before us but discover and appropriate those eternal and inexhaustible resources which are ours because we are His.

God may be calling us as he called Abraham, to leave old and familiar places and go forth, not knowing where we go, but if we dare to follow Him with unquestioned obedience, we have the divine assurance that He will bring us to a better country. The church needs many things, but above all else, it needs men and women who will set the trumpet of the everlasting gospel to their lips and proclaim the sovereignty of God in the all-sufficiency of Christ.

Wesleyan Christian Advocate, January 10, 1957, p. 4.

Dr. J.W. Lambuth Bishop Walter Lambuth

Reverends Frank Moorhead, Rembert Sisson, Bishop Moore,
and Reverend L. Bevel Jones III.

Editors Note: The Rev. L. Bevel Jones III, was elected to
the episcopacy in 1984. In 1974, at the death of Bishop
Moore, he was one of the ministers chosen to speak at
Bishop Moore's funeral service.

CHAPTER SIXTEEN

A Mission to Belgium and Germany

JULY AND AUGUST 1958

Cherbourg, France
July 15, 1958

These notes are being written while our ship, the RMS *Queen Elizabeth*, is in the port of Cherbourg. We have enjoyed five wonderful days at sea. The sea has been gentle and the crossing of the Atlantic without incident. In a previous article, I attempted to express my appreciation of the RMS *Queen Elizabeth*. To spend a few days on board, surrounded by the excellent service the English know so well how to dispense, is my idea of a real holiday.

I left Atlanta on Friday, July 4th, for Washington, to take part in the National Convocation on Evangelism. Thousands of Methodists from all over the United States had gone there to re-emphasize this original passion of Methodism. It warmed my heart to see how effectively and wisely our General Board of Evangelism was leading our church to interpret its mission to "Tell to sinners round, what a dear Savior we have found." The sessions were held in the Uline Arena, which accommodates thousands. The weather was hot, and the acoustics were poor, but day after day throngs crowded in to study how to make Methodism more skilled in winning men to Christ.

I was given the high honor of being the preacher for the closing service on Sunday night. The service was held in Griffith Stadium, which, as most of you know, is the baseball park of the Washington Senators. Despite rain in the afternoon, some fifteen to twenty thousand people packed the stands. I stood in a specially arranged pulpit out on the field and preached as best I could to this great congregation about "Life's Inevitable Choice." Others will evaluate the service, but I can say honestly it was for me a fine opportunity to present the claims and challenge of Christ, and I had a good time doing so.

The day we sailed from New York witnessed a traffic jam along the waterfront. The RMS *Queen Elizabeth,* the SS *United States,* the SS *Constitution,* and the MS *Vulcania* - all of the mighty ships, were sailing the same morning. More than ten thousand passengers were trying to get from their hotels to these ships. Never have I witnessed such traffic confusion. Everybody, led by the taxi drivers, was nervous and shouting at each other. We were a long time traveling a very short distance. Then suddenly we were out at sea, and everyone settled down to the luxurious quiet of this mighty ship.

We were hardly on our way before friends and acquaintances of other days and places began to appear. Should I attempt to name them all, it would make a long list. Most of them disembarked here at Cherbourg and will spread-out all-over Europe. The one place to which all of us will be going sooner or later is the World's Fair in Brussels, Belgium.

Last night while listening to the world news, the shocking announcement of the pro-Nasser camp in Iraq came through. It ran like an electric current throughout the more than two thousand passengers. I understand that the country has been taken over by a revolutionary regime.

The borders have been sealed and all airports closed. Long before these lines are read in the United States, the full facts will be known; but even now it is apparent that we may have commitments in Iraq that will call for some decisive action by our government. My traveling companions, the Rev. John Wilson, and the Rev. Tom Whiting are scheduled to visit Syria, Jordan, and Israel. They will not proceed to these troubled spots unless the "all clear" signal is given.

I was in India two years ago when England and France undertook to put Mr. Nasser in his place, but our American government, for good reasons I am sure, refused to assist England and France, and as a result, their armies and navies were withdrawn. This left Nasser as the undisputed leader of the Arab world. In my humble opinion, he is a dangerous leader, a sort of Pharoah in shirt sleeves. Many of his ambitious actions remind me of Hitler's earliest days. I should not be attempting to interpret what happened in Iraq last night; my only reason for doing so is that in that part of the world a titanic struggle is going on between Russia and the Western Powers. No one would deny that the rich oil fields in that part of the world are at the bottom of the power struggle. To say that and nothing more would be an over-simplification of what is undoubtedly the most explosive situation in the whole world at this moment.

As I write these lines, I can look out through the porthole and upon the green hills of France. Yesterday was Bastille Day in Paris. Gen. Charles de Gaulle reviewed his troops in Paris during the morning and then flew to Toulon for a review of the French Navy in the afternoon. So far as I can tell, his assumption of power has brought tranquility to France.

My prayer is that it may prove to be a permanent blessing for this sorely tried nation. We must not become too impatient with France. In World War I, this nation lost a million, four hundred thousand men in battle. Her losses in World War II both in men and morale have never been added up. Should France break up completely, it would be a terrible blow to Western solidarity. Russia would most certainly move in and that would be equivalent to having a burglar inside your house.

Editor's Note: The 14 July Revolution, also known as the 1958 Iraqi coup d'état, took place on 14 July 1958 in Iraq, and resulted in the overthrow of the Hashemite monarchy in Iraq that had been established by King Faisal I in 1921 under the auspices of the British. King Faisal II, Prince 'Abd al-Hah and Prime Minister Nuri a-Said were executed by the military.

As a result of the overthrow of the Iraqi Hashemite dynasty, the *coup d'etat* established the Iraqi Republic. The coup ended the Hashemite Arab Federation between Iraq and Jordan that had been established just 6 months earlier. Abd al-Karim Qasim seized power as Prime Minister until 1963, when he was overthrown and killed in the Ramadan Revolution. (Wikipedia)

At Sea
July 15, 1958

Our ship is due in Southampton late tonight. We will remain onboard until early tomorrow morning and then take a train up to London. The thrill of coming to England never leaves me. While on this voyage I have read again Volume 3 of Sir Winston Churchill's *History of The English Speaking People.* His treatment of how we achieved our independence, and of our historic conquest of a continent could not be fairer if the writer had been an American.

Truth is, we are one people. When England is sick, America is sick, and vice versa. God has bound our two great nations together for the good of mankind; and what God has joined together, let no short-sighted politician put asunder.

This visit affords us only four days in London, and that I regret. John Wilson and Tom Whiting will be under the careful guidance of my dear friend, the Rev. Edward McLellan, who is so well-known and loved in America. Much of my time will be spent in the home of Frank Salisbury, a world-famous portrait painter. Some friends of mine have arranged for him to do a portrait of me, and I will be "sitting" for this painting. Mr. Salisbury is famous for his portraits of John and Charles Wesley. It is not clear to me how I got into such distinguished circles, but I accept it as another one of the many blessings showered upon me that I neither merit nor deserve. On Saturday, July 19, we will fly from London to Brussels where I am to preach in the Protestant Pavilion, on July 20th, at the World's Fair. In a subsequent article, I shall have something to say about my days in London and of my return to Belgium, where I have presided over their Annual Conference twelve times. For me, Belgium is a "second home" and I shall be thrilled to greet old friends once again. Meanwhile, to the friends in Georgia, who are for me the dearest people on earth. I send my affectionate greetings.

Brussels, Belgium
July 21, 1958

After four crowded days in England, we arrived in Belgium on Saturday, July 19. One can hardly imagine a weekend in which more international turbulence is packed. We were hardly off our ship before the news of President Eisenhower's decision had set tremendous forces at work. The English people were quite excited over what part of Great Britain would play in this new struggle and what the ultimate result would be. The conservative party, led by Mr. Harold MacMillan, immediately put England at America's side. The Labor Party, which is the opposition party, cautiously announced its refusal to approve, but there was none of the violent objection which was so evident two years ago during the Suez Crisis. It gives me personal satisfaction to see our two great nations acting in such complete unity.

Editor's Note: In response to the crisis in Lebanon, Eisenhower responded by authorizing *Operation Blue Bat* on July 15, 1958, in the first application of the Eisenhower Doctrine in which the US announced that it would intervene to protect regimes that is considered to be threatened by international Communism.

Operation Blue Bat
The 1958 Invasion of Lebanon, July 15, 1958

While I write these notes, it is difficult to get the picture in focus. Russia has asked for a conference, but what our answer will be, I do not know. I would guess that we will insist that the United Nations send in a military force large enough to prevent Russia's penetration of the entire Middle East. If someone does not challenge Russia's slow, but steady expansion, soon Russia and Egypt will stand sword in hand at the crossroads of the world and the rest of us will have to pay the toll. I felt we could have demonstrated more force when Nasser grabbed Suez, but that is now history. Now that our president has made this momentous decision to prevent a third world war, I feel all good Americans should stand by him. The Middle East is an explicit part of the world, and our national policy must deal resolutely and realistically with the challenge of Russia unless we want atheistic communism to dominate that part of the world.

Coming to Belgium is almost like coming home. Since 1934, I have had intimate contact with the life and work of our Methodists in Belgium. There is not a more virile and evangelical section of world Methodism than our little church here. It is ably administered by my good friend, Bishop Ferdinand Sigg, who resides in Switzerland, and my longtime comrade Dr. William G. Thonger, who is the General Superintendent. Georgia Methodism has long thought of Belgium as our "Parish Overseas." Many of our Georgia churches contribute to the work here. If my readers could see the churches and institutions which they have helped to build and sustain, there would be no need for further exhortation to keep up the good work. Only yesterday I inspected the Susanna Wesley Residence, a home for the aged. It is being used just now as a hotel to accommodate the innumerable visitors who crowd Brussels for the World's Fair. In October, more than fifty bright, comfortable rooms will be available to some elderly people, who otherwise would live out their last days in dark and dreary surroundings.

Sunday morning, at 9:30 a.m., found me in the pulpit of our Wesley Church where throughout the year a service in the English language is maintained. The sanctuary was filled with eager worshipers. I hardly realized there were so many here, where French is the language, who depend upon this service in the English tongue. Following the church service, I was tendered a reception in the social hall of the church, and there I met a large company of dear friends. Here were missionaries of our church, some I had commissioned either on their way to the Belgian Congo or just coming out after several years' service for furlough. It gave me special pleasure to meet two charming young ladies from Georgia, who are over here serving as hostesses in the United States Pavilion at the World's Fair. One was from Eatonton, and one was from Augusta. That they would find their way to church when a thousand other attractions bid for their time impressed me very much.

The chief purpose of my visit to Belgium this year was to preach in the Protestant Pavilion at the World's Fair. It is not easy to describe the Pavilion except to say that standing as it does among the extravagantly beautiful and expensive buildings erected by nearly fifty nations, it does not suffer by comparison. This Protestant Center was organized and built by the Federation of Belgian Protestant Churches. Friends in America have contributed generously to the cost. The exquisitely beautiful sanctuary, which seats several hundred, was filled yesterday afternoon. Dr. Thonger presided, the music was impressive, and I gave them the best sermon I could about the Savior of the world. This World's Fair depicts in a thousand ways the scientific achievements of our age, but these gadgets will destroy us unless we use them in the spirit of the Lord, Jesus Christ.

It would require the extravagant superlatives of a Hollywood movie writer to describe the magnificence of the World's Fair. When President Theodore Roosevelt was asked to describe the wonders of the Rocky Mountains, he replied, "To do so would bankrupt the English language." Nearly fifty nations have called upon their best architects and poured out vast funds to erect buildings that will in some measure depict the strength and ideals of the nations. All these buildings are extremely beautiful, and to describe them is not possible.

America and Russia have huge buildings facing each other. I inspected both of them today. Each the credit to the nation whose name it bears. To say that I was completely satisfied with the United States of America Building would not be true. It shows our scientific advance marvelously, but it seemed to leave out those intangibles but impressionable values such as love of freedom, the worship of Almighty God, and the opportunity America offers an everywhere-worthy man. I failed to see a Bible or church spire. This is not a criticism, but only a wish that somebody had said to the world, "We believe our secular civilization is made secure by our spiritual ideals."

In Belgium, you see no Protestant cathedrals. There are none. The buildings in which evangelical Christians meet for worship are small, in general, off the main street. Maybe you have heard people say that Protestantism does not suit the Belgian people, the evangelical faith being too steady and austere of the Belgian character. Such statements are untrue. They stand in contradiction with historical facts. The truth is that there was a time when the Lutheran and Calvinist Reformation flourished in this part of the world. This land is the home of the two first martyrs of the Reformation. On July 1, 1523, Henry Voes and John van der Esschen died at the stake on the Grand Place in Brussels.

You may also be interested to know that the wife of John Calvin was a native of this country, probably from Liege. Indeed, it must be said that quite early at the time of the Reformation, the people of this land responded in large numbers to the preaching of the pure gospel. But at that period of history, the Lowlands were Burgundian territory, ruled by Emperor Charles V and his son Philippe II. Both considered that they had been divinely commissioned to oppose fiercely the advance of the Reformation.

Despite the courageous struggle of the "Beggards", this opposition prevailed and when the Duke of Alva arrived in this country to stifle heresy, more than one hundred thousand refugees fled from the Southern Lowlands to seek liberty in more hospitable countries: England, France, and Germany. This number of refugees in itself is evident proof of how very wrong is the statement that Protestantism does not meet the aspirations of the people Belgian.

The truth is that in this country, at the time, there seemed to have been particularly favorable ground for the spreading of the gospel. After the period called the "Spanish Fury," that is to say the ruthless intervention in Zeeland and Brabant of the Spanish mercenaries, it seems as if the Southern lowlands were about to conquer their liberty.

From 1578 to 1584, there existed in Ghent a Calvinist Academy, and in many sections of the country, an important majority of the population had given their adhesion to the new religious teaching. Unhappily, the troops of the Duke of Palma conquered one city after the other for the King of Spain. The last stronghold, Antwerp, fell in 1585.

The consequence was new immigration in which at least a hundred thousand people (some say as many as three hundred thousand) left the country. Most of them fled north and settled in Holland. Dutch Protestants thus have a serious debt of gratitude for their Belgian brethren because it is not the least among them who chose to leave their country. These immigrants, it can truly be said, made a tremendous contribution to the prosperity of the Northern Republic (Dutch) and helped considerably to make possible its "Golden Century."

In the year of our Lord 1958, Belgium has two hundred ninety-seven Protestant congregations, mostly in the large towns and industrial regions. Six more or less important churches, next to a larger number of smaller groups, give their aid to the Belgian Bible Society, the Protestant Army and prison chaplains, the teachers of religious classes in schools, and occupied a dignified place in the Belgian community.

In a friendly atmosphere with the authorities, the liberty was obtained to let the voice of the gospel be heard in the official schools, in the Army, and on the national and regional radio and television broadcasting systems. In our age, the Protestant churches in Belgium have a task that they cannot possibly fulfill in their own power. They desire to live among the people, not in a secret society or strange sect, but as a group that understands its responsibility for the whole population as described in the gospel as "a city on a mountain" and a "light in the candlestick."

Who gave them the power to offer their lives and possessions during the Reformation? What generated the power of Protestantism in the 19th century to make a new start? It is the Living Lord, the King of the church, our only Master. On this day also, the only aim of the evangelical, Protestant churches in

285

Belgium is to proclaim Him. We believe that small Belgium has a great task of service to fulfill in the whole world. But we also believe that this can only be brought about if the Belgian people are prepared to listen to the voice of Jesus Christ and are prepared to live in the presence of God's Word given to all mankind.

Tomorrow, we go to France, and I hope to have something to report on the recovery of the great people under General De Gaulle.

Bishop Moore with Dr. Elmer T. Clark, Assistant Secretary to the General Board of Mission (1926-1938) and editor of *World Outlook* (1939-1952)

Frankfurt, Germany
July 30, 1958

It is difficult for me to remember that less than a month has passed since good-byes were said in the United States. We have hurriedly visited England, Belgium, France, and Switzerland, and are now gazing upon the incredible recovery of Western Germany.

Our days in Paris were too crowded. Because we were able to be there again before sailing for home, we limited ourselves to the nearby places of supreme historical importance such as the Arc de Triomphe, Napoleon's tomb, Notre Dame Cathedral, the Place de Concord, and others too numerous to mention. Everyone seemed to be waiting for General De Gaulle to work a miracle in the weary economic and political conditions, which have slowed France down to a very slow pace. One does not like to approve of dictatorships anywhere at any time, but France needs strong determined leadership, to give it the stability of purpose and a clear sense of direction. General De Gaulle seems to be moving in the right direction, both in France and in Algiers, which has long been a trouble spot.

England is showing incontrovertible evidence of slow, but certain recovery. It is difficult for us in America to realize the enormous cost both in men and money, which two world wars brought to England and France. The announcement by Queen Elizabeth II that her son, Prince Charles, who is a fine lad of about ten, had been declared to be Prince of Wales gave great satisfaction to all the people of the British Commonwealth. The *London Express*, in an editorial, stated the situation in the following concise manner:

"In a schoolroom in Berkshire, among the end-of-term litter of used exercise books and empty ink pots, a small boy bears the news made public that he is to be the Prince of Wales. His classmates sit around him as he listens. Until this moment he has been their friend. Now comes a sharp reminder that one day he is to be their King. There can be few in Britain who remain unmoved by the manner of the announcement. There can be none who do not with all their heart wish that God may bless the new Prince of Wales. May it be long before he reigns. And when he does, may it be asKing of a Britain that is proud and great and free."

Wherever we go in Europe the matter of paramount importance is the tensions in the Middle East. The hard realities of that political situation are slowly coming to the surface. The Eisenhower Doctrine, pronounced at the time of the Suez Canal, was misunderstood in many places when it was first announced. It looked at the time as if we had abandoned our longtime allies, England and France. But now that the tide of Arab nationalism is running so high that Mr. Nasser seeks to make himself another

Hitler, we are beginning to see that the British and American governments must have a common policy or that vital part of the world will fall into the hands of Russia and her allies. Be it far for me to intimate that I know what should be done, but I am convinced that Egypt and Russia are prepared to gamble heavily on bringing the heart of the world under the totalitarian control of their philosophy of life. What I hope for is the continuance of our present demonstration of Anglo-American unity and cooperation.

When we look at the forces at work in Lebanon, Jordan, Egypt, and Syria, not to mention larger nations, we see that the furnace of life has been heated hotter than we have known, and the most obtuse person cannot but realize the tremendous import of what is happening and what will happen in that part of the world. No one wants it, but we must deal with dictators from a position of strength.

The Reverends John Wilson and Tom Whiting, who are my traveling companions, have been compelled to change their plans to visit the Holy Land at this time. They will travel instead during the last two weeks of their stay in Italy and Austria and go again to France. I have found them to be the most delightful traveling companions, and it will be with a bit of sadness that I say goodbye to them tomorrow when they leave for Vienna and Rome, and I go to Freudenstadt, Germany, for a hard-working meeting of the World Methodist Council.

But let me get on with my travel experiences. One must make a leisurely visit, maybe several of them, to fully appreciate Switzerland and the fine people who compose this interesting little nation. Switzerland's history is conspicuously different from that of other European countries in which kings and rulers have succeeded each other from century to century. This is a federal state, built up of differing elements, all living at peace with each other. Here one finds differences in language, culture, and customs, but despite all these, a happy God-fearing, prosperous, liberty-loving people. Only yesterday I gazed upon a sacred spot – a single grass-covered meadow where in August of 1291, the Swiss Confederation was founded. During the several hundred years, which have intervened, the Swiss has won a name for courage and industry. If there is a country in all the world where the scenery is more wonderful, the people more courteous, and life more wholesome, I have yet to see it.

With my two traveling companions we travel by air from Paris to Geneva. Here is a great international city. Again, I looked upon the elaborate buildings erected under the inspired leadership of President Woodrow Wilson. While onboard the ship crossing the Atlantic, I had time to read a recent book written by President Herbert Hoover which recites the extraordinary leadership of President Wilson. If the world had only followed the inspired leadership of this Great American, the world might have stayed out of the jungle of World War II and all the world chaos which followed the signing of the armistice that November day in 1918. One has such thoughts while looking at the League of Nations buildings in Geneva.

Always in Geneva, I pay a visit to the Reformation Monument. We who are Protestants do not pause often enough to evaluate our heritage of religious freedom. Our debt to leaders such as John Calvin, John Knox, John Wesley, and others, is beyond calculation. We gaze into fairer skies and live in a world of freedom and opportunity because others suffered and died to secure for us these liberties.

The next five days will be spent at Freudenstadt up in the Black Forest section of Germany. There I will sit down with Methodist leaders from all over the world. Our one concern will be to keep our great Methodist Church creatively and redemptively in contact with men and human society. In a final newsletter, I hope to evaluate this significant conference. On August 7, I board the RMS *Queen Elizabeth* at Cherbourg, France, for the return voyage to those I love best and seek to serve.

Image from the Reformation Wall or Monument in Geneva

Editor's Note: Bishop Moore referred to *The Ordeal of Woodrow Wilson* by *Herbert Hoover,* McGraw-Hill, 1958

Freudenstadt, Germany
August 3, 1958

Tomorrow, I say goodbye again to Germany and the wonderful people called Methodists who live here. For nearly a week I have been their guest in this quaint city of Freudenstadt, and while I have been busy with an important church conference, there has been time to look at the magnificent recovery of the national economy which has taken place since the end of World War II.   My duties brought me here immediately after the downfall of Hitler and the victory of the Allied armies. Then the ghostly ruins of war were to be seen everywhere. The lovely city in which these notes are written – like nearly every other German city – was more than eighty percent destroyed.   Now evidence of war is hard to find, factories are humming, and one sees on every hand the signs of national recovery and prosperity. How they have found material and labor not to mention funds for such a gigantic rebuilding I do not know. Naturally, I am speaking of Western Germany. The old Germany has been divided, and the eastern portion is completely under the domination of the Russians.   I am told that the recovery and rebuilding in that zone is nothing like here in the Western Zone.

One of the most interesting phases of a visit to Western Germany is the absence of any reference whatever to Hitler. I visited Germany often during his disastrous reign and saw him strutting on the stage of history promising to build a Germany that would last forever.

Today this name is only a memory, and no one thinks even to mention it. Such has been the experience of many rulers throughout the ages who sought to rule without honoring and obeying Almighty God. As was said four thousand years ago, it is true still that God works in mysterious ways his wonders to perform.

In the last, fleeting hours of Adolf Hitler's tyranny – as Hitler was putting a bullet through his head – his deputy, Martin Bormann, fled and was last seen darting down a Berlin street already under fire from Russian tanks. He was never seen again; it was assumed that a shell blew him to bits. In any case, he was not mourned; on his hands was the blood of millions, including children.

But he, too, had children – ten of them – and the youngest, a skinny boy of fifteen, Adolf Bormann – named for Hitler – wandered onto a farm in Austria, where a Catholic family sheltered him, and where he worked for two years in return. At seventeen, he decided to study for the priesthood. At Innsbruck the other day, at twenty-eight, he was one of twenty-six deacons ordained in the Jesuit Holy Trinity Church. For nine years he has been preparing in the Order of the Sacred Heart of Jesus, dedicated to mission work around the world. Young Bormann, now a bearded monk, has asked to be sent to the Belgian Congo.

And so it comes to pass that the son of the man who preached the anti-Christ – who denied the very existence of human brotherhood, and he who put his fellowman to fire in torture and the gas ovens – will now go forth into the jungles where primitive men are struggling for the light and bread. He obeys the old command of the Master, "Go and teach all nations."

The World Methodist Council is composed of all the branches of Methodism. Our church is at work in sixty-five nations, and it has been estimated that not less than forty million souls proudly bear the name Methodist. The Council meets once every five years, but the Executive Committee meets annually. Last year we were in London, this year in Germany, and to my great delight, the Council will meet in September 1959 at Epworth-by-the-Sea. Already our lovely Georgia Methodists Assembly has gained the attention and won the admiration of Methodist people literally around the world. Georgia will hear much of this gathering as we approach the time for the meeting in our state.

We have had present for our sessions this week representatives from England, Australia, New Zealand, South Africa, Ceylon (Sri Lanka), Canada, Switzerland, Germany, Sweden, and the United States of America. To sit with these delegates has been a rare experience. For one thing, it has been a good lesson in geography not to mention the opportunity of hearing first-hand reports of world events. Our sessions have been held at Teuchwald, which is a beautiful mountain hotel, somewhat like Lake Junaluska. Here the Methodists operate a first-class hotel, not luxurious, but clean and comfortable. In addition, there is operated a Sanatorium for the sick and weary may find the best medical attention.

I rose early this morning and went by auto to Stuttgart where I was met by Pastor Eissek of the Methodist Church at Waiblingen. At 9:30 a.m., his lovely church, which seats about four hundred or five hundred, was filled with worshipers. The pastor served as my interpreter, and I did my best to preach the everlasting gospel. Dr. Dow Kirkpatrick, who has been with us for the Council Meeting went with me to this service, and after the sermon, he and I assisted the pastor in the Service of Holy Communion. It was a blessed time of Christian fellowship and served to remind me that the Methodist people are one people.

Tonight, I will fly from here to Paris, France, and on Thursday go onboard the good ship RMS *Queen Elizabeth* for the voyage homeward. Bishop and Mrs. Fred P. Corson of Philadelphia will be my traveling companions. We are due in New York, on August 12, and I plan to hurry home and get under a pretty heavy workload for the balance of August.

These "travel letters" have been written, "on the wing." They have not been intended as serious reports of people or things but simply jotting down day-by-day experiences and impressions. On the first trip one makes to Europe, he feels qualified upon returning home to write a book. A little knowledge of people and their culture and institutions is apt to make one dogmatic. However, the more one learns about real-life understands the day-by-day pressures under which another person lives loses all of his dogma, and no longer seeks to play the role of the prophet.

The most evident thing everywhere is that life is strenuous and uncertain for most people, the only safety and satisfaction to be found either by men or nations is in a humbled reliance upon the goodness and mercy of God. Unless our help comes from Him, it will not come at all.

To generous people in Georgia who have honored me far beyond my worthiness, I send my genuine affection. To serve you is not drudgery but a dear delight.

Editor's Note: This chapter was transcribed from Bishop Moore's original manuscripts held by the Arthur J. Moore Methodist Museum, St. Simons Island, Georgia.

The Protestant Pavilion at the Belgium World's Fair.

Bishop Moore preached at the Pavilion July 1958

CHAPTER SEVENTEEN

Another Mission Trip to Asia

February and March 1959

After weeks of hurried preparation, I boarded a TWA plane in Atlanta at noon on February 25. We enjoyed a nice, uneventful trip across this vast continent we call America. Although the schedule called for only two stops, the flight required almost eleven hours. Upon arrival in San Francisco, I came immediately to the Californian Hotel.

This is a modern sixteen-story hotel that is owned and operated by the Methodist Church. It is as good a hotel as I know, and one is assured of elegant accommodations. After a few hours of sleep, I arose early to have breakfast with the Rev. Pierce Hayes who served many years as one of our finest missionaries on the mainland of China. He was appointed some time ago by the late Bishop Ralph A. Ward to travel throughout the United States soliciting funds for the erection of some much-needed churches and schools in Taiwan (Formosa). Now that Bishop Ward has gone, the work being done by Mr. Hayes is of even greater importance. I have requested him to continue in the same capacity and I sincerely hope some of those who read these lines will respond to his appeal.

At 10:00 a.m. this morning, I will go onboard Pan-American Flight No. 5 for the long flight across the Pacific Ocean. We are due in Honolulu at 4 p.m. this afternoon. There we will have four hours to stretch our legs and get ready to settle down for an all-night flight from Honolulu to Tokyo.

We are scheduled to refuel the plane at 3:45 a.m. tomorrow at Wake Island. This tiny island is located in this vast ocean of water and is always a good thing to behold. We will remain at Wake Island for only one hour and then fly on to Tokyo, Japan, where we are due to arrive at 10 a.m. Incidentally, we will cross the International Date Line somewhere between Honolulu and Japan.

It will be Wednesday night when we leave Honolulu and Friday morning when the sun comes up. So Thursday, February 26th, will go out of my life and I will be minus a whole day until my return flight when we will observe the same day twice. This is only one of many varied experiences one encounters when he goes wandering about the wide world.

Practically all of March I will be busy in Hong Kong and Taiwan trying to give supervision to our Methodist work there. The days and much of the nights will be taken up in conferences, meetings with pastors, boards of trustees, and government officials to ascertain the problems and possibilities before us and how to cope with them.

All of China is very much in the thought of the world at the present moment. It is not possible to know much about what is taking place on the mainland. The Iron Curtain has practically shut us off from our people who remain there. However, hundreds of thousands of Christians have succeeded in getting away from the clutches of atheistic communism and are now living in Taiwan and Hong Kong. They have built schools, and churches and re-established their Christian institutions. They need and must have our help.

All of China is passing through one of the most turbulent periods of its long history. Christianity and communism are locked in a struggle for survival. Generalissimo and Madame Chiang Kai-shek are loyal and faithful Methodists and the church in Taiwan has a marvelous opportunity. If we are all faithful, the Christian church may witness a great triumph out there. There are unparallel difficulties, but there are also staggering opportunities.

No ebb and flow of the tides of history can ever cancel or modify the Great Commission Christ gave to His church. The gospel is not for an age but for the ages. It is not always a quiet world to which we are sent, but we can always be certain that He goes with us. We are not to brood over the problems and difficulties. Instead, we are to discover and appropriate that eternal and inexhaustible resource that is ours because we are in the King's business.

The belief that my people in Georgia are upholding me with their prayers will give me strength and courage. I hope to write more at a later time.

Wesleyan Christian Advocate, March 5, 1959.

Hong Kong, China
February 28, 1959

This is Saturday morning in Hong Kong. Since boarding a plane in Atlanta Tuesday afternoon, I have flown more than eleven thousand miles, visited briefly Hawaii and Japan, skipped the entire day of Thursday (on account of crossing the International Date Line), and am now in far-away Hong Kong hard at work.

The journey has been almost without incident. Modern planes are comfortable and fast and can generally avoid the roughest weather; never-the-less there is some strain in spending almost three days high in the air, crowded into one place, listening to the hum of mighty motors, and "watching the world go by." I have not yet learned how to get much sleep while in the air and the result was a weary man when our plane landed in a fog early this morning.

My weariness soon gave way to exhilaration when I observed a large company of friends, Chinese and missionaries, who had come to bid me welcome. One could hardly count any task as unpleasant where he is to labor with such congenial fellow workers. In this company of friendly colleagues were many with whom I had lived and labored while serving as bishop in Shanghai from 1934 to 1940. Since then, the world has passed through a catastrophic convulsion and China has been at the very center of the catastrophe. Here are friends who have seen the China they loved fall into the hands of plunderers. The ideals and spiritual values by which they and their ancestors had lived for centuries have been torn up by the roots. To breathe the air of freedom and live where one has dignity and opportunity, they have fled, most of them penniless, into this haven of safety. By their heroic sacrifice, they have re-established their homes, built humble churches, and are taking their part in building a safe, friendly, free world.

One of the first persons to greet me was an American-trained pastor, who was educated in the United States. He has not seen his wife for nine years and recently, at last, she was able to get across the border and join her husband. Their children are still in Communist China, and we all pray for the day when this fine family can be reunited.

Thus, one gets a glimpse of what has and is happening to millions of people who live on the mainland of China. If all the heartbreak and tragedy represented by those who have suffered so much could be tabulated, it would shock us into some determined action. Alas, there is little we can do except to help them with the education of their children and help them provide places of worship. This the Methodist Church is doing in a remarkably fashion.

It is now Monday, March 2nd. I had hoped to write these sketchy lines and rush them back to friends at home. My plans and work have been disrupted by many tokens of kindness shown to me by these wonderful people. Take yesterday (Sunday) as an example. I began the day by preaching in our Ward Memorial Church, which has been designated as a memorial to the late Bishop Ralph Ward. The services are being held temporarily in the Y.M.C.A. I suppose there were three hundred present. The music rendered by the choir was excellent. There were more men than women present and practically every person there had left home and business to escape the tyranny of communism. I was impressed by two fine-looking young Methodist students from far-away Sarawak. Here in a big, wicked city they had found a Christian atmosphere and many friends to help them. Following the sermon which had to be given through an interpreter, we observed the Sacrament of the Lord's Supper. One of the tasks to which I must address myself is to find some friends with which to help these loyal people build a house of worship. They are giving generously out of their poverty. In fact, at the service yesterday they received two offerings. One for operating expenses and one for the building fund. I was told this was a regular procedure.

From four to six yesterday afternoon, I was warmly welcomed at a large union service in another church. We had tea and spring rolls, and then a long service of speeches. My heart was again comforted by the sight of a large congregation, many of whom I had known and labored with while I was Bishop for the Church South in Shanghai. Then last night I went to a typical Chinese Feast with a fine group of leaders. Fitted in between all these engagements were several personal interviews. Thus, you can see how a letter which was started on Saturday is being finished Monday night.

Today at noon, I was honored to be the guest at lunch of His Excellency, the Governor, Sir Robert Brown Black and Lady Black at Government House. There was typical British formality but a warm cheerful atmosphere which I greatly enjoyed. Hong Kong is a British Crown Colony, and one moves faster and better when acquainted with high Government Officials.

Speaking of Hong Kong, the following information concerning the city may be of interest. The British Crown Colony of Hong Kong is situated off the southeastern coast of the Kwangtung Province of China, east of the Pearl River estuary, about 41 miles east of the Portuguese Colony of Macau. The total area is about three hundred ninety-one square miles and includes: (1) Hong Kong Island (thirty-two square miles) and harbor were ceded to the British Crown in 1841, on which the capital city of Victoria is located. (2) the Kowloon Peninsula on the mainland up to Boundary Street (three and a quarter square miles) and Stonecutters Island (a quarter sq. mi.) which lies in the harbor, became part of the Crown Colony under the Peking Convention in 1860. (3) The New Territories as well as 198 adjacent islands in the vicinity of Hong Kong Island were leased from China on July 1, 1898, for ninety-nine years.

Hong Kong Island is irregular in shape, rocky, and deeply indented by sea and narrow valleys. It is eleven miles long from east to west and varies in width from two to five miles. The highest point is Victoria Peak which is one thousand eight hundred nine feet high. The main business center, which has helped to make the Colony modern and prosperous, clusters around the foot of the Peak. Between the Island and the mainland lies the natural harbor of Victoria. Almost land-locked, it covers an area of seventeen square miles and is from one to three miles wide. Embraced by mountains on all sides, it is said to be one of the most beautiful and busiest harbors in the world and is capable of taking ships drawing up to thirty-six feet.

The ceded territory of the Kowloon Peninsula consists mostly of flat land and low hills. However, most of the hills have already been levelled and the rock and soil removed from the hills were used to extend the land by reclamation from the sea.

Hong Kong is one of the most densely populated areas in the world. The total civilian population is estimated to be two million seven hundred thousand (nearly seven thousand to the square mile). Ninety-nine percent of whom are Chinese. Over two million of the inhabitants are living in the thirty-six square miles of the Urban area (Hong Kong Island and Kowloon), the remaining are living in the New Territories, including the floating population (boat dwellers) and the inhabitants of the one hundred ninety-eight islands in the vicinity of Hong Kong.

Hong Kong lies just within the tropics, but it enjoys four different seasons which is unusual in the tropical region. A mild, dry, sunny winter lasts from November to February. In the early spring, humidity starts to rise, and the weather is occasionally overcast. Mist and fog are usually confined to March and April, light rains are frequent, and the weather is damp. Summer is the rainy season which lasts from May to September. Eighty percent of the annual rainfall of 7.05 feet occurs during the summer.

In subsequent letters, which will be written if time can be found, I shall attempt to describe what our Church is attempting to do in this fabulous city where history is certainly being made.

The Florida Methodist, March 15, 1959, p. 12

Hong Kong, China
March 6, 1959

This city of three million population is excited over the arrival of His Royal Highness, the Duke of Edinburgh. Everywhere there are signs of the elaborate preparations being made for his coming. His pleasing personality and cordial manner are well known and from the highest to the poorest, he will be given the hospitality of the city.

But one does not need to wait for the arrival of royalty to discover unforgettable personalities. There is something exciting associated with nearly everyone over here if the story can be procured. As I have stated in another article, much of Hong Kong's population is composed of those who have fled from the mainland of China to live with dignity and freedom.

Some were able to escape with family and fortune intact, but the vast majority here represent those who left loved ones behind and come out with only the clothing upon their bodies. Last night at dinner I sat with the children and grandchildren of one of Methodism's former great leaders in China.

He served the church there with great distinction and died recently as a result of the heavy load he was forced to carry. Some of his children are still in China; some are in America, and some are here. One of the devastating by-products of this tragic revolution in China is what happens to families – to little children.

It is something less than pleasant to listen to people tell of how long it required them to get a permit to leave, or worse still, their frightful experiences as they secretly slipped across dangerous borders. In Hong Kong, a drama is unfolding of major proportions with all the lights and shadows of danger and death mixed with unforgettable courage.

Here one learns of the fresh assault being made just now against the organized church on the mainland. Until now the churches that remained open have been under police surveillance, but now many more of them are being closed. Reports, which I believe to be authentic, show that in Shanghai where there were two hundred churches there are now only twelve. In Peking, eighty-six have been reduced to four, while in Canton only eight are left out of the forty-eight. The same old story of atheistic communism either using or destroying the Christian church is being re-enacted.

Yesterday I gave much of my time to a close-up study of several of our Methodist institutions. Early in the morning, I addressed the students at the Methodist College. Seldom have I seen better buildings or spoken to a more responsive student body. This is an institution in which Methodism both from Great Britain and America cooperates in financial support and missionary personnel.

Following this occasion, I spent some time inspecting our roof-top churches and schools. The city of Hong Kong has constructed many low-rent apartments and into these have been crowded thousands of homeless refugees. In one small room, an entire family must live. Some small rooms have as many as seven people in them.

Into these congested areas, our church had come with two magnificent services. Upon the flat roof of one of these buildings, we are at present operating a church, a school, and a milk station. Fortunately, the climate is mild, and we can carry on our activities in the open air. We have provided a chapel and some classrooms on the roof of the building. While I was there yesterday, children were being given milk for their bodies, knowledge for their minds, and the gospel for their souls.

I have not seen a more Christ-like ministry anywhere. Tomorrow morning, I am to visit and preach at Chung-Chi College. This is a Grade A college operated by several of our protestant churches. The plant which would compare favorably with our best church schools in America is entirely new. No words of mine could overstate the educational service being rendered by this lovely institution.

Two new church-building enterprises are of the utmost importance, and I wish to lay them heavily upon the hearts of our people in the United States. They are Ward Memorial Church and North Point Church. In each congregation, there are some three to four hundred devout and generous members. But in the very nature of things, they are not prepared financially to buy land and construct buildings. These two churches, like all of our other Methodist institutions here, were born in the faith and vision of Bishop Ralph A. Ward. He gave his life for them. Now that he has passed to his eternal reward, we who remain must preserve and promote that for which he lived and died. I can say in utter sincerity that I do not know any place in the wide world where one could place his or her tithe and see it yield larger demands in Christian character.

In the above paragraph, I have indicated what is my greatest concern. It will not be physically easy for me to give episcopal supervision to the work of our church in Hong Kong and Taiwan.

I have more than one man can carry. But by putting my body under added pressure I can do what is required in that field. My greatest concern is where I can find funds with which to support these wonderful projects. Bishop Ward had nearly a half-century of service behind him and had built up a group of loyal supporters. By some means, this financial support must be maintained, or the work will be endangered.

It is my purpose to appeal to American friends to stand by the work both here and in Taiwan (Formosa). I will go there next week and be confronted as I am here with staggering opportunities before me and inadequate resources in my hands.

I have been in Hong Kong for a week and into these hurrying days I have packed about as much work as any single week my life ever knew. In all the varying demands of this assignment, I am sustained by the knowledge that what we call "missionary work" is nothing less than the attempt to carry out the dearest wish of the heart of Christ. His will must be our delight.

The Florida Methodist, April 1, 1959, p. 2

Editor's Note:
On several occasions Bishop Moore mentioned attending a Chinese Feast. It is said that there were "Thirty-Two Delicacies," in the feast, referring to exotic ingredients used for the banquet.

Taipei, Taiwan
March 9, 1959

After nine crowded days in Hong Kong, I boarded a turbo-jet plane early Saturday morning for Taiwan, or Formosa as it is known in America. When I arrived in Hong Kong, I was already weary due to strenuous days at home before leaving on this mission. The nearly three days of continuous flying added to my weariness. My schedule while in Hong Kong was enough to test the endurance of any man. However, I was able to meet all my engagements which included not less than a dozen "Chinese Feasts"; and when I went on board to start my flight to this interesting nation, I was still able to go, sustained by the knowledge that I was on the King's business.

The flight over required about three hours and it was on one of the fine aircraft of the Hong Kong Airways. We left early; were served a nice breakfast; spent the time looking down on the broad ocean waters, and by 11:00 a.m. we were coming in for a landing in this Capitol City. I must confess that my emotions were stirred. Here on this island are ten million people living under the government of Generalissimo Chiang Kai-shek. From 1934 to the time of Pearl Harbor, I was the Bishop of the Methodist Episcopal Church, South, with headquarters in Shanghai.

During my first three years in China, there was unmistakable evidence of unity and progress under the leadership of this gifted leader. There was something like the spirit of a spring morning in the air.

One heard on every hand something about the New Life Movement. A nation was being remade. Then came the invasion of China by the Japanese Army and confusion, struggle and destruction became the order of the day. That struggle widened until Pearl Harbor stabbed America awake and we were caught up in World War II.

I have never been able to arrive at any satisfactory explanation of what happened on the mainland of China at the close of nearly ten years of war. I have a strong suspicion that we in the United States misread the significance of the forces which were out to break the rule of General Chiang Kai-shek and to deliver China into what was then called on an "agrarian reform" movement. I have no desire to assess blame at this late date, but surely if we had loyally supported the Generalissimo, who for nine years had successfully withstood the aggression of Japan, we could have prevented China from falling under the domination of a ruthless, communistic regime. What has followed is fairly well known. We exchanged the mainland of China with a democratic government that was friendly to democracy and Christianity and saw one take over which is opposed to our free way of life.

Generalissimo Chiang transferred his government to the island of Taiwan (Formosa) and was followed by some two million fellow Chinese who were determined to keep China free and democratic. What they have accomplished in economic improvement, progressive education, democratic ideals, and religious liberty is not fully known to the rest of the world and must yet be told.

Well, I am about to write an article on Free China, while what I started to say was that my emotions were deeply stirred as the plane came in for its landing. Gathered on the field were many Methodists – both missionaries and Chinese, together with these were some highly placed officials of government who had come to extend an "official welcome."

I was soon through customs and on my way to the Government Guest House, where for the next ten days I am to be the guest of the nation. My quarters are most comfortable, and I am grateful for such bountiful hospitality.

Yesterday was the Sabbath and my engagements called for sermons at 8:30 a.m., 11:00 a.m., and 7:30 p.m. The first was in English to a congregation of Americans and Chinese and several other nationalities. There was approximately one hundred present and I have not been to a more lovely and worshipful service. At 11:00 a.m., I preached in our main Chinese Church. This happened to be the sixth anniversary of Methodism beginning in Taiwan and the organization of this church. There are today approximately seven hundred members.

They all seemed to be present yesterday morning when I preached. The lovely building, which houses both the Chinese and English-speaking congregations was erected with the help of the churches of the Philadelphia Area under the direction of Bishop Fred Corson. The Chinese people, however, gave most sacrificially. Adjoining the church building is the Water of Life Clinic.

It was started by the late Dr. Edward C. Perkins who for more than forty years served as a medical missionary on the mainland. He has since died, but the evidence of his wonderful service as a Christian doctor abides.

Upon my arrival in Taipei, I was greeted by General J. L. Huang, a distinguished Christian leader, and a highly placed government official. He had kindly arranged a tour of the island with some American businessmen. Because it was a most gracious gesture on the part of the government and in addition allowed me to see the entire country and visit some of the chief cities, I hastily rearranged my schedule to make this trip. By going with General Huang and his party, I will also have a chance to visit both Taichung and Tainan where we have churches and missionaries.

It is now Tuesday, and I am back in Capitol City. Today I am to get my first sight of Soochow University which we helped to build on the mainland. Dr. Y. C. Yang, the beloved President in other years, was well known in American circles. He has now passed from the tyranny of the present rulers of the mainland and is at home with God. The old university buildings are being used by the Communists.

In Taiwan, there are many Soochow graduates, and they are determined to rebuild this grand old school. A splendid site of sixty acres near the limits of this Capitol city has been secured and two new buildings have been erected.

Day and night classes are conducted also in a large building near the centre of the city. I shall have more to say about Soochow University in a later letter. While on the southern part of the island, I spent some time with the Rev. and Mrs. Carlisle Phillips and their three fine children. They are among our finest missionaries. Their home church is our Druid Hills Church in Atlanta. Highly trained, deeply devoted, and sacrificially dedicated to Christ and His Church, they are rendering a magnificent service in Taiwan, which is a city of more than three hundred thousand.

Along with their officials, they entertained me with a lovely "Chinese Feast." While together I inspected the splendid location which they have acquired for a church site. One of my resolutions while with them was to do all I could to persuade some group in America to see to it that these sacrificial missionaries and Chinese people have a place of worship. They are now in a rented hall. The Chinese congregation has given and will continue to give sacrificially. I have reason to know that Dr. Rembert Sisson and the fine people at Druid Hills Church are interested in this worthy project, and I shall present it to them when I get home.

This letter is far too long and the editor of the *Wesleyan Christian Advocate* as well as the editor of *The Florida Methodist* may be forced to edit it a bit. When one stands face to face with a brave people, living in exile, trying to rebuild their institutions, and seeking to preserve their glorious culture, he is simply overwhelmed by the staggering need. Free China needs and deserves our understanding and our help not only in economic and military assistance but religiously as well. Let us keep them in our thoughts and gifts. Best regards to all the dear folks in Georgia and Florida.

The Florida Methodist, June 1, 1959, p. 2

Taipei, Taiwan
March 12, 1959

Because Nationalist China occupies such a commanding place in the thought of the day, and especially in the United States of America, I have thought it might prove of some value if I would put on paper some factual information concerning Taiwan or The Republic of China as it is now known.

The word "Taiwan" means "island beautiful." Its history is known as far back as the seventh century. Although it is better known as Formosa, the Chinese call it Taiwan. I have been told that the word is also sometimes used to describe a "Terraced Bay," but more say the word means beautiful island.

According to the latest census, the population approaches ten million souls and is increasing at a rapid rate. The morning paper announced that there were thirty-one thousand babies born last year in this city alone. More than two million liberty-loving Chinese followed General Chiang Kai-shek to this island when the Communists took power on the mainland.

Just across a narrow body of water, the Soviets are attempting to remake Old China after the hard pattern of atheistic communism. Here in Taiwan, there is austerity and struggle but freedom, democracy, and an atmosphere friendly to Christian ideals. But let us look at some of its histories.

The end of World War II opened up a new page in the history of Taiwan. Per the Cairo Declaration, the island was restored to Nationalist China following the surrender of Japan in 1945. Thus ended fifty-one years of colonial rule under the Japanese, who seized the island from China after the First Sino-Japanese War of 1894-1895.

Despite a century of Japanese occupation, the native Taiwanese retained most of the Chinese customs and traditions. The overwhelming majority of the local people are of Chinese extraction, linked with the mainland Chinese by blood, language, and family ties. Their forebears mostly came from the seaboard mainland provinces.

The Taiwan Chinese have always kept their lunar calendar as a symbol of the Chinese civilization. They worship their Chinese gods largely from the Buddhist and Taoist cults. But in recent years, Christianity is becoming more and more popular on the island. Even high up in the mountains are found Christian establishments, bringing the gospel not only to the civilized people but to the aborigines, too.

Since the day the Chinese flag was raised on top of the governor's office, the Nationalists have been laying a firm foundation upon which to build. In 1950, a year after President Chiang Kai-shek retreated to the island base, the Nationalist government granted self-rule to the local people. Except for the governor, all other local administrators in Taiwan are elected by popular vote. Voting rates have been unusually high, averaging around seventy-five percent and in some areas approaching ninety percent.

Following the restoration of Taiwan to China, the Nationalists quickly started an island-wide program to teach the native Mandarin, the standard spoken language of China. In every nook and cranny on the island, new schools and classrooms have mushroomed. One out of every three dollars spent by the local government goes to supporting the island's universal education program. Over one-seventh of the province's population, or upwards of ninety percent of all school-age children, are now taking elementary courses in Chinese public schools. Illiteracy has dropped to below ten percent, an all-time low among Chinese provinces.

Shortly after the Chinese took over the island in 1945, there had been some dislocation in the island's economy. Lack of understanding between farmers and landlords slowed down farm crops while the population expanded steadily. The local industries, developed under the Japanese, were virtually paralyzed because of wartime bombings. Runaway inflation on the mainland, sapping the Nationalist treasury, also cuts deeply into the economy of Taiwan.

The Nationalist government by grim determination has gradually restored economic stability and improved the living standard of the islanders. A mild agrarian land program has greatly helped in rural areas. The Nationalists have pushed a three-phase program to entitle every farmer to own the land he tills on easy terms. Conservatively estimated, a farmer on the island of Taiwan is now earning about fifty percent more than what he did before the rural reform.

Strides made in defense by the Nationalists have been impressive. The Nationalist army remnants, pulled out by President Chiang after the fall of mainland China into Communist hands in 1949, have in the last eight years been whipped into one of the best fighting units in the Far East.

Modern American weapons shipped to Taiwan by the United States have changed the backward outlook of the Nationalist forces. President Chiang's troops, formerly equipped largely with World War II arms, now have heavy tanks, long-range guns, and the latest anti-aircraft guns. Rigid training has kept the troops alert and combat-ready all the time.

The United States, by a mutual defense pact signed with the Nationalists in December 1954, is committed to helping defend Taiwan against Communist attacks. Washington has set up on the island the United States Taiwan Defense Command, which is authorized to direct American military operations in this region shoulder-to-shoulder with the Nationalists.

At the same time, units of the United States Seventh Fleet are constantly patrolling the Taiwan Straits against possible Communist invasion. The latest demonstration of American determination to keep the Nationalist defenders armed with new weapons is the stationing on Taiwan of a ground-guided missile unit, capable of firing both conventional and atomic warheads. Relations between American servicemen and civilians and the ten million Chinese population on this island have been generally warm and friendly.

Several thousand American officers and men of the United States Military Army, appear to have won the confidence of the Chinese soldiery. The unfortunate May 24 riots of 1957 in Taipei ruffled for a brief time the otherwise cordial relations between the Americans and Chinese peoples, but all seems harmonious at present.

The Nationalist government and the general public here were quick in denouncing such vandalism and deploring such acts as a national dishonor to China. A friendly atmosphere between the Chinese and Americans quickly returned after this shocking outburst of emotions in Taipei.

The important role that women in Free China can play to maintain the traditional Chinese family system which the Communists on the mainland are making every effort to overthrow was pointed out by several Taipei newspapers in special messages commemorating Woman's Day. "Happy Home Movement" now being sponsored by Free China's womanhood has particular significance at present as a counter to the Communists' communization program aimed at uprooting the family.

Among the various factors that contribute to the formation of a happy home in Free China are a husband and wife who work together for the support of the family and the other looking after affairs of the household.

The Communists are pursuing an inefficient system of production by slave labor and are using women workers to supplement the labor force that Communist society provides, and to mobilize this female workforce, they have gone to the length of seeking to destroy the family system. The people on the mainland, now forced to separate from their wives and children, know better the value of family as the foundation of human happiness.

It is reported in Taiwan that the brilliant Chinese culture, established on the principle of morality, has vanished on the mainland under the rule of the Communists. The Communists seek to destroy human nature, undermine family relations, make husbands and wives, brothers and sisters suspect each other, and create hatred between parents and children. They drive apart from the members of every family. Women on the mainland are seeing the suffering which is stretched to the limits of human misery. Lately, the Communists' communization program has gone a step further by turning every person in the family into an independent being. With parents separated from their children and husbands from their wives, all homes have well-nigh vanished.

This is only a fraction of the history of these exiles, many of whom are separated from home and members of their families. It is more than a struggle to hold an island, it is a brave attempt to defend and preserve the Chinese culture, and millions of them think no price is too great to pay if only they and their children can be free.

The Florida Methodist, April 15, 1959, p. 2

Editor's Note:
A Chinese mob, protesting the acquittal of an American soldier who killed a Chinese civilian, sacked the American Embassy and the United States Information Service buildings and injured several American citizens.

Bishop Moore with an unidentified group of ministers in Asia.

Taipei, Taiwan
March 14, 1959

Nearly three weeks have passed since I arrived in Hong Kong. In three more days, I board an airplane here in Taipei for the long but happy flight homeward. These have been exciting but happy days for me. Hour after hour has been spent listening to missionaries and national leaders explain the strategic importance of this part of the world.

I have visited every church and institution of learning with which Methodism has any connection on this island. It has seemed wise and helpful to have conversations with a large number of persons who occupy high places of leadership. All this seemed necessary to bring this whole picture into focus so that I might have an intelligent understanding of my duties in planning the Christian strategy here at these "Crossroads" of the world.

From time to time – always in great haste – I have tried to put down on paper some of my experiences, observations, and convictions. These articles have been written in great haste and flung back to friends in America. There have been five or six of them, and I have not yet seen in print the first one, which was written as I was about to leave. I can only hope my story has been clear and that my telling it has enabled my readers to better understand this part of the world. These letters have sought to be nothing more than the "human side" of my work during these weeks of strenuous toil.

In this concluding article, I have decided to say a few words about some of the unforgettable people I have met and some of the moving experiences through which I have passed.

First, my sincere tribute must go quickly to the late Bishop Ralph Ward and his devoted wife, Kathryn. Ralph Ward spent nearly all his life on the mainland of China, first as a missionary and later as a bishop. He was imprisoned in Shanghai for a long period, and we now feel never recovered physically from that cruel treatment. When released he did not seek the retirement to which he was entitled but followed "his" people to Hong Kong and Taiwan where he labored to preserve and expand the church. As the Chinese would say, "He carried it on his body."

What Methodism has today in this section of the world is the direct result of the faith and fidelity of Ralph Ward and his equally devoted wife Kathryn. It is not surprising that one of our rapidly growing churches in Hong Kong is to bear his name and the chapel at Soochow University here in Taipei is to be known as the Ward Memorial Chapel.

No one can overstate the power of a dedicated ministry such as these fine servants of Christ have rendered. I am honored to be in such a succession.

Second, I must record my sincere thanks for the hospitality I have received. In Taipei, I have been a guest of the government. A comfortable room with every attention needed has been mine. In Hong Kong, I was a dinner guest of His Excellency Governor, Sir Robert Brown Black and Lady Ann Black. In Taipei, our United States Ambassador Drumwright and his charming wife graciously received me at the Embassy. All these acts of hospitality were not extended to me as a person but to the church I represent. Methodism has a good reputation out there.

I cannot refer to those who serve in high places and not express with equal gratitude the reception I have received at the hands of our Methodist people.

They have heard me gladly and cheered me with the warmth of their hearts and homes. Years ago, I put the missionaries on a high pedestal, and these out here justify the reverence I hold for missionaries everywhere. We need desperately some additional missionaries.

Third, one day this week I was invited to preach to the "Prayer Group" which was organized and directed by Madame Chiang Kai-shek. Madame Chiang has not returned from her recent trip to New York, but her friends gave me a warm welcome. Many of the most prominent Christian women of Taiwan were there.

The atmosphere was simple, friendly, and spiritual. After I had preached, they asked for special subjects of prayer. These were all listed on a blackboard, and then we spent a long season in earnest prayer. This was about the most genuine "Prayer Meeting" which I have shared in a long while. Things are being shaped by the believing faith of these devout women.

Fourth, while here I have flown over this entire island and from the window of an airplane looked down upon the beautiful mountains, the bustling cities, and the endless fields of growing rice. Millions of acres have been irrigated, and I understand that since the present government took over the yield of rice has increased by thirty percent. This has vast significance for the life and prosperity of the ten million people who reside here. We hear about social and economic gains that the Communists claim to have brought about on the mainland. I wish equal publicity could be given to what Chiang Kai-shek's government is doing on this island.

While everyone here lives for the day when the mainland will be liberated from the Communists, they are not negligent in making this island a more prosperous place of residence. The general rule of life here is austerity, but there is much evidence of good government and an increasing supply of the necessities of life.

Fifth, in both these fields – Hong Kong and Taiwan – we face as a church unbelievable opportunity and at the same time struggle with inadequate equipment. The great need is for additional missionaries and more well-trained Chinese pastors. So much needs to be done, so many doors of creative service stand wide open, and yet we are attempting to meet them with very little money and a handful of overworked missionaries. Surely there must be some way to arouse our big, comfortable Methodism in America to rush up some reinforcements. I have gladly accepted these additional responsibilities and will give to them all I have, but Soochow University can never be built, the memorials to Ralph Ward will languish; Chinese people will die without hearing the gospel, and a brave government that also needs and will welcome spiritual reinforcement will be disappointed unless the church in America hastens to give a few of her sons and daughters and some of her wealth to preach and teach the gospel. If we really mean it when we sing "Publish Glad Tidings," then we ought to know that a wide-open door and a people are waiting to hear these glad tidings.

It is difficult to live amid this scene of a military operation and not become deeply concerned about the questions which engage the attention of everyone. This nation is girding itself against what it considers to be a deadly enemy dedicated to its destruction. Not only does the dream of eventually recovering their homeland sustain these people but they also realize that across a narrow strip of water is an implacable enemy who might at any time seek to destroy them. In the light of these facts, one cannot but approve of their fierce determination to defend and preserve themselves and ultimately deliver their homeland from the threatening Communist regime.

It should always be remembered that the United States of America has a real stake in affairs in this part of the world. It is unthinkable that we should be neutral in the presence of such a grim struggle. There are only three choices before us as far as I can see:

A. Isolationism - To stay at home and live our own luxurious life. That is hardly a choice because we either meet and defeat this enemy outside our shores or watch it slowly move nearer until at last, it is upon us.

B. Give our understanding and assistance to Generalissimo Chiang Kai-shek and his Anti-Communist Republic of China, for here is a nation devoted to democracy and one which is our proven friend, or

C. Make some agreement with the International Communist Regime which has ruthlessly invaded and subdued the mainland of China. To me, the latter would seem a gross betrayal of the "Freeway of life" everywhere in the world.

Mr. Walter S. Robertson, Assistant Secretary of State for the U.S.A., made a pronouncement in Ottawa, Canada, on March 14 which in my humble opinion states clearly what is and should be our firm position. Here are some excerpts from his address:

"It is the policy of the US to meet this pervasive
threat (of Communism) by helping to build up
the military, political and economic strength of
our Far Eastern allies and friends as rapidly as
possible. This the sole purpose of our
mutual Security programs in these countries."

"On the one hand, our policy is to face up to
the realities of Chinese Communist objectives,
opposing the further spread Chinese
Communist Influence and power. On the
other hand, as a principal means to this end,
our policy is to keep alive, support, and
government, firmly oriented to the free world.
As a foil and a challenge to the fanatical,
aggressive, hostile, and threatening

international Communist regime
of Peiping, an implacable enemy dedicated to
the destruction of all the foundations upon
which a free society rests."

"American policy is based on three major
considerations; the security Interests of the
US; American interest in helping other Asian
nations maintain their national independence;
and the long-range interests and future
orientation of the Chinese people themselves.
Let no one say that representation is
being denied to 600,000,000 mainland
Chinese. The fanatical Marxists of Peiping
come no closer to representing the will and
aspirations of the Chinese people than the
puppet regime of Budapest comes to
representing the will and aspirations of the
Hungarian people... After nine years of
Communist power in China, less than 2% of
the Chinese belonged to the Communist
Party. The Reds had kept themselves in
power by bloody purges and the liquidation
of some 18,000,000 persons.

"The Anti-Communist government of the
Republic of China is a symbol of Chinese
opposition to Communism, the only rallying
point in the world for non-Communist
Chinese – the only Chinese alternate focus
of loyalty for millions of Chinese on the
mainland, on Taiwan and throughout
Southeast Asia. If the Republic of China
should be liquidated, it would
extinguish the beacon of hope of millions of
mainland Chinese. Taiwan's ten million
would be delivered to the slavery of the
mainland and the twelve million overseas
Chinese would automatically become

increasingly dangerous cells of infiltration
and subversion in the countries where they
reside."

Sunday afternoon
March 15, 1959

Within the past twenty-four hours, I have had an unusual
opportunity to meet and talk with Generalissimo Chiang Kai-
shei. I was honored yesterday afternoon by his invitation to tea
at Chilin, which is the residence of the President. This
comfortable but not palatial home is located on a mountainside
in a beautiful garden. When we approached the residence,
"security police" were in evidence but otherwise, my visit was
as friendly and informal as calling on a good layman in Georgia.
We were received most graciously at the door and made to feel
quite at home. Servants in long white Chinese gowns moved
silently about the spacious reception room.

The place is typically Chinese, but I could detect many
touches of Western style. Madame Chiang is still in New York,
but evidence of her creative skill and love of beauty could be
seen in the exquisite furnishings. I was told she made many of
the drapes with her own hands.

The Generalissimo is now 73 years old but as I watched him
approaching down the corridor, he had the swing of youth and
the bearing of a soldier. He greeted me with extreme cordiality,
and we were soon plunged into a lively discussion of world
events. We then turned to a discussion of Methodism. The
Generalissimo and Madame are both devout Methodists. He
chided me tenderly because our church has not done more in the
way of churches and schools for his people, and I promised him
we would strive to expand our work.

For fifty-five minutes we discussed a great range of subjects.
Perhaps more than any other man in the world he is the symbol
of resistance to atheistic communism. He is of course America's
time-tested friend and ally. Despite all the buffeting of war, he
has never broken his word to the United States or to anyone else.
No one knows what prizes the Japanese and Russians have
dangled before his eyes, but he refuses to be bought.

The refreshments consisted of delicious cake and coffee. The Generalissimo does not smoke or drink. I was deeply moved by his simplicity and courage.

This morning (Sunday), I was invited to be the preacher in "The President's Chapel." It is a lovely, beautifully decorated chapel located on the grounds near the residence. The entire congregation is made up of those who occupy the very highest positions of government. The Generalissimo entered the chapel ten minutes before service time and took his seat near the pulpit. He entered heartily into the singing of the hymns, recited the creed, and when I read the scripture lesson, he turned to it quickly in his own Bible which he had in hand.

It seemed wise to me to make the sermon informal and thoroughly evangelical, I, therefore, preached on Peter's reply to Christ: "Thou hast the words of eternal life." This is not the place to repeat the sermon, but I tried to say to all who were present that Christ is the answer, that He alone speaks with the accents of a timeless moral universe, and that all our unuttered longing and undeveloped capacities are fulfilled only in Christ. I preached with complete liberty and with a preacher's joy. The Generalissimo was the first to take my hand and say to me some gracious but undeserved words of commendation.

An hour after the service was finished, a high official in Government brought to me from President Chiang a lovely piece of ivory with my name engraved on it alongside his own. I shall treasure it always. No man can know this great leader and not be impressed by his personality and devotion.

Thus ends another Sabbath Day. I shall now get some sleep as the next two nights and days will be on the flight home. I board a plane at ten a.m. tomorrow morning and will touch down at Okinawa, Tokyo, Honolulu, San Francisco, and best of all Atlanta. Love to all.

The Florida Methodist, May 1, 1959, p. 2

Editor's Note: Certain parts of this chapter were transcribed from Bishop Moore's original manuscripts held by the Arthur J. Moore Methodist Museum, St. Simons Island, Georgia.

The Bishop's last passport photo.

CHAPTER EIGHTEEN

A Final Mission Trip
To Asia

September 30 - November 4, 1959

San Francisco, California
September 30th, 1959

At noon on Tuesday, September 29, I boarded a modern airplane and left Atlanta for San Francisco, and today, I fly out of San Francisco on an ultramodern plane across the Pacific Ocean to Hong Kong, China. This trip is in connection with my duties as Presiding Bishop of the Hong Kong-Taiwan Area. It will require approximately seven weeks and I will return to the United States in time for the meeting of the Bishop's Council in Phoenix, Arizona, on November 17-20. If all goes well, I will reach Atlanta late in the afternoon of November 21.

My time will be divided as follows. The first two weeks will be spent in Hong Kong, which is today one of the most fabulous cities in the world. Methodism is there and very much alive. I shall fling back more detailed accounts of our Methodist activities while I am in all these countries. The latter half of October will find me in Taiwan (Formosa) where the Hong Kong-Taiwan Annual Conference is to hold its sessions. Delegates will gather in Taipei, on October 22-25 for a most important conference. It is relatively easy to meet here in America and make elaborate plans for the church and its expanding activities. It is quite something else to carry on the work in places where life is austere and among millions of people who are refugees. However, I could tell a thrilling story of the faith and generosity of the Methodists out there that would put some of us to shame.

The first week in November will be spent in Japan where I go as the official representative of the Council of Bishops to share in the Centennial Celebration of Protestantism in Japan. While there, I will preach three days in evangelistic services in Palmore Institute, one of our fine schools, so ably presided over by a fellow Georgian, the Rev. John B. Cobb. On Sunday, November 1, I will preach in our leading Japanese church in Kobe and that afternoon will dedicate a beautiful chapel at Kwansei Gakuin University, built to honor our great Bishop Walter J. Lambuth. This is one of Japan's finest Christian universities and has nearly ten thousand students. November 2-4 finds me in Tokyo, the nation's capital, participating in several significant celebrations.

It was as late as 1854 that an American Commodore, Admiral Perry pushed open the unwilling doors of Japan. In the century that has followed, Japan has grown so mighty that it dared to wage war against America. Their defeat was a humiliating experience for them but out of it has come a new nation with democratic ideals

Methodism has played a valiant role in the history of Japan, and I am highly honored to be the messenger from the American Methodist Church to our fellow Methodists in that vital part of the world.

I have written in some detail about my responsibilities in Japan but in fact, my chief duties are in Hong Kong and Taiwan. In these two countries, we face staggering opportunities and overwhelming problems. We have at least a half-dozen building projects underway, and they involve large sums of money. I am not alone responsible for the wise expenditure of these funds, but for what is even more difficult, the securing of these funds. In Hong Kong, we are building new churches, doing additional low-rent housing projects for refugees, and a new primary school. In Taiwan, we are building a university. Soochow University was a proud university on the mainland before the Communists came. Now, these loyal Chinese Methodists are rebuilding their Alma Mater in the land of their exile. It is already a growing institution with more than a thousand students. The building of a chapel and other important additional buildings weighs heavily upon my heart.

As I started out on this long and difficult missionary journey, my mind goes back to the General Conference of 1934 when I was assigned to supervise practically all of the overseas work of the Methodist Episcopal Church, South. Twenty-five years have rolled by, and I have not yet found an end to these missionary responsibilities. In addition to all I have tried to do in the USA., I have also carried the work of the church far in difficult places upon my heart and shoulders. It has not been a burden but a privilege. I am conscious of my imperfections, but I know I am a better man and a more sincere Christian as a result of these duties out on the ends of the earth.

As I begin this long journey, I do not go alone. The Lord and Leader of the Church said a long time ago, "Lo, I am with you to the end of the world."

I decided what kind of creature I wanted to be. I desire above all things else that my sermon shall always deal with the central certainties of our faith. I want to bring "good news." The good news about God, about the Savior of the world; good news about his power to forgive sin and vanquish guilt; good news about the ultimate triumph of righteousness and the subjection of the world, the flesh, and the devil; good news about the transfiguration of sorrow and the withering of the thousand bitter roots of anxiety and care; good news about the stingless death and the spoiled and beaten grave. This means the whole gospel for the whole world.

I covet most earnestly the prayers of all my friends that I may have "journeying mercies" and that my health and strength will in some measure be equal to my responsibilities.

Wesleyan Christian Advocate, October 8, 1959, p. 9.

Hong Kong
October 7, 1959

It is easy to affirm that this is a small world. That statement has been often upon my lips. If one is attempting to point out how distance has been annihilated, then the statement is correct. But despite all the modern and rapid means of transportation, and they are almost unbelievable, this is still a big world. At least that is the way I felt while in the air for almost thirty-six hours of flying enroute from Atlanta to Hong Kong. The Pacific Ocean is still a mighty big body of water whether you cross it by ship or by airplane.

On board a modern Pan-American plane, I left San Francisco at ten o'clock on Wednesday morning, September 30. After several hours of uneventful flying, we were on the ground at Honolulu being greeted by a group of dear friends. The three hours there afforded time for a good visit and a delicious dinner with these friend.

Somehow it always seems to me that the longest and most difficult part of the journey begins when one says goodbye at Honolulu and takes off for Japan. Hawaii is, after all, a part of the United States and people and things are of one's own kind. Beyond there one goes toward new nations, new currency and many different languages, but nevertheless, friendly people.

We flew nearly ten hours out of Honolulu above the broad expanse of the Pacific Ocean until three o'clock the next morning. Well, in fact, it was not the "next morning" because we had flown over the International Date Line and an entire day had vanished into the unknown. It was Wednesday night when we left Honolulu and Friday morning, ten hours later when we put down at tiny Wake Island. It is such a small bit of land in the vastness of a wide sea that one can but wonder how the pilots locate it.

We had some coffee and orange juice and after we had stretched our legs a bit we were off for Japan, another eight hours away. I have never learned to sleep very well on a plane. A tragic and almost fatal experience while flying some years ago did not cause me to "give up" flying, but ever since, I feel better to stay awake and see that all goes well.

At six thirty Friday morning (Thursday back home) the sun was coming up out of the east to banish the darkness and make us feel safe and secure in Japan where we landed at seven thirty.

The International Airport at Tokyo is one of the finest and planes to and from every corner of the earth are all around the place. Customs examination and passport formalities were soon over and I was in a comfortable automobile headed for the Imperial Hotel down town. The day was cloudy and rainy and after I had telephoned a few dear friends, I went to bed to get some of the sleep which had eluded me on the plane.

The first week in November will find me back in Japan participating in the Centennial Celebration of Protestantism and at that time I will write more about that fascinating country. One word should be said now. We came into Japan on the very heels of one of the worst typhoons ever to strike in this part of the world. Signs of destruction were evident in many places-ships had been washed upon the shore and more that 5000 had lost their lives. Vast schemes of relief by both government and interested persons were manifesting the humanitarian spirit of that noble people.

It required another night of flying from Tokyo to Hong Kong and that is how and where I spent Friday night. I was eager to get here and start my work and it was a pleasant sight when this extravagantly beautiful city of Hong Kong came into view about six the morning. Several of our missionaries and Chinese Christian leaders gave me a royal welcome.

Custom examination was hardly more than a formality and soon I was in my room at the Peninsula Hotel. By the way, the ride from the airport to the hotel was in a nice station wagon driven by the Rev. Lonnie Turnipseed, one of our finest missionaries. The car was gift to him from the fine people of First Methodist Church, Newman, Georgia.

As I go about the world and see what the gifts of our people in the USA mean to so many people in the ends of the earth, I find myself wishing they could see how much good these gifts are doing. Practically all my travelling this week has been this automobile, which was made possible by Brother Peter Manning and his fine people. God bless them all.

This travel letter has been so very informal and personal that no place has been left for an account of the work our church is doing here. That will follow in another letter. Suffice it to say that I am rushing from one duty to another.

Sunday morning last, I preached at eight thirty and eleven. The first service was in Wesley Village, a housing project where nearly three hundred refugees have found shelter, home, a school and a church. The church membership number ninety-nine and ninety-five were in their pews when I stood to preach. Nearly two hundred children were downstairs in Sunday School. I doubt that many of our American congregations could report such a large percentage of their memberships present an any given service. But I shall say more about Methodism in Hong Kong in my next letter.

Last Sunday, brought me a new kind of experience-unlike any I have ever known. It seems that one of the airlines reported in Atlanta that I did not take my scheduled flight out of San Francisco. Mrs. Moore naturally wondered where her husband had gone, and was a bit troubled. She called the Peninsula Hotel here in Hong Kong to know if I had arrived. By some strange coincidence they reported that I was not registered. This, despite the fact that I had been registered for more than twenty-four hours. That kind of report naturally added to my families' concern. Then I was called to long distance to hear Mrs. Moore's eager and slightly excited voice. I hastened to assure her that the report about missing my plane in San Francisco and not having arrived in Hong Kong were "gross exaggerations." It was good to hear her voice and to know all was well back home; but I cannot understand who gave out such misleading information. It is good, nevertheless, to be loved and missed when you are out of sight.

The weather in Hong Kong is about what late September was in Georgia. It is a lovely season here and autumn bids fair to reveal the wonders of God's handiwork. Love to all.

The Wesleyan Christian Advocate, October 22, 1959, p. 1

Hong Kong
October 12, 1959

This is one of the most spectacular, picturesque, and fascinating cities in the world. The wonderfully blue harbor is crowded with modern steamships, Chinese junks with their brown butterfly sails, and British and American ships here and there – all this constitutes a moving panorama. This beautiful harbor is surrounded by majestic mountains whose slopes are covered with modern buildings. All of this is in contrast to the innumerable squatter villages housing hundreds of thousands of refugees who have fled the Communist scourge on the mainland and have come here to breathe the air of freedom. The island is about eleven miles long and its width is from two to five miles. The harbor area covers about seventeen miles and once one crosses over from the city of Hong Kong, he is on the Kowloon

Peninsula and only a few miles from the border of Communist China. My hotel is just across the street from the railroad terminal in Kowloon and from my window I watch trains leaving for Red China. Naturally, there are not many passengers.

Hong Kong is a British Crown Colony and is administered by a Governor, assisted by an Executive Committee and a Legislature. The principal languages spoken are English and Cantonese. However, many of the refugees speak Mandarin. That means to serve the people we must be skilled in three languages.

The Methodist work here is approximately a hundred years old and was originally related to Methodism in Great Britain. Our particular branch (American) of Methodism was not here until the capture of the mainland by the Communists and the coming of vast numbers to this city of refuge. Among these exiles are many of our Methodists. Naturally, we followed them with missionaries and every possible help we can offer. Our relationship with the English Methodists is most cordial and cooperative. Generally speaking, the English work is done in the Cantonese dialect and ours is with Mandarin-speaking people.

We have three flourishing congregations at the moment and two outposts where we conduct worship services. We have two large housing projects where we offer shelter to the homeless while they make a new start in life. One of these projects is known as Wesley Village and one is known as Asbury Village. At Wesley, we have eighty-three apartments and at Asbury, which has just been completed, we have one hundred thirty-one apartments. Let no American reader get the idea that these are spacious dwellings. We average more than four persons to a room but in crowded Hong Kong, such quarters as these are considered most desirable.

Last Sunday I inspected a new primary school built with help from the Women's Division of Christian Service. There are twelve large classrooms and an assembly auditorium. We have a capacity of five hundred and forty pupils and on opening day one hundred and fifty applied for admission. No doubt, we will have to turn down many applicants at the beginning of the next term of school. The building is modern in every respect and we can point to it with pride as an institution of the Methodist Church.

We have two flourishing congregations, as I said above. One is known as Ward Memorial Church and one is the North Point Church. One congregation worships in a converted garage building and the other meets in an auditorium at the Y.M.C.A. One of the pressing responsibilities which I inherited from Bishop Ralph Ward when he fell at his post was to secure funds with which to construct two church buildings to house these rapidly growing congregations.

It has been estimated that the cost of these two new church buildings will amount to $225,000 American dollars. The people in America, during the last two years, have responded generously and if I can secure twenty-five thousand additional dollars, we will let contracts. As I write these lines, I saturate them with a prayer that churches and individuals who read what I write will be moved to help complete these needed projects and will mail checks to me to help. A little help will enable us to reach the desired goal for which so many have prayed and labored for so long.

The Annual Conference will be held in Taipei, Taiwan (Formosa) October 22-25. I will leave Hong Kong shortly for that wonderful land where another heroic struggle for freedom is taking place. Bishop Hobart Amstutz, from Singapore, has accepted my invitation to come and visit the Conference. Delegates from Hong Kong will fly over to Taipei and be quartered at our Methodist Assembly known as Wesley Grove. The problems and possibilities with our Methodist work in this part of the world are so colossal that one has to strive diligently to maintain a spirit of faith – not simply faith in God's goodness and mercy but in His identification with His church and a conviction that if we are faithful to Him we will not fail. If we believe in the sovereignty of God we must believe in the ultimate supremacy of righteousness.

The words of a previous poem are often in my thinking these days:

"At morn, at night, in earth and heaven
Be thou my first and last."

My next letter will be from Taiwan and must be written during the crowded days of the Annual Conference. Until then, God bless you.

The Wesleyan Christian Advocate, October 29, 1959, p. 1

Taipei, Taiwan
October 17, 1959

If my memory is correct, my last notes were written from Hong Kong. After eleven busy and fruitful days there with our Methodist people, I took what is known out here as The Mandarin Flight from Hong Kong to Taipei. It was an uneventful journey except for the knowledge that we were flying approximately one hundred fifty miles off the coast of Communist China. The fighting forces of these two nations are constantly clashing both in the air and on the land. The Civil Air Transport or "The Orients Own" as it is known out here, is attribute to General Claire Chenault who founded it. It is a first-class air service with uniformed attendance; all reading matter in English; and of course typical, and to me objectionable, alcoholic refreshments.

As soon as my plane was cleared by immigration officials, I was warmly welcomed by a group of dear friends, both Chinese and American missionaries. I was once again the recipient of precious hospitality in a quiet, restful atmosphere, but I knew that everything and everybody on this island is living and sacrificing for the preservation of the freeway of life in the maintenance of the precious heritage bequeathed to them by his or her Chinese culture.

The island of Taiwan, or Formosa, as we know it in America, is separated from the mainland of China by one hundred twenty miles of water. In 1949, Generalissimo Chiang Kai-Shek and his retreating armies, weary from nearly nine years of a fierce struggle with the Imperial forces of Japan and in the very hour of their victory was set upon by a Communist army, came to Taiwan that they might regroup themselves and return some happy day to regain the mainland from the Russian influenced Communist Armies. That was in October 1949 – ten years are gone by but the hope of returning to their mainland still burns like a light in the darkness.

There are no words at my command with which to describe the transformation wrought during these ten years in the social, economic, and political life of Taiwan. We hear often of what the Communists do to improve the welfare of the common man but what has been done here to improve living conditions, provide an education for the young, and establish a stable government does not receive the publicity it richly deserves. On every hand, I see evidence of high morale and an ability to meet difficult problems with heads up and with high courage.

The recent typhoons have brought Taiwan frightful destruction of property and some loss of life. I will preach next Sunday in Taichung where at least fifty percent of the crops have been wiped out. The entire nation is on an accelerated austerity program to provide funds for relief and rehabilitation.

It was my high privilege to say to Madame Chiang Kai-shek at her famous woman's prayer that her fellow Methodists wanted to help the unfortunate victims of these disasters. Before leaving the states, I secured from our Methodist Committee on Overseas Relief the sum of five thousand dollars which has been placed in the hands of Madame Chiang for relief. In a letter addressed to the gifted lady, I wrote, "Your fellow Methodists in the United States follow you and the Generalissimo with continuing interest in earnest prayers. Your successes are ours. The sorrows of your people move us to do what we can to render them some assistance." Needless to say, this gift has been gratefully received. Practically every newspaper has carried notices of the gift of American Methodists in the relief of human suffering.

I must speak once more of Madame Chiang's prayer group. Twice have I spoken to it and its power and influence grows upon me. In this group, the wives of the most influential government leaders are to be found. The wife of the president, the vice president and almost every highly placed official came together to sing hymns, read the Scriptures, receive prayer requests, and then went down upon their knees in prolonged prayer to seek God's help. With us last week was a highly placed

American General and his wife. They joined in the hymns and seem to be at home in this atmosphere of praise and prayer.

Once again, I am being entertained by the government while here. General J. L. Huang is my host. He is president of the Board of Trustees of Soochow University which is being built on this island. The general was my guest in Atlanta this past summer. He is a graduate of Vanderbilt University and is known as a great leader and the most genial host. While he was in the states, Oklahoma City University conferred upon him an honorary degree of Doctor of Laws. He is an earnest Christian and is at the very center of practically every significant movement taking place in the nation. Before I leave, we are to have a groundbreaking ceremony for a new men's dormitory at Soochow University. It will house one hundred fifty students. A well-known foundation in America gave one-half the cost and the Board of Missions advanced the other half in the belief that our people through Advanced Special gifts, would contribute the other half. I am confident that our missionary-minded people in the States will not only provide the funds needed for this dormitory but that speedily they will help me build the proposed chapel on this campus which is to be a memorial to the late Bishop Ralph Ward. He gave his life for this work and I must not rest from toil until I complete what he so nobly began. If one's heart could speak and feeble words could convey their meaning, I am sure these funds would be forthcoming and that right soon. Surely, I will rest better when I know they are in hand.

A dedicated Christian layman in America has already given funds with which to build a Christian Student Center on the campus of Soochow University. When the appointments are read next Sunday, I will appoint the Rev. Frank Smith, a fine young preacher from the Florida Conference, as chaplain to the more than one thousand students enrolled in Soochow. I am eager to get the student building erected as soon as possible so that Frank Smith can have a base for all of his Christian activities. Christian Emphasis Week held last spring with the students resulted in approximately sixty decisions for Christ. It is not easy to carry on a wise and winsome Christian crusade on college campuses in American schools and it is more difficult out here where such a large percentage of the students are non-Christian. However, we are doing our best to build a first-class Christian college at the center of this great nation where there is now a ten million population.

These notes were started three days ago. It is now Tuesday, October 20. During this time I visited Taichung, preaching to a fine Chinese congregation and also to a large English-speaking congregation composed of missionaries and U.S. Government officials and employees. I made a firsthand examination of some of the recently flooded areas and watched brave but poor people attempting to gather up their earthly possessions (not much was left) and build a new roof over their heads. The disaster was wrought by two successive typhoons with high floodwaters that exceed what newspaper reports had prepared me to expect. I was made doubly proud to be a part of a church that has an organization such as the Methodist Committee for Overseas Relief which can play the part of the Good Samaritan alongside all the broken roads of the wide world.

Tonight, I go to be the guest for dinner with Generalissimo and Madame Chiang Kai-shek. They have shown me many courtesies and I look forward to this evening with them. They gladly acknowledge that they are my parishioners and I am honored to be their Bishop. Here are two of the principal characters in this wide-world drama and it pleases me that they plan their part with Christian faith and high courage. Maybe in a subsequent letter, I shall give a brief account of my visit to these gifted leaders.

Wesleyan Christian Advocate, November 5, 1959, p. 9.

October 26, 1959
Taipei, Taiwan

We closed the Taiwan-Hong Kong Annual Conference last night and the final business item, as in all Annual Conferences, was the reading of the pastoral assignments. The number to be appointed out here is small compared with the large Conferences in America, but the problems are the same. The task of sending the right preacher to the right appointment has always been a solemn task for me. Preachers, whether they be in America or out on the mission field, always amaze me with their cheerful obedience to the marching orders of their church. There is no better system of ministerial assignment than ours, and there are no more capable and consecrated ministers to be assigned than Methodist preachers. God bless them all.

The Conference sessions were held in a lovely small assembly known as Wesley Grove, which we have acquired and developed on the edge of this capital city. All the delegates, both Chinese and missionary, were quartered here and it added greatly to our fellowship. This was only the fourth session of this Conference and much of our time was spent perfecting our organization and planning for new activities.

I have discovered, long since, that holding a Conference where you work in another language is more wearying than one at home. During this Conference, I had one interpreter translate what was being said on the floor and another translate what I said into Chinese. Fortunately, they were good interpreters and everything went smoothly. I recall years ago while preaching in Warsaw, Poland, speaking through an interpreter who knew but little English. We got through the sermon poorly and then proceeded with the Sacrament of the Lord's Supper. Anxious to use this young preacher in the service, I turned and said, "Please dismiss them." Meaning those who were kneeling at the altar. He looked frightened and hurried from the church leaving me without an interpreter. Later he returned to say he had not understood me, had thought I had said, "You are dismissed." He thought I had discharged him right in the midst of the service!

One of the highlights of our Conference was a significant mass meeting on Sunday afternoon at Soochow University where we broke ground for a Christian Student Center Building and the men's dormitory. Several hundred persons, including many highly placed government officials, were present. This lovely old university stood for more than a half-century on the mainland and was the pride and joy of the Methodists in the southern states. Many of the alumni are now in Taiwan and with extraordinary courage and generosity are rebuilding their Alma Mater. I must hurry home and secure at least seventy-five thousand dollars with which to build a chapel on the campus in honor of the late Bishop Ralph Ward.

My stay in Taiwan has brought me to a new appreciation of the importance of Taiwan, not only for the Chinese but as part of our military defense against an aggressive atheistic communism. If we were to forsake Taiwan, Japan, Okinawa, and the Philippines, our line of defense would have to be based in Hawaii. Enlightened self-interest tells us to stand by our allies in this part of Asia or see all of Asia go communistic.

It would be impossible for me to exaggerate the many courtesies I have received while here. I have been quartered in a comfortable guesthouse with every provision for my needs. General J. L. Huang, one of China's great leaders, who was my guest both in Atlanta and at Lake Junaluska last summer, has anticipated my every need and left me forever in his debt. He is the President of the Board of Trustees of Soochow University and under his inspired leadership, the Chinese in Taipei has given one million Taiwanese dollars to erect a magnificent dining hall and gymnasium at Soochow University.

It was my high privilege to be invited last Tuesday night to a dinner given by Generalissimo and Madame Chiang Kai-shek. One is not inclined to write in detail concerning the hospitality of those who invited him into their homes, but this occasion was so gracious and cordial that I dare to mention a few details.

The Presidential residence is a large house situated in the midst of a beautiful park. The Generalissimo and Madame Chiang spend all their time here except for brief vacations in the summer when they move to a more modest bungalow up in the mountains where there are hot springs and a cooler climate. There were several guests present at the dinner party to which I was invited. I shall not list them except to say they represent the very highest levels in the Chinese government and our armed and civilian forces stationed on this island.

The Generalissimo and Madame Chiang mingled freely with their guests before we were seated for dinner. I had time for an uninterrupted conference with the Generalissimo. He was especially thankful for the gift of money which I brought from our Methodist Committee on Overseas Relief and intended for the victims of two severe typhoons. I was given a place of honor at the side of Madame Chiang and directly in front of the Generalissimo where we had a chance to talk during the dinner hour. When we were seated Madame Chiang rose and said, "Bishop Moore is our bishop and our friend, and I request that he pray for us." Such an evening adds up to an unforgettable experience. The simple faith of these two world leaders and their open acknowledgment that they are Methodists made me proud of them. A lovely photograph of the two of them with their signatures below a simple line of personal friendship will hang on the walls of my study for a long time.

Today I fly to Japan where for a week I shall take part in the Centennial Celebration of Protestantism in that nation. Once again, I shall be with old friends for it was my privilege to supervise the work of the Methodist Church, South, in Japan for nearly eight years. Many of the missionaries and Japanese Christian leaders, whom I knew then, have passed on to their heavenly rewards but many remain. It is a heartening thing to see this nation rising so rapidly from the ruins of war, and pause to celebrate the arrival and activities of the Protestant churches. The world is coming at long last to see that no group has done so much to keep a topsy-turvy world in balance and to spread the joyful tidings of man's redemption, not to mention the spread of education and medical science, as have these men and women who left the comforts and safety of home in response to him who said, "Go ye into all the world."

On November 4, I start the long flight homeward. One more of these "travel letters," and I will be in my office in Atlanta. Already my heart is there and my body longs to be.

Wesleyan Christian Advocate, November 12, 1959, p. 1

Tokyo, Japan
November 4, 1959

After more than a week of travel and observation in Japan, I am prepared to say that present-day Japan is a miracle. At the end of World War II, this nation was prostrate. Its cities were in rubble, its ships at the bottom of the sea, its economy wrecked and its people humiliated by as severe a defeat as ever came to any people. But with initiative and hard work for which the Japanese are famous, they have rebuilt their nation so that today one finds a new philosophy of cooperation which enables this country to take its place in the family of nations. When I registered at the Imperial Hotel in Tokyo, I could hardly secure a room due to the crowd gathered from all over the world for an International Trade Conference. Of course, a vital part in all this rebuilding has been played by the United States of America and for that I am proud.

Perhaps my friends back home would be interested in the schedule of work I have carried during the last nine days. Let me hasten to say that I have not been here as a tourist. I have scarcely known ten days into which were crowded more exciting and delightful responsibilities. Here is a list of some of these duties:

October 26: Arrived in Tokyo and was met by a delegation of Japanese church leaders and missionary colleagues.

October 27: Traveled by train from Tokyo to Kobe – a journey of twelve hours. Kobe was the center of the activities of the Methodist Church, South, and it is in this part of Japan I feel most at home. To be the house guest of John B. and Theodora Cobb, two of the grandest missionaries in the world, was worth the journey.

October 28-30: I conducted evangelistic meetings in Palmore Institute, Kobe, and spoke daily at Kwansei Gakuin, one of Japan's truly great universities, founded by the late Bishop Walter Lambuth.

November 1: I preached at 11:00 a.m. in the large Japanese church which stands on one of the main thoroughfares of Kobe. That same afternoon I spoke and dedicated the Lambuth Memorial Chapel located on the campus of Kwansei Gakuin University where there are two thousand students.

This lovely chapel is the gift of a Japanese citizen who happens to be a Korean and a Buddhist, but out of his appreciation for what the church has done for his son, he made this most generous contribution. The chapel is a thing of beauty and would lend dignity to any college campus in America. Walter Lambuth, son of early missionaries to China and later a Bishop of the Methodist Episcopal Church, South, came to Japan in 1886 to assist his honored father in opening up Methodist work. Later he founded Kwansei Gakuin which, as I have stated, is become one of the greatest universities in the world. In later years, after the good Bishop had opened up our mission in the heart of Africa and carried on worldwide ministry, he came back to Japan to hold an Annual Conference and died while here. If there is any person in the world who doubts the lasting values of foreign missions, he should have been with me here in Japan during the past week.

All Christian groups in Japan are celebrating this year the one-hundredth anniversary of the beginning of Protestantism in this land. Celebrations have been going on all over the Empire for a year and will reach their grand climax here in Tokyo this week. It is my high honor to be here as a representative of the College of Bishops and as President of the Board of Missions. Time and time again during my visit my heart has been warmed and my pace quickened by this outpouring of thanksgiving for what our churches have been able to do. Protestantism is still a minority group in this nation of ninety million, but its influence far out-runs its numerical strength. One of the highlights of this celebration has been the awarding of certain high Japanese decorations to some of our missionaries who have lived and worked out here for nearly a half-century. Miss Mabel Whitehead of Alabama and Dr. Roy Smith of Illinois are two worthy Methodists who were included in this honor list.

Those who know me best know that I am never so happy as when engaged in evangelistic services. Evangelism is not the only business of the church but it is and must continue to be, the main business of the church. Under the skillful direction of Brother John Cobb, I preached twice daily to the eleven hundred students at Palmore Institute. The preaching was straight evangelistic preaching and was aimed to bring students to an immediate decision for Christ. They listened with eagerness and I am glad that a large number of them signed cards signifying their acceptance of Christ. It was a glorious sight to see the Japanese president of the school exhorting the students to confess their faith in Christ. All those who have been moved in a decision will be organized into Bible classes and carefully instructed for baptism and church membership.

One day last week I drove up a tall mountainside to stand reverently at the grave of Dr. J. W. Lambuth, the first of our missionaries to come to this part of Japan, and the father of Bishop Walter Lambuth. My, what a man of faith and courage!

Carved on his tombstone are his last words: "I die at my post." Whenever I visit the scenes of such great adventurers for God, I cry out to God to impassion Methodism to give her sons and daughters to the cause of missions.

The celebrations here in Tokyo have taken on national dimensions. Christian leaders from every part of Japan as well as delegations of Japanese Christians from California, Hawaii, and other parts of the world swelled the crowds. Added to these are many missionaries and official representatives from the Mission Boards in the USA. I am honored to be the spokesman for the Methodists.

Tonight, at seven, after a series of receptions, banquets, and church services attended by thousands, I board a huge British jet plane for the flight to Honolulu, where I will stop for a day and night. I made my first journey to Japan by ship in September 1934, exactly twenty-five years ago. Practically every year since, except for the war years, I have been coming to Asia. My first journey required more than twenty days by a ship. These air jets span the Pacific in a few hours. It all takes one's breath away.

The church has been good to me in many ways; none greater than allowing me to spend so much of my ministry out here. So many years have passed since I first came out here that I am now in the category of an "elder statesman." Everywhere I have gone old friends have greeted me and at no time have I felt like a stranger. So far as I know this should be my final missionary journey, although I have thought that once or twice before. Be that as it may, I shall always be thankful for having had a small share in the Christian missionary enterprise in one of the most stirring and challenging periods of history. Someday, when I have quiet and free time, I may attempt to write something about my experiences as a Methodist Bishop traveling a worldwide circuit. If ever I do, the title of the book will likely be, "On Business for the King." Whether the book is written or not, my life has been infinitely blessed by my missionary service. I hope my course is not yet finished and I could hardly claim to have "fought a good fight" but I do say humbly and proudly that I have "kept the faith." There is no sanity, no satisfaction, and no salvation for this bewildering world apart from Jesus Christ. Christian missions are not for an age but the ages.

After arriving in America, I go first to Seguin, Texas, where I will preach for five days in a revival, and then back to Phoenix, Arizona, where the Council of Bishops will be in session November 17-20. If all goes well, I plan to arrive in Atlanta Friday evening, November 20, spend the weekend quietly with my dear family then plunge into the many duties awaiting me in Georgia and Florida. For all of God's journey mercies and the love and support of friends, I am deeply grateful. *Wesleyan Christian Advocate*, undated clipping

IN MEMORIUM

Bishop Arthur J. Moore
(1888-1974)

Martha T. McDonald Moore
(1884-1964)

Bishop Arthur J. Moore

by Frank O. Salisbury

Arthur James Moore

(1888 – 1974)

by Bishop Roy H. Short

Arthur J. Moore was elected to the episcopacy by the 1930 General Conference of the Methodist Episcopal Church, South, from the pastorate of First Church, Birmingham. He was only forty-one years old and had a meteoric rise to prominence. He had already been pastor of two great churches – Travis Park in San Antonio and First Church, Birmingham. He also had a striking career as an evangelist. His name had become a household word in much of Southern Methodism. His first episcopal assignment was to the supervision of the small and widely scattered Southern work in California, Arizona, and the Pacific Northwest.

In 1934 the Church, South found itself deep in the depression. It was losing three bishops by retirement and lost active bishops by death during the previous quadrennium. The decision was made not to elect any new bishops and to double the assignments of the bishops remaining active. Bishop Kern was returned from the Orient for assignment to home service, and Bishop Darlington from Europe for the same purpose. The Episcopal assignment of the entire mission field of the Southern Church was placed on the shoulders of Bishop Moore, and he carried it for six years. In the years to come, he was to know more assignments for temporary service to mission fields than any other bishop of the church.

In 1940 he was assigned to the Atlanta area, which he served for the next twenty years. He was a native son of Georgia, where he was born on December 26, 1888, in Argyle. He grew up in Georgia, was converted there, and began his ministry in the South Georgia Conference. The two great Georgia bishops of that period, Bishop Candler and Bishop Ainsworth were in a sense his spiritual fathers. They gave him great encouragement throughout their lives.

Bishop Moore was particularly active in the affairs of Emory University, in the establishment of Epworth-by-the-Sea, and the promotion of all Georgia conference educational and other institutions. He also furthered the work of Paine College, long a joint enterprise of the Christian Methodist Episcopal Church and the Methodist Episcopal Church, South.

Everything in Georgia Methodism in the last 40 years still carries the mark of Bishop Moore's influence and will continue to do so for years to come. The whole of Georgia regarded him as one of its first citizens. It is indeed fitting that Atlanta should have been the final resting place upon his departed this life on June 30, 1974.

Bishop Moore was principally a preacher, with a warm heart. His preaching was scriptural, fervent, and deeply moving. He had an unusual command of the language, and words flowed from his lips and pen in a torrent of beauty. Vast audiences waited upon his preaching. One of the striking facts about him was that he was such a master of speech when his schooldays had been so limited. As a young man, he was a railroader, as his father had been before him. He was largely self-taught; an avid reader, and a close follower of current affairs. He had no earned academic degree, but the day came when great educational institutions showered honorary degrees upon him.

Following his retirement, he went back to his first love, evangelism, and followed a full schedule of evangelistic meetings all over the country that would have taxed the strength of the far younger evangelist.

Bishop Moore's companion interest was missions. As a young man, he applied for missionary service but was turned down by the Mission Board of the Church, South. He lived to see the day when he was bishop of the very fields to which he sought once to go as a missionary. He served as president of the Board of Missions of The Methodist Church for twenty years. He never visited Cuba, perhaps because it was nearby, but he visited every other mission field of the church. His feet walked literally in the far places of the earth. On countless occasions, the Council of Bishops or The Board of Missions sent him on special missionary journeys. He raised millions for missions, and the map of the world was stamped upon his heart. He used to say that should he find himself stranded overnight in almost any large city in the world, he would be able to call someone he knew who would open the door of their home in hospitality to him. The statement was no exaggeration.

Bishop Moore was a large man with striking blue eyes that seemed to have in them the element of wonder. He moved with a rapid gait and never seem to tire. All his movements were quick. He had a genial and warm disposition, and his emotions ran deep. He cultivated friendships and was particularly popular with laymen. He challenged them for the Kingdom and usually met with a ready response.

Bishop Moore was a strong personality. Without purposely doing so, he dominated any group he was in by the sheer weight of his personality. He always had something to say, and he spoke his mind freely on any and every occasion. He was fully self-confident. Bishop John Branscomb, whom he loved devotedly, and he loved him, used to refer to them humorously in his absence as "King Arthur." Bishop Moore was aware of this, and it afforded him amusement. The term did not miss the mark too far. He was not, however, an autocrat. Rather, he was simply an unusually strong man.

He spoke often in the Council [of Bishops]. In his active days, he had much to do with determining whatever work was done. He will long be remembered as one of the greats of the episcopal body.

Short, Roy H. *History of the Council of Bishops of The United Methodist Church 1939-1979.* Nashville: Abingdon Press, p. 239-241.

Bishop Moore is greeted by at the Atlanta airport as he returns from Korea on one of his special missions. On the Bishop's right is his long-time friend Dr. Louie D. Newton, pastor of Druid Hills Baptist Church. On his left is Dr. James H. Rushbrooke, of London, President of the Baptist World Alliance.

Bishop and Mrs. Moore posing with friends, along with Mr. and Mrs. Asa G. Candler, Jr.

Martha Tabitha McDonald Moore
(1884-1964)

Power Behind the Bishop
by Helen C. Smith

To say that Martha McDonald Moore was the power behind the bishop is in no way to denigrate the man. Highly publicized, world-renowned Methodist Bishop Arthur J. Moore was the first to admit it, says W. Wardlaw Moore of Atlanta, one of the Moore sons. "My mother was a great woman. She moulded the entire family. Everything my father accomplished is due to her. She was a very quiet person, that she drove him on when he wanted to quit and he admitted this."

Wardlaw Moore goes on to describe how his mother was a schoolteacher in South Georgia when she met his father who was working on the railroad. At that time Moore was a "backsliding Baptist with no interest in the church" because he had been "readout" for rejecting a church summons to answer charges of dancing. The story goes that Moore had not been dancing, simply watching others indulge, but he was indignant that the charges had been made at all.

But when he took Martha McDonald for his wife, she was determined to get him back into her fold, a strongly Methodist one where children were encouraged to pray and speak out in church gatherings at an early age.

Moore was to recall years later: "I was married to a lovely girl from a devout family and she gradually began to pull me into the church. We went to a series of Methodist meetings at Waycross and at one of them I experienced a great awakening, spiritually and intellectually, much more than release from sin and hope of heaven."

That was the beginning of a dual ministry. Moore without theological training soon had a circuit of eight rural churches in McIntosh County. A woman parishioner was so impressed with his preaching she put up her money to send him to Emory at Oxford.

In the meantime, her son relates, his mother also spoke somewhere nearly every Sunday. "She was a great speaker, and in great demand everywhere. She always talked about the Christian home and family. Those were her things."

And with her husband on the road so much of the time, Mrs. Moore was left to carry water, wood, and supplies upstairs to the second floor, two-room apartment which served as their first parsonage, a far cry from one of the Candler homes they were to live in later in Atlanta.

Moore's advancement was swift and he was referred to as the "boy evangelist." In time, the Moores had five children, of which one daughter died as a young child. Three sons and another daughter all grew to adulthood and became involved in church work.

Moore's career took him to many parts of the world including China, Africa, Japan, Korea, and Belgium. Sometimes his family would go with him, and whenever Mrs. Moore was able to go, she was also much in demand as an accomplished speaker in churches and missionary outposts. She wrote articles for various national publications and was awarded the Doctor of Laws degree by LaGrange College. She became the recipient of many honors including Atlanta's Woman of the Year in Religion.

But perhaps it remains for a daughter-in-law to heap the highest praises on Mrs. Moore. Lynda Moore, the wife of Wardlaw who is treasurer of the North Georgia Conference, says this of her mother-in-law: "She was my second mother. She was one of the kindest people I've ever known. Never in all of my life did I see her upset or mad. She never said one unkind word to her family or anyone else. She gave advice when needed or when asked for, but she never scolded."

Lynda Moore recalls also that her mother-in-law was a petite, pretty woman with blue eyes and a great love for pretty hats. She entertained frequently, sometimes a hundred or more persons at a time without letting [it] bother her a bit. However, she did have help.

Around 1940 the Moores moved into a large, red brick home on Decatur Road. It was originally built for the late Bishop Warren A. Candler. It was purchased upon the death of Bishop Candler. The Moores also had a home at Epworth-by-the-Sea, which Bishop Moore had founded on Saint Simons Island. This home was sold after Mrs. Moore died in 1964 after a prolonged illness.

The Bishop, who was still living at the time, had inscribed on a white marble monument that she was the bright star in his life, leading him homeward from his travels in faraway places.

Another memorial to her is the Martha MacDonald Memorial Moore Chapel at Magnolia Manor in America, Georgia. The Chapel has many stained-glass windows depicting women in the Bible. A Chapel at the Protestant Radio and Television Center in Atlanta is named for both Bishop and Mrs. Moore.

These are the big memorials to a woman who is also surely remembered in the hearts of many, such as the "beggar lady" and the "lace lady" her daughter-in-law tells about.

"Mother would never turn anyone away from the door, ever. Every week she would pile up the beggar lady with groceries from the pantry and buy dozens of thin washcloths with crochet around them from the lace lady. We never used them. When we asked her why she wanted to do this she told us: "You don't turn anyone away. You might be turning away the Lord.""

Smith, Helen C., *The Atlanta Constitution*, May 30, 1976, p. 171.

Editor's Note:
Martha McDonald Moore passed away on August 17, 1964 following a prolonged illness. The Bishop recorded her passing in his pocket diary as follows"

August 17 – Mother Goes to Heaven

August 18 – The funeral will be Thursday. We are overwhelmed by kindness. Martha was a saint and is with God.

August 19 – Her service is directed by Bishop Costen Harrell, Rev. Eugene Drinkard, and Rev. Rembert Sisson. A triumphant service.

August 21 – We walk in faith but with a sense of our loss.

August 22 – We visit Westview [Cemetery] very often.

August 23 – Quiet day at home, no desire to meet crowds yet, but I mean to carry on as she would expect me to do. I thank God for her wonderful life and her influence over me.

August 29 – Doing my best to adjust to the fact that Mother is not here.

September 1 – My spiritual and physical adjustment to the greatest loss I ever sustained. It is difficult to realize that Martha is not here and that I must walk without her. God will keep me.

Bishop and Mrs. Moore probably
at their home in San Antonio, Texas.

Mrs. Moore often greeted the Bishop at the airport upon his arrival home. This photo is from the late 1950s.

On September 1, 1964, the Bishop sent the following letter to friends announcing the passing of his beloved Martha.

Dear Friends.

My dearly beloved Martha walked triumphantly into God's house on Monday, August 17th. You can imagine how lonely the children and I feel.

For more than fifty-five years, her unfaltering faith, her compassionate heart and wise judgments have been for me an unfailing source of inspiration and courage. She was a woman of extra ordinary faith. There was about her daily living a freshness of intelligence and a response to the needs of those about her, which made her life full of singing cheer. She was a woman of rare gifts, unfailing in her fidelity to her Master, her family and to an innumerable company of friends, who stretch literally around the earth.

We who walked close by her side can never cease to be grateful for her radiant asinging soul and Christlike compassion.

In these months of serious illness, her brave beauty and victorious faith were as clear as sunlight. In her final written word to those she loved best, she said, "I neither fear death, nor dread to die." In this earthly life she lived in God, now in that land where shadows never darken, she lives with God. In life she held "her own" securely in her love. Now that she is away for a little while, we shall hold her forever in our undying affection and loving memory.

Telegrams, letters and remembrances have come from her friends around the wide earth. To make individual acknowledgments of all these is manifestly impossible. Therefore, this note is an expression of our sincere gratitude. We of the family will strive to walk with larger hope and braver step until we greet her in the morning of the fadeless day.

With great gratitude.

Arthur J. Moore

Addendum

Several important items were discovered after *The Bishop Is In a Hurry!* was organized for publication. To omit these letters and articles was inconceivable. The article by Laura Wheeler was moved to the addendum since it was not a letter from the Bishop. Also included here are two of a series of letters written by Homer Rodeheaver. They were written while he was traveling with Bishop Moore in the Belgian Congo in 1936. Unfortunately, the remainder of the series is lost. An article published in *The Florida Methodist* so succinctly outlined the Bishop's life and career. Finally, the week of publication a letter was found written to Bishop Moore from the Executive Council in China detailing the damage to Methodist properties in the Japanese invasion of China in 1937. The letter dated March 24, 1938, is part of the Roger Gramling Collection at the Arthur J. Moore Museum, St. Simons Island, Georgia.

Bishop Moore Visits the Congo
by Laura N. Wheeler

After the General Conference of 1934, news reached the missionaries of the Congo Mission that Bishop Arthur Moore was to be our bishop for the quadrennium, there was great rejoicing. We had not had an official visit since the spring of 1930, and so very naturally we hope for a visit from Bishop Moore at an early date.

When we learned that he had almost literally been given John Wesley's parish, "the world," and that he would not be able to visit us before late in the second year of his administration, our hearts sank within us.

Dr. Cram came in August 1935, and thus filled in the gap. We were grateful for his visit. We were all very happy when we received a letter from Bishop Moore saying that he had completed plans for a visit to us in the spring of this year and that he would be accompanied by Mr. Homer Rodeheaver and Mr. E. M. Sweet, of Stockton, California.

On April 30 Bishop Moore and Mr. Rodeheaver alighted at Luluaberg, our nearest airport. They were met by a group of missionaries with Mr. Sweet, who had made a detour through India and Palestine while Bishop Moore was visiting the work in Europe, and had arrived on our mission field two weeks in advance. Two days' travel brought them to our mission. The joy in the hearts of the missionaries and native Christians could not adequately be expressed.

Perhaps the natives, with their innate ability for demonstration, came much nearer to the missionaries in expressing their joy.

After visiting four districts and getting an insight into the work, Bishop Moore convened the first regular session of the Congo Mission meeting at Wembo Nyama on the evening of May 18. Our organization, which was [organized] by Dr. Cram last year, calls for an annual Mission Meeting in which the native pastors who are members of this body and lay delegates chosen from among the native Christians, have a part, and following that meeting immediately, the Missionaries' Meeting, which takes care of business which is as yet out of the realm of the native mind. This year marked the real beginning of these annual meetings.

No one in the homeland, except those few who have been missionaries, understand what were the feelings of the missionaries in the opening hours of the Mission Meeting as we saw our native preachers and layman take their seats within the bar of the Conference and have their first experience in taking part in such a meeting. We felt exactly like parents watching the development of their natural children, for our natives in their inexperience and simplicity are just like children, and we missionaries have the feeling of parents in our attitude toward them.

During this Mission Meeting, which lasted two days and a half, Bishop Moore preached twice each day, and his messages were interpreted by one of the missionaries. At each session, Mr. Rodeheaver delighted us all with his music and song leading. The natives were very much pleased when he sang in their native tongue, but even more so when he taught them to sing in English the refrain of "Walkin' in Jerusalem Just Like John." He also instructed all in song leading.

Bishop Moore with native pastors ordained at the
Conference in June 1946.

The Mission Meeting adjourned at noon on Thursday, and the Missionaries' Meeting convened that afternoon, continuing through the Sunday night service. Bishop Moore preached twice each day, but this time only to the missionaries, and we were greatly blessed indeed under his sincere gospel preaching. Again,

Mr. Rodeheaver inspired, delighted, and instructed us in the ministry of song. Only in the Sunday morning service bid the natives again [take] part. That service was the climax of the whole week. The large Lambuth Memorial Church was packed with natives. The sermon was of course interpreted for them, and the music was in the native tongue. After the sermon, four of our natives were ordained deacons.

In our Mission Meeting last year, when Dr. Cram led us in the reorganization of our work, and our meeting this year, we feel that we have indeed made history. The foundation of our branch of the Protestant church in the Congo is now taking shape.

In the Mission Meeting this year there were three high points. The first one was when on the first morning of the meeting Bishop Moore received the first-class into full connection. There were twelve of these native preachers, and they were all men who had been preaching for several years and men in whom we have confidence and whom we love.

The second high point was at the closing service of the Mission when Bishop Moore presented to the Women's Missionary Society of Wembo Nyama, a beautiful silk banner that was made by the Women's Missionary Society of China and sent through Bishop Moore to their sisters in the Congo. The banner was sent with a letter that gave expression to their Christian love and goodwill.

At Bishop Moore's request, the banner will be held from year to year by the society which makes the best record. So, the presentation of this banner will be an annual event at our Mission Meeting. For those of us who are struggling now in laying the foundations for Christian womanhood among our people, this event was significant and prophetic.

The third and highest point was the event of the Sunday morning service already mentioned in the preceding paragraph – the ordination of deacons and of the preachers who had been admitted into full connection. We missionaries saw the four stalwart men, whom we felt had proved their fitness to receive this responsible office in the church, standing before the altar and the Lambuth Memorial Church as the first of the regularly ordained, our hearts were filled with praise and gratitude to God.

To us, the ceremony was most impressive. We commend these men to the prayers of the church at home. It is true that Bishop [James] Cannon had ordained our oldest preacher, Kimbulu Charles, in the spring of 1930. But as we had no organization as a Conference at that time and no Course of Study this was out of the regular order. The ordination, this year, was the first regular ordination. I am sure that Kimbulu Charles appears in the picture with the four who will be ordained this year.

And now, as we look back upon this meeting which we feel was truly memorable, we give thanks – as we did many times during the meeting – to our Father in Heaven that he allowed Bishop Moore to be with us just at this time; his spirit of comradeship throughout the whole stay, his sound gospel preaching, his strong leadership, and what his wise counsel meant to us, only eternity will reveal. May God in his providence allowance have Bishop Moore's firm, brotherly leadership through many years!

We are truly thankful, also for the visit of Bishop Moore's companions, Mr. Sweet and Mr. Rodeheaver. In the two weeks Mr. Sweet was visiting us he endeared himself to all. When the natives learn that he had come to visit us at his own expense, just because he was interested in our work, they were very much impressed. They gave him the name "Unagi," which means "the lover." Mr. Rodeheaver made us laugh and he made us sing. We need to laugh much more here, and we need to sing much, but we often get too busy to do as much as either of us needs. We hope that others who may be able to make missionary tours will include the Congo field and their itineraries.

World Outlook, November 1936, p. 4

Rainbow-Graphs Letter #4
by Homer Rodeheaver
Luhota, Belgian Congo
May 6, 1936

I am writing this in the little mud rest-house of Luhota, a primitive village of mud huts, inhabited by about four hundred and fifty natives. Mr. Davis, of Minga, brought us over here.

Here's our schedule. Tonight we will sleep in the rest-house, get up before daylight, go down to the river, and antelope hunt. Then, get in one of the big native canoes and do some picture "shooting" of elephants and hippopotami. Mr. Davis is one of the best hunters in this country, and he can locate the game if anyone can.

Just before coming here, we visited Minga. On our arrival there we were met by a fine group of missionaries. Mr. and Mrs. Davis and Mrs. O'Toole, the nurse, are due home on furlough. I have invited them to be my guests at Winona Lake. Miss Fareman, one of the nurses, has just returned to take Mrs. O'Toole's place.

At Minga there is a splendid home for girls, with Mrs. Davis in charge; also a leper hospital, as well as a General Hospital. The leper hospital has been supported by the Mount Vernon Methodist Church, Washington, D. C. The equipment is poor and inadequate, but they are carrying on magnificent work despite these handicaps. All that they received for the splendid work is about $3.00 a year for each leper.

I wish you could see the little girls in their home. They wear very simple little one-piece dresses, and are very proud of them. The method of punishment at home is to take away the dress and compelled the disobedient child to wear a narrow strip of cloth, with nothing above the waist.

This morning, at 5:45 a.m., Miss Parker called me. I dressed hurriedly and took the trombone to the little church. After a blast or two on the trombone, I wish you could have seen the natives piling out of the village, dressing as they ran. In five minutes the church was completely filled. We conducted a service and then took some pictures. Later they sent a committee to Miss Parker, requesting her to ask Bishop Moore to appoint me to their village. It's not often a candidate can get a call with just one sermon. They knew that the bishop appointed the others, and thought he could appoint me.

While writing this there was a great commotion in the village. We heard the beating of the drums and saw a man rush out with an upraised spear. His head was covered with a terrifying headdress. Other natives ran for their spheres, and soon the street was filled with wild, gesticulating men and women. It certainly looked to us like a tribal war, but we soon learned that the kind natives were simply putting on a little "show" for the visitors. We took advantage of this opportunity to get some unusual pictures.

Just now, while sitting here in front of the rest-house, a boy came and told us of a deep place in the little creek where we could swim. We hurried down to the creek, the native boys carrying our guns and camera and a mat on which we can stand when dressing. O, boy! It was refreshing and cooling.

As we returned from the swim, the sun was setting in a gorgeous splash of red, and the rising moon looked like a great golden ball with a filmy silver frame. Words fail me in describing the splendor and beauty of the scene. When we reached the hut, Mahala, the black boy, had set the table out in front of the hut, in the moonlight. The palm trees outlined against the sky, the tropical foliage, the little black naked boys, and the stall wart Blacks with their skin like polished ebony, all contributed to making this a never-to-be-forgotten picture – such is seen as one reads about and thinks of only in terms of descriptive fiction.

And here we are, amid this glorious setting – Africa, with its romance, drama, tragedy, beauty and charm, squalor and dirt, all mixed together. What a harvest field for the Christian church, if the folks back home could realize the needs and furnish these missionaries with the proper equipment and sufficient means to reap the harvest.

Next, we took the trombone and walked to the main street, which is the village center. After a few calls on the instrument, we were circled by these ebony-skinned people, with their bodies glistening in the moonlight, and their forms silhouetted against the sky. What a sight! I have been in many strange meetings, but none to compare with this. I sang some spirituals; they began to hum, and but for the barrier of language we were again back in Tennessee, Alabama, or Georgia. They were courteous and attentive. The boys rushed to carry chairs for us. I delivered a short message, which was interpreted by Mr. Davis, after which he prayed.

We returned to the hut, and on the way, we met a man who had found a little songbook we had dropped in the village ten miles away. He had walked, or run, the entire distance to bring it to us. We gave him a franc. He was very happy and started back to his village at once.

On one trip, the missionary remembered something he had left and one of the villages he had visited. He stopped at the next village and told the man to go back – a distance of about thirty miles – and bring the missing article to us. The messenger returned with it the next day.

When we find the native on the road with a split stick or piece of bamboo, or reed with a loop in it, we know he is a dispatch-bearer; having no pockets, he carries the message in the split of the stick or loop of the reed.

This morning we had another interesting experience. We ate breakfast by the light of the moon, in front of our hut. Anxious to get to the river early, we arose before daylight. Mahala had breakfast ready, and we were soon on our way. We drove as far as we could in the open Chevrolet, the first car to go over this new road. The tall grass overhung the road and sifted into the car and onto our clothes. At the end of the road, we walked through the thick grass to the river, climbed a tree, located the hippos, and crawled through the grass until we got a rather close view of them. Then we got into a wateau, – a long canoe hollowed out of a solid tree. This one was at least forty feet in length. The natives poled the canoe around a little island, where we were able to shoot some closer pictures of the hippos. These animals look rather ferocious as they stick their heads out of the water and snort and blow. The natives who carried our guns and cameras, etc., were happy to get the two francs which we gave them. Incidentally, the missionaries are very careful about tipping the natives too generously. The house servants asked the missionaries not to accept money for them; they want to feel that they are doing something for us.

The hut had already been swept by the natives. Mr. Davis brought along some Montgomery-Ward cots, and after securing poles for our mosquito nets, we slept in style and comfort.

After the hunt, we started for Tunda. The accelerator pedal on Mr. Davis's car became disconnected, and he could only feed with his choke. At one particular spot, only would the car perform, and that was between sixty and eighty kilometers an hour. Of course, most of my friends who have ridden with me will say, "Well, what are you kicking about; that's normal for you." Yes, over the roads in Florida, Indiana, or Illinois, but these roads are made about twenty miles an hour. We surely did some bouncing.

On our arrival at Minga, the missionaries held a reception, at which Bishop Moore, Mr. Sweet, and I were the guests of honor. All of the missionaries joined in a delightful dinner party on the lawn of the Lewis home. About five hundred children from the schools, Chief Tunda and four other chiefs, and many of the natives were present. After dinner we gathered in front of the porch; Bishop Moore spoke to them briefly, and I played, sang and entertain them with some tricks of magic. They were amazed over "Willie Jones" and the flags. It's a real joy to do things for people who are not worldly-wise, and thrilling to watch them as they view something for the first time.

Last night we slept in a very comfortable bed in one of the cottages. This morning I took the cameras and made a picture of Dr. Lewis while he operated at the hospital. The doctors back home would naturally think that it could not be done in a place like this — just a bare mudroom. Dr. Lewis does have an electric light, from the Delco system, the first one I have seen in Africa. He also has a sterilizer, given him in the United States, brought across the river in canoes fastened together, and carried here by sixteen natives. But I believe the doctors in the United States would soon forget the porcelain floors and walls of the hospitals if they could have watched this clever surgeon start the incisions. The alert black boys, who assist him, and the anesthetist are all under the watchful eye of Miss Mary Moore, a trained nurse. If the picture is a good one, you will see all of this operation, and the eight-pound fibroid tumor which Dr. Lewis took out the chief's wife, one of three of the wives of the same chief, all of whom are here for operations. The chief himself is here too. You don't wonder at that, do you?

If the people at home can only see how faithfully and efficiently these missionaries work, they would be more generous in helping to carry forward this humanitarian work. The hospitals and schools are the great contact forces for the people. There is a fine school year for the boys, which is directed by Miss White, and another for the girls, directed by Ms. Parham. Somehow or other these simple black people reach into my heart as you know other people in any mission field.

As Mr. Davis and I were sitting in front of our hut in the moonlight the other night, we noticed a little black chap, about ten years of age. He'd been hanging around ever since we reached the village. All the men had gone to their huts. The sentry sat by the fire, but this little black fellow, with his great wistful eyes, remained long after the others had left. I asked Mr. Davis to call them over. We learned that his mother was dead and that he wanted to become a Christian, and there in the African moonlight we prayed and dedicated him to God in Christian service in Africa, with my promise to pay for his education if he proves worthy. Time will tell!

Homer A. Rodeheaver and Bishop Moore

Rainbow-Graphs Letter #5

by Homer Rodeheaver
Wembo Nyama, Belgian Congo
May 17, 1936

Traveling fifteen hundred miles in Fords and Chevrolets with these faithful missionaries, over the bumpy roads of this section of Africa, brings a realization of the difficulties with which they contend.

First, let us take up the matter of intercommunication. The stations are seventy-five to one-hundred-fifty miles apart, there are no telephones, and in some cases no roads except native paths. If one does not have access to an automobile, the only way is by bicycle or native runner. Over some of the paths, the runners can outdistance the bicycle.

A cable or wireless sent to us at Luluaberg, the nearest airport and radio station, must be forwarded by automobile or runner to Lusambo, a distance of about one hundred miles, then to Wembo Nyama, an additional one hundred fifty miles. When the missionaries communicate with other stations, they are compelled to wait for an answer until the runners can take the message to its destination and return. And so the first big problem is that of roads.

Mr. Wheeler, of the Tunda station, is quite a builder of roads. He takes a sack of salt, goes out on the native path, and by paying with salt gets hundreds of natives to cut the brush, dig up the rough spots, fill the holes, cut the poles for the bridges, and soon he has a road over which an automobile can safely travel. Some of the committee asked him the probable cost of building a fifty-mile section of road. Much to their surprise, he told them it could be done for $250.00 and also stated that he had built some of them at a lesser cost.

Mr. Wheeler has pioneered many miles. The government has taken over some of his roads, made further improvements, and assumed the care. As the roads are built, small villages are concentrated. These villages are accessible, and thus the missionaries can reach them with the Gospel message, and a good road builder is therefore as necessary in carrying the message as a preacher. However, these missionaries in many instances are both.

We next reached the headquarters of Mr. Reid, at Kondala. He is the Presiding Elder of that district. Fifty-one native preachers, under his supervision, work regularly in that many villages, and they reach out and touch eighty-five villages with the Gospel message. Each pastor must be a consecrated Christian. A prayer meeting is conducted in the native church at 5:00 a.m. or 5:30 a.m. each morning and the church is usually filled; this does not interfere with their work.

At the headquarters at Kondala, Mr. Reid has a school for boys and girls, and a catechism class for the older Christians. As these children finish their native schools an opportunity is given to them to enter one of the station schools, and it is at the station schools that the boys and girls meet each other. Marriages are arranged between Christian boys and girls, and Christian homes are established. Those who desire to take up a Christian work may enter the Normal and Bible School where they are prepared for teaching and preaching. The annual cost of maintenance at the school for each girl is as low as $8.00, and that of the boys is approximately $15.00 each.

One of the greatest contributions that can be made to this mission work would be a radio system enabling the workers to talk with each other. This would require a mechanical genius to erect the radio station and operate it for a time. He might also devise a hand-operated spinning machine and loom that would spin and weave threads small enough to make gauze for the hospitals. One hospital has been compelled to wash the old dressings and use them over again. This genius need not be a preacher at all, that he could in this way make a vital contribution to the work. The raw cotton is here, labor is plentiful and cheap, and all that is needed is a directing genius.

Another need is for a builder who can mix the native clay and sand in such a way that the brick will be permanent. All the wooden houses are now attacked by ants and rapidly destroyed. The roofs of the houses are of grass or tin, and another need is for a man who can make the right kind of roofing tile.

We have just returned from a meeting in the village of Wembo Nyama, the chief who was decorated by the Belgian government for having saved the lives of many white people when the blacks attacked them many years ago. Alex Reid has built a church in the village, a substantial brick structure with a seating capacity of about six hundred. The natives did the work and the total outlay in cash was three hundred francs, about eleven dollars in our money. Doesn't this give you an idea of the tremendous contribution some skillful artisan could make to this great work, even though he never preached a sermon?

Most of the missionaries over here may be classed as inventors. For instance, the hospital at this station has no electric light. When Dr. Sheffey has an emergency operation to perform he is compelled to use a kerosene lamp and a flashlight. As you know, ether is flammable, and the lamp must be placed at a distance sufficient to avoid the danger of explosion, yet close enough so that the doctor can see to operate. What would you do under such conditions? The doctor used the flashlight as an emergency light.

And now let me write briefly concerning the destructive white ants. I saw one house the other day, just two years old, yet when I hit the porch post with my hand the dust flew out from thousands of ant holes; the post was a hollow shell. If some chemists were to come over here and extract from certain plants or minerals a substance that would serve as creosote and make the posts and timbers used in house construction impervious to the deadly ravages of these white ants, he would make an outstanding contribution to the progress of this country.

This part of Africa is a paradise for the horticulturist or botanist. Fruits of all kinds are plentiful. Imagine, avocados and pears for every day, not just when our California friends send them; papaya and grapefruit for breakfast; and oranges and tangerines in abundance. There are twenty-two different kinds of fruit on one mission compound. Rice is also plentiful and cheap, and the millet is wholesome. The bounteous supply of fruit, coupled with the fact that the boys and Ggrls work in the gardens, is the reason for the low cost of maintenance.

The first night we were entertained in the home of one of the missionaries, we were greeted by a huge scorpion on the wall. Mr. Stiltz caught it in an envelope, and put it away in a jar is one of the many varieties found here. There is one very persistent little inset they call a "jigger;" not the "chigger"– but a "jigger." It is a little black insect that jumps like a flea and is about the size of a large flea. It usually bores into the bottom of your foot or between your toes; it crawls inside and lays its eggs. In a short time, the spot begins to swell, and the only way out is a minor surgical operation. Someone must go in with a knife or sharp pin and dig the jigger and its family out. I saw them take some out of the feet of the children in one of the hospitals, and it was not a very pleasant experience.

The children in the Mission homes have regular days for "jigger inspection." Of course, every time your foot itches a little, your imagination can easily conjure up "jiggers." Bishop Moore thought he had them. We took off his shoes and socks, examined his foot carefully, and sure enough, there were three little black specks. We called the black boy who is a "jigger" expert. He came with his knife, but when he started to operate we found that what we had supposed were "jigger spots" were merely three little black specks that were easily brushed off. Naturally, we were all disappointed, including the Bishop. We had hoped to witness a "jigger operation" on a Methodist bishop. However, Mr. DeReiter accommodated us. He took off his shoe, and we discovered a little swelling. The black jigger surgeon dug in and out came the little black animal that was causing the trouble. Confidentially, I think Mrs. Moore and I saved the life of the Bishop, for she made me promise faithfully that I would get some sulfur and put it in the Bishop's boots and shoes. This I did, and carried it from London, despite my excess baggage, and when we arrived here, true to my promise, I put some in the Bishop's boots; but up to date, he has not entertained any jiggers.

There are many large animals here. Just a few days ago at this station, Dr. Sheffey heard a loud commotion among some of his black boys. Upon investigation, he found that a python had crept into his goat-house and swallowed two of his goats. The huge reptile was found in the corner of the house, too heavy from the weight of the goats to move. It was an easy matter for Dr. Sheffey to take his gun and shoot the Python, dissect the goats, (no, they were not alive!), and give the natives a feast both of goat and python meat. They tell us that snake meat is very tasty. We haven't as yet tried any of it – not that we know of.

Traveling through this country one wonders why we never see any horses, mules, or cattle. These animals would be of inestimable value in the cultivation of farms, and for transportation purposes over the paths. The milk, too, would be wonderful for the children; all that is used here is canned. The makers of canned milk are a blessing to the missionaries.

There are no horses, mules, or cattle here because of the dreaded tsetse fly, which causes sleeping sickness and is greatly feared. Someone who could discover a way to eliminate this insect would make a valuable contribution to the life, prosperity, and happiness of these people. They keep only such animals as can be taken into the house with the family. They have goats and sheep; and by the way, the sheep here have no wool. Wool is not needed to keep the animals warm, nor do the natives need woolen garments – we might term this "economy of nature."

To the uninitiated, the social customs of the country are unique, yet to avoid offense they must be carefully observed. For example, while we were in a conference the other night with some of the native preachers in one of the station guesthouses, a man walked in with a goat. At first, we rather resented the intrusion, but the missionaries soon discovered that the goat was a present from the chief of the village to the "Wangi Bischopp." Of course, the Bishop didn't want the goat. He had no fear that anyone could get his goat, but he just had no use for it. Furthermore, it was going to be "dreadfully annoying," and it would be in the way. I refuse, don't you know, to take care of it, for it is not my present; it was from one chief to another, and no one could properly care for it but the Bishop himself; but he was a railroad man and without experience in caring for goats. If Arthur, Jr., had been with us, we could've turned the goat over to him, but he was back home in Texas. It, therefore, became not only a diplomatic, homiletic, theological, ecclesiastical question, but an important social problem as well. A delicate ethical question was involved. The Bishop thought he could refuse with thanks, but the missionaries told him this particular chief had great power, had been a friend to the Mission, and it would not be good policy to offend him, as the Bishop surely would do if he refused to accept the goat. To complicate matters still further, we soon discovered, by certain calls back and forth, that there was a little goat involved – a son or daughter of the Bishop's goat. The Bishop now had not one goat, but two, and one of them almost too small to travel. After a "palaver" it was decided that there was only one way out of the dilemma: the Bishop must accept the goats.

The Bishop then discovered another requirement of the social customs, that is, when one chief accepts a present from another chief, the gifted are supposed to give the giver a present of even greater value. Of course, the final credit would then depend upon which one sees the other first. In our case, the chief of the village saw the Bishop first, and in spite of the fact that he did not want the goats, and had no way to care for them, as we drove through the village the next morning the chief was waiting. The Bishop, with the cheery, friendly Methodist smile, handed him sixty francs. As I saw the chief smile, it seemed to me he must've been a Baptist, doubtless rejoicing in the thought that he was getting ahead of the Methodist bishop. If the Bishop had been a guest in the chief's house, he would've given him one of his fifty wives, and that would simplify matters for the chief; but since he was not the chief's personal guest the problem was the Bishop's. If someone were to write a volume on "The Bishop's Goats," it would afford an opportunity of explaining many interesting African customs.

Perhaps you are wondering what became of the goats? The chief had been sent through the country to Wembo Nyama, about fifty miles, where they are holding this Methodist conference. I saw the poor little innocent things here on the compound, and since Abraham and Isaac are not here, I fear the animals will be sacrificed on the altar of Methodist epicureanism during the Conference, to give strength to these native preachers and enable them to go back to their stations to start a crusade against the custom that would present such a problem to a visiting Methodist bishop. There is one thing, however, that I must say in favor of the goats: They do have noses, but they do not smell.

Speaking of smells, it would require a separate letter to properly handle the subject. The odors are many and varied in this country – from the flowers and other things, and the people. A missionary, even though blind-folded, could probably recognize by the odor what country he was in! Seriously, the odor is not really offensive when one becomes used to it.

Here, there certainly are unusual possibilities for color photography. The color of some of the flowers and shades in the forest and jumbles are magnificent; gorgeous orchids growing wilds; another large golden-yellow flower growing plentifully on large bushes, a flower with shape and coloring much like the golden lily we so rarely see in our hot-houses and flower exhibits during the Easter season.

Mr. Stiltz, of this mission, has cataloged more than a hundred different species of trees and bushes. I've not seen a tree over here similar to those in the United States. One is called the "elephant medicine" tree. Under it, they find where the elephants had chewed the bark and spat it out. From another tree, they extract the poison which they put on their darts to kill animals. Sap obtained from one of the trees, when mixed with sand, makes a kind of cement that hardens quickly. And from yet another tree the witch doctors and medicine men secure the poison with which they mixed the potions to kill people. Still another species produces an insecticide that will kill insects, and if that genius ever comes to Africa, he will probably find close at hand the very material needed to exterminate these pests, thus making it possible for the native to raise cattle mules, and horses, thereby increasing the agricultural possibilities.

Speaking of insects, driver ants move across the roads and fields in battle formation, like soldiers. They seem to be well organized and have their officials direct their columns. I hope to shoot a picture of one of these columns if I can.

The boys and girls here do not worry about clothes; especially is this true of the boys. The women in some villages wear very small pieces of cloth. One of the ladies said that a man's handkerchief would make four Sunday dresses for some of the women, but judging from some that I have seen there would be cloth to spare if only four were made.

The natives are much like overgrown children. Magic fascinates them tremendously. Just a little disappearing thimble will intrigue them. The more pretentious bits of magic seem marvelous to them. We are always very careful to explain that they are not the arts of witch doctors or medicine men, for I find that some of the simple tricks of magic have been used by the witch doctors and medicine men.

Attending this conference is one very famous woman witch doctor, who once had great power among the chiefs and natives because of her witchery. She was converted in one of the evangelistic meetings held by Alex Reid and is now an ardent Christian. After her conversion, she visited the chiefs and natives and explained her trickery, at the same time giving her testimony, and has been invaluable in helping the missionaries in their evangelistic work. I hope to secure her story more in detail before leaving for home. Her name is Mama Walu. Here, all the women are "mama."

This village and station are named for Chief Wembo Nyama. He lives in the village in a rather nice house. He is the chief who was kind to Bishop Lambuth when he first came here, and he is the man who donated the ground for this compound. Mr. Reid has agreed to help him build a brick house for himself. The natives will do most of the work, and the expense will not be as great as it would be for a brick house in our country. It is in the village of this chief that Mr. Reid built the fine brick church, previously mentioned in this letter, at an expenditure of about ten dollars in our money.

The only other request from this chief is that they give him a bicycle. Mr. Sweet, a personal friend of Bishop Moore, who is also traveling through here, spoke to the chief about having seen his picture with Bishop Lambuth, holding the little native baby. Mr. Sweet expressed his appreciation and told the chief that the people of America had been praying for him. The chief warmed up to Mr. Sweet and became quite friendly. They walked arm in arm through the village, and then Mr. Sweet discovered the reason for this warm display of friendship – the hope that he would give the chief a bicycle. He told the missionaries that he would be willing to make a public profession as a Christian if they would get him a brick house and a bicycle. I have promised to take some pictures of him and some of his wives, although I am not contemplating any kind of a trade with him.

The custom of buying wives is the great curse of Africa. A little girl may be contracted for when she is a baby, and when the missionaries try to get the girl for training or any kind of service, the parents will say, "we have been eating on her body already," meaning that money or property has already been deposited on the contract. We have found but one woman servant who has been trained in a Mission home, and she is the wife of one of the boys, who also works there.

Somehow, a way must be found to give these girls a chance to develop and do more than the menial work of the fields. Some of them would make find nurses and workers in the homes. The great problem is that the girl belongs to the father and not to herself. She is a chattel to be traded or bartered. To a certain extent, the problem is being solved by matching up some of these boys and girls in the Mission homes. The Christian girl is married to one of the Christian boys who will go out to be a native pastor, and thus establish a Christian home with one wife. These mission homes for the children are doing great work. Think of being able to pay all the necessary expenses to provide for a girl in one of these homes: $8.00 for a girl and $15.00 for a boy annually. At the request of Bishop Moore, four men made contributions toward the expense of my trip over here. I'm going to invest this money in some of these boys and girls. It is a splendid investment, one that will pay large dividends in Christian training and service.

The hospitals make tremendously vital contacts. As I watched Dr. Sheffey, with his native assistance under the direction of Mrs. Sheffey, the head nurse, so very efficient yet handicapped through lack of equipment, I thought that our people back home should find some way to a supply the necessary equipment since these workers are giving their very lives of these people. In each of the hospitals, there are from forty to sixty cases on the surgical department waiting list.

What a wonderful thing it would be if the American Medical Society or some foundation would provide the funds and equipment, and send a group of young surgeons over here to assist the self-sacrificing doctors and nurses. What a wealth of experience would be theirs, and what a magnificent contribution this would be to the great work of the missions here! In one year over here these young doctors would receive more practical operative experience than they could secure at home in five years' practice. However, it would be necessary for them to bring their material and instruments. Dr. Sheffey is compelled to handle an emergency operation in the most adverse conditions. To heat the water for sterilizing, a fire is lighted under an improvised boiler and blown with a crude bellow.

You must see these two pictures to understand the difference between a heathen and a Christian home. First, let us look into one of the heathen native homes before the missionaries came. The wife is about to become a mother. The house and grounds are dirty; the sheep and goats are mixed up with the children in the house and yard. Unclean and undernourished children in loincloths and the younger ones are seen with nothing but a little string around them; the husband is lazy, and the wife gathers and prepares the food.

The husband frequently beats his wife if the food is not ready when he wants it. The son and father sit in the front of the house when eating, while the wife takes what is leftover and scurries behind the house to eat. The time arrives when the baby is to be born inside the house. The father washes his feet and hands, and the native "granny," or midwife, takes the dirty water to the laboring mother, who drinks it to obtain strength from the father's body for the child and herself.

Then they pour cold water on the frail, newborn babe, to toughen it and make it strong. The methods of the midwife are the crudest kind. The father ties a charm around the baby's neck to ward off disease, and then places an idol under a shed in the yard to ward off the evil spirits. The baby develops a sore throat, whitewash is applied to the baby's neck; they call in the witch doctor, who goes through all sorts of incantations to frighten away the evil spirits. The witch doctor puts medicine under his or her fingernails, and when the hand is rubbed over the baby's body it causes irritation, and the parents think the witch doctor has power. No wonder the baby dies! Next, we see the wild funeral orgies; we hear the beating of the drums and the wailing of the people. The members of the family cover their faces and bodies with whitewash.

Compare this with a Christian home, after the missionaries came. House and grounds are clean and neat. We see a family with clean, healthy children going to a prayer meeting at daylight; the father plays with the children while the mother pounds the grain and prepares the food. They all sit around the pot or the table, the blessing is asked, and they eat all together.

The time comes for the arrival of the baby. The prospective mother is carried to the Mission hospital in a hammock. She has sanitary care; the baby was born strong and healthy. At the hospital the mother is taught how to properly care for herself and the baby; and when the baby is sick the Mission doctor or nurse comes, proper treatment is prescribed, and if necessary the child is taken to the hospital. As the child grows, it is taken into the native village school by the native preacher or evangelist, where it is taught practical principles of Christianity; and as it proves itself worthy it can be sent to the Mission school, where under ideal surroundings is taught how to live the Christian life. Christian boys are matched with Christian girls, and thus Christian homes are established.

One of the greatest difficulties in working with the girls is the frightful custom of contracting for their marriages soon after, sometimes even before, birth. Yesterday I was taking some pictures of the little girls in the home here. We could hear the drums and the wailing of the mourners just across the swamp. A prominent man of the village had died. Miss Zickafoos brought out a girl, probably twelve years of age, and told me that this girl had been the child-wife of this man who was being buried. The Mission folks had redeemed her from this man for one hundred twenty-nine francs, which he had paid to her father, and now she is being raised under the Christian influences, and may eventually become one of the future workers of Africa among her people.

We had a "revolution" here last week. I doubt if any of you could have guessed what caused it. There are over one hundred boys in the school here. While the Bishop and I were at dinner, in the home of Mr. and Mrs. Anker, a committee of six boys from the school came to call on the Bishop. He met them, and with Mr. Anker, as the interpreter, he listened to their spokesman, a bright lad of about fifteen years. The boys were dressed in the native fashion of the school with just a strip of cloth, made of burlap, wound around their waist and dropping down a little more than halfway to their knees. The school furnishes this piece of cloth, food, and a place to stay. The boy pays a little on his books and a few francs for tuition.

The cause of the "revolution" was this: the boys heard that in the other mission schools at Minga and Tunda, conducted by Anne Parker and Miss White, the boys are also provided with a pair of pants in addition to the customary grass sack, and these young lads were striking for pants. Like strikes in other places, they had not considered everything. They did not realize that Mr. Barden, in charge of the school here, was taking care of one hundred boys without pants; and that out of the same appropriation other schools were taking care of only fifty with pants. Nor were they aware – that Miss Parker and Miss White were furnishing the pants to their boys out of their meager salaries or private funds. None of this mattered to these "revolutionary" boys; if others had pants, they wanted them too. The next morning there was quite a flurry of excitement. In the meantime, these few leaders organized the entire school, which came en masse to demonstrate to the Bishop their lack, and in great need, of pants.

Mr. Barden was determined that they must not bother the Bishop; they were equally determined to personally present their plea, so around and around, first one side of the compound and then the other, the strange pants-less group would break out. Mr. Barden, on his bicycle, would head them off at one point and then another. Finally, a small group broke through.

The Bishop told them he would not talk with them until they came in regular order and made their complaint through Mr. Barden. After consultation, the leaders decided that was the best thing to do, and marched back into their school building. At the request of Mr. Barden, the Bishop went over for the conference. The boys were very quiet. He asked for their spokesman. They discussed the matter. The Bishop tried to explain to them that the appropriation was not large enough to do all that he would like to do. He endeavored to convey the idea that they had formerly agreed that they would rather have more boys with less equipment, but they could not get the idea of pants out of their minds. The matter of "appropriation" was just a word to them, and it was too long to understand anyway. They seem to think there should be no limit to money in America. With his usual poise and common sense, the Bishop soon convinced them it was foolish to strike against an organization that was unselfishly trying to help them.

They went back to their work, and since then everything has been quiet on that particular front. There is a smoldering fire, however – that undying longing for something the other fellow has, whether it is pants, automobiles, power, or more territory – will continue until the pants are supplied.

Deep down in the heart of this Methodist Bishop remembering his boyhood days, there is also a longing for pants for these boys, and I have a suspicion he will find some way to provide them.

Mr. Sweet and I were willing to furnish the pants but we must have law and order. It is one of the greatest lessons they must learn, obedience to a governmental authority, and the method and proper channel through which to make their appeals.

When Miss Parker and Miss White came over to the Conference this week, we told them of the "revolution" which had been started because their boys had pants, and these had none. But I feel sure the boys will get their pants – not because of the revolution, but because of the real need. History records many revolutions that were necessary before the real needs of the common people were recognized. The particular question of pants or no pants may seem trivial, but the principal back of it is a vital one.

Mr. and Mrs. Barden have done monumental work in building up the school helping to make these people independent in their thinking. Mrs. Barden plays the piano exceptionally well, and Mr. Barden has a fine tenor voice that would be in demand in any church choir in our country. He teaches music and has done splendid work here in this particular department.

Every group must learn a certain number of songs, and all the boys must learn to direct, so they can help when they go out into their villages. That is the secret of fine group singing. They sing some of the great hymns without books and also love to sing the gospel songs, such as "Jesus Loves Me" and "The Great Physician." They have had a great time learning "Sing and Smile and Pray," which has just been translated into their language.

Most of all, they seem to find great joy in learning some of the Negro spirituals. Only two or three have been translated, so I've taught them "Walk in Jerusalem" in English. They do remarkably well. I am convinced that if they will learn the spirituals, they will carry forward the gospel message in song.

These mission evangelists are spirit-filled men and women. This is also true of the doctors, nurses, teachers, and mission workers; they are devout and consecrated and do their work in prayer and faith in God. I predict that this section of Africa is on the verge of a great spiritual awakening.

-Homer Rodeheaver   1 Corinthians 14:15

Bishop Moore and Homer A. Rodeheaver

The Thrilling Story of
Bishop Arthur J. Moore
from
The Florida Methodist

On April 26, Bishop Arthur J. Moore went to Waycross, Georgia, for a week of revival services that marked the 50th anniversary of his conversion at the altar of the First Methodist Church of that city. Noting that significant event, the *Wesleyan Christian Advocate* published the following account of the Bishop's conversion and ministry. Now that he is again the presiding Bishop of the Florida Conference we are sure that many of our readers will enjoy this bit of personal history.

When the 21-year-old Moore went to the revival service in 1909, he was a railroad flagman, married for two years, and the father of a son. At 14, he had been "readout" of the Baptist Church for peeping boylike into a room where a dance was in progress. For this sampling of worldly joys, he was summoned by the board to explain his erring ways. Resenting what seemed to him an unfair accusation, he refused to go, and his name was removed from the church membership list.

Before his conversion, he had attended church and had not been an irreligious boy. But said Mrs. Moore, "I was deeply interested in church membership and I wanted to be completely proud of my husband. I tried quietly but persistently to bring him to membership, and I will never forget my joy and pride the night he rose and went down to the altar."

"On that night in 1909, after a sermon preached by Doctor Charles Dunaway, the young railroader had no sense of impending change. Yet something in the sermon moved him to go down to the altar and seek membership in the church on profession of faith. "A bronze plaque at the church now commemorates his conversion. Young Moore had no thought then of becoming a minister. However, he became a lay worker, seeing to it that the church was cleaned and that cooking fires at the summer camp meetings were supplied with wood. Soon he was doing some lay speaking in the small, country churches.

About six months after his conversion, the Presiding Elder got permission for Arthur to leave his job temporarily to go down to Saint Mary's and preach for an elderly minister named John W Simmons, who was critically ill. "You've got it in you. Pray with Doctor Simmons and preach," were the Presiding Elder's orders.

The people like the young preacher so well at Saint Marys that they ask that he be sent to them as their regular minister. However, when he applied for and was granted a License to Preach, he was assigned to a circuit of seven isolated rural churches in McIntosh County. People still talk about the visits of the enthusiastic young minister to all on the old broken-down white horse.

Thus began a ministry that has won thousands to Christ. The success he had at Jackson Chapel on that first seven-point circuit is characteristic of his later ministry wherever he went. The first time he preached at the church, every unsaved soul in the community - 23 in all - joined that night. Then followed several years as District Evangelist, then Conference Evangelist, in which time he organized almost 100 churches

Mr. and Mrs. Elisha Thorpe, of Townsend, Georgia, gave financial assistance so that their hopes for Arthur Moore could come true. His contemporaries at Emory college recall how he studiously poured over his books and took time out only to play on the baseball team and an occasional game of tennis, with his two small children playing on blankets behind the tennis courts.

Travis Park Episcopal Church, South
San Antonio, Texas

While in school he preached in churches around Atlanta. Then came the time when the Bishop said he was ready to take a large charge. He was assigned to Travis Park Church, in San Antonio, Texas, and later to First Methodist Church, Birmingham, Alabama. In these two churches in a period of ten years, he won 6000 persons to membership.

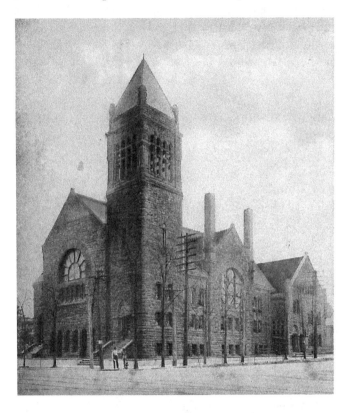

First Methodist Episcopal Church, South
Birmingham, Alabama

In 1930 at the General Conference in Dallas, Texas, he was elected bishop on the first ballot. Throughout his episcopacy, he seems to have been kept on "circuits," never having just one geographical state or country but sometimes as many as seven or eight.

These circuits have included Arizona, Montana, California, Washington, and Oregon (the Pacific Coast area) from 1934 to 1940; China, Japan, Czechoslovakia, Belgium and the Belgian

Congo, Poland, and Korea, 1934 to 1940; the Atlanta area, 1940 to present time; the Geneva, Switzerland area, central Europe and North Africa, 1952 to 1953 and his most recent additional assignments, Florida and the Hong Kong- Taiwan area.

It will be a homecoming for the busy bishop when he arrives in Waycross for a week with old friends and a re-sharing of the gospel he preaches with such strong conviction. But those who know the bishop well know that he won't unpack his suitcase to stay any length of time.

The Florida Methodist, May 15, 1959, p. 2

Editor's Note:
Regarding the Bishop's episcopal election, see the editor's note on p. 24.

Shanghai, China
March 24, 1938

Dear Bishop Moore,

We send you the following information concerning destruction or occupation by the Japanese military of our Mission property. Many places damaged, and churches thought to be destroyed, such as Woosung, Quinsan, etc., are not reported here. We report only verified facts.

SHANGHAI:
1. New Chapei Church burned
2. Ten new houses next to Chapel Church burned. (Parsonage not burned)
3. Old Law School occupied by the Japanese (transport company) without permission.
4. Margaret Williamson Hospital property occupied for a period and looted.

NANZIANG:
1. Girls' School burned.
2. Kindergarten burned.
3. Parsonage bombed, but not entirely destroyed
4. Miss Peacocks' home destroyed (burned)

    5.   Church floor partly burned.

TAICHANG:

    1.   Large church completely destroyed.

    2.   Two parsonages completely destroyed.

    3.   Primary school building completely destroyed.

    4.   Woman's Center occupied by Japanese military and horses.

CHANGSHU:

    1.   Front part of S.U. Primary School building destroyed, and buildings looted.

    2.   Chapel destroyed.

    3.   Faith Johnson School and old buildings damaged by bomb.

    4.   Wesley Smith home occupied and looted.

    5.   Louise Avett home occupied.

    6.   Doors, windows, floors and materials of new church being built taken.

SUNGKIANG:

    1.   Main buildings of Susan B. Wilson School bombed and burned. New Primary building damaged.

    2.   Eight bombs dropped on West Sungkiang Center, making direct hits on Susan B. Wilson School for Girls, and on Hayes Wilkins Bible School Building, and doing considerable damage to residence of W. ( ) Burke, Hayes Wilkins Home, Bible Woman's Home , and residence of J. H. H. Berckman, and to small buildings of Christian Center.

    3.   Grace Church bombed, and since Jan. 8 looted of all pews and wood-work, and now being used as a stable for Japanese horses. Parsonage occupied by Japanese military.

    4.   All of our remaining Sungkiang property looted, and things that remain are still being taken. The Japanese authorities still deny Bro. Burke permission to go to Sungkiang for relief work.

CHANGCHOW:

1. New clinic of Stephenson Memorial Hospital burned.
   New single doctor's residences bombed and burned.
   Two married doctor's residences bombed and burned.
   Main building hit by two bombs doing serious damage,
   but buildings can be repaired, though at large expense.
   All hospital and residence buildings looted. All 245
   beds taken, medical books destroyed, x-ray equipment
   taken or deliberately damaged.
2. Carriger Memorial Church occupied by Japanese
   military; parsonage damaged from bomb.
3. New home for aged women destroyed.
4. Bible Women's Center, primary school and Alice
   Green's home destroyed.
5. North-gate School center and Miss Leveritt's home
   occupied by Japanese military.

HUCHOW:

1. Virginia School buildings occupied by Japanese military;
   library books reported burned as fuel.
2. Haitao Church stripped of floors and all word-work.
3. Huchow Institutional Church center occupied by
   Japanese military, part of it for stabling horses.
4. Huchow Hospital used as hospital by permission.
   Manget and Henry trying to return.
5. Virginia School Home looted: floors, doors, windows
   of Estes' house taken.
6. Wushing Middle School occupied by Japanese military.

SOOCHOW:

1. Soochow University still occupied by Japanese military.
   All University buildings looted. Cline Hall and Allen
   Hall damaged by bombs.
2. Whole property of Laura Haygood Normal School
   occupied by Japanese military.
3. Soochow Hospital buildings taken over by Japanese for
   a hospital, but without asking permission. Dr. Rice and
   Dr. Thoroughman residences looted. Our doctors

have done everything they could to return, but have been refused permission.

4. West Soochow Church occupied and reported looted of pews. Davidson School occupied. Atkinson Home and Dowdell Center occupied by Japanese military.

5. Henry's house bombed, badly damaged.

6. Atkinson Academy occupied by Japanese military.

Our missionaries are trying to secure permission to return to their stations, but this far little hope has been offered. The terrible experiences of workers and members are beyond belief and can only be suggested in other report.

Sincerely yours,

EXECUTIVE COUNCIL

by Z. T. Kaung, J. H. Berkman, S. R. Anderson